C000183411

Alastair Vere Nicoll runs a renewable energy business and lives in London with his wife and two children. This is his first book.

www.ridingtheicewind.com

RIDING THE ICE WIND

By Kite and Sledge across Antarctica

ALASTAIR VERE NICOLL

Foreword by
BEAR GRYLLS

I.B. TAURIS
LONDON · NEW YORK

Published in 2010 by I.B.Tauris & Co Ltd
6 Salem Road, London W2 4BU
175 Fifth Avenue, New York NY 10010
www.ibtauris.com

Distributed in the United States and Canada Exclusively by Palgrave Macmillan,
175 Fifth Avenue, New York NY 10010

ISBN 978 1 84885 306 5

A full CIP record for this book is available from the British Library
A full CIP record is available from the Library of Congress

Library of Congress Catalog Card Number: available

Typeset by JCS Publishing Services Ltd, www.jcs-publishing.co.uk
Printed and bound in Sweden by ScandBook AB, Smedjebacken

Foreword

Riding the Ice Wind is the tale of a wild gamble, an adventure so ambitious that few have even attempted it, let alone pulled it off. It is the very honest, human tale of a journey to the coldest, windiest place on earth for nearly three months of indescribable hardship and pain.

People think adventure is romantic. But romance dies pretty fast in temperatures of -45°C. In truth, people have no idea how people like Al and his team can endure the trials of difficult expeditions. Such journeys are always hard to explain. Often it is easier to move the subject on. I understand that feeling well. 'Been away recently, have you?' It is a question that cannot be answered in 30 seconds over a pint. But it is answered beautifully in this book.

A heart-led account of one of the longest, hardest polar journeys of recent years, *Riding the Ice Wind* is a testimony to the fact that enduring hardship isn't about bravado but about a quiet, at times faltering, daily decision to endure. What impressed me most about this journey was the team. They succeeded simply because they worked together so well, although such words don't really do their achievement justice. Their story isn't one of stiff upper lip, but rather a strong resolve to do their part, and more, and never to complain. That is real courage. Getting on and enduring, with a smile.

I know all of the team, except David, and I am so full of admiration for them, as men, as friends and as adventurers. Al is always shy of being called an 'adventurer', as if he feels he hasn't earned the title. This book tells a different tale. Al, you have an adventurer's spirit through and through, trust me. I have known Al since he was 13 and I have realised over the years that he possesses a rare quality that life often rewards. Toil. Toil, sweat and tears. Hard work, never quitting. And of course he possesses the eyes of a dreamer, one of T.E. Lawrence's all-important 'dreamers of the day'.

Al, Paul, David and Pat have my greatest admiration. Now go home and enjoy a beer, please.

Bear Grylls

Contents

Illustrations

Images 1, 4, 6, 8, 9, 10, 12, 13, 14 © Paul Landry
Images 2, 3, 5, 7, 11, 16 © martinhartley.com
Image 15 © Conrad Dickinson
Image 17 © Lyndsey Young

Antarctic Route Map

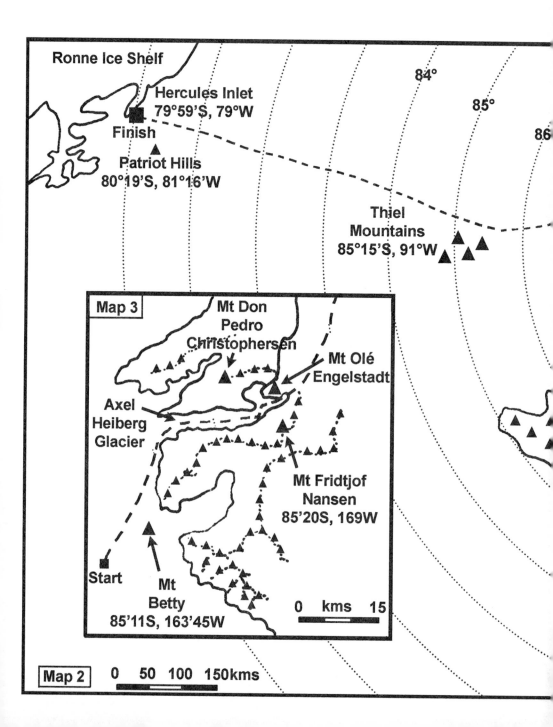

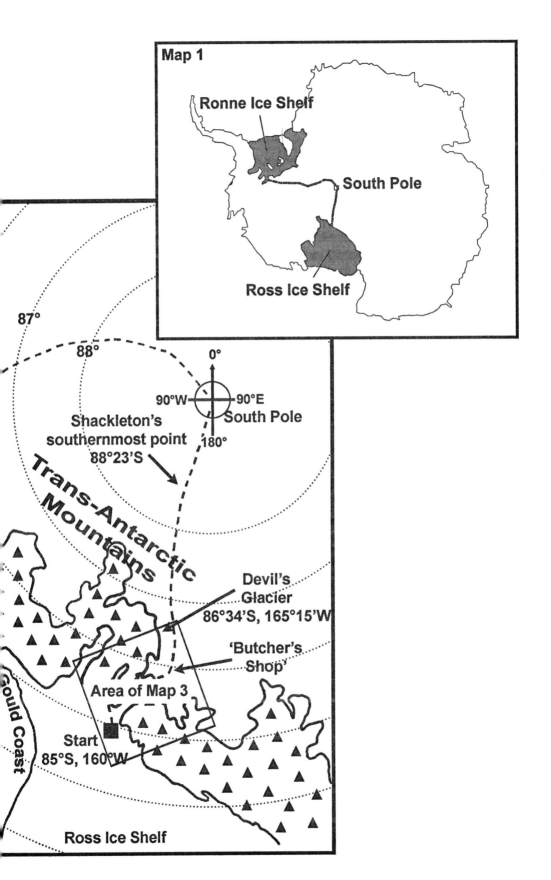

Map 1

Ronne Ice Shelf

South Pole

Ross Ice Shelf

87°

88°

0°

90°W — South Pole — 90°E

180°

Shackleton's
southernmost point
88°23'S

Trans-Antarctic
Mountains

Devil's
Glacier
86°34'S, 165°15'W

'Butcher's
Shop'

Area of Map 3

Start
85°S, 160°W

Gould Coast

Ross Ice Shelf

Introduction

Life is not about finding yourself; it is about creating yourself . . .
George Bernard Shaw

We are all familiar with the phenomenon of the mid-life crisis. We can instantly recognise its distinctive and incongruous couplings – the uplifted blonde with the down-slung grey, the slow body in the fast car, the ostentatious outfits but the thinning plumage – but we are less familiar with its quarter-life counterpart. A decade after leaving school and looking ahead to a life of repetitive drudgery like a goldfish in an aquarium, those hitting their late twenties or early thirties can often also face their own, quieter, crisis of direction. While the mid-life crisis is essentially Epicurean – characterised by indulgence – the quarter-life crisis is more Stoic. Rather than wanting to be in society, it wants to be outside it. It wants to get its kicks from something of substance – rather than from substances. It aspires to reinvention rather than reliving.

After my first five years of professional life, I felt a little empty – as if nothing in the current circle of my existence had the capacity to truly stir me. Admittedly, to feel restless after such a comparatively short period of working life sounds somewhat pathetic – despite the fact that for most juniors such a period of apprenticeship inevitably involves repetitive and uninspiring tasks with little responsibility – but it is precisely this brevity, the feeling that you have only dipped your toe into 'real' life but have found it unbearable, which leads to the quarter-life crisis. It is worst for those who have excelled at school and university and who expect and have got used to standing out, or have been funnelled by that very success into professional careers that are the most unromantic and laborious. Your future spreads out before you and can seem so interminable, so dull, so filled with routine tasks – each successive day the same as the next, the career ladder so hierarchical, and promotion won by time-serving, conservatism and petty politics. It is the world of precedent – you learn by copying what those have done before you, all risks nullified. The formula of each year punctuated only by the odd holiday spent going to the same overcrowded and rapidly melting ski-slopes.

The crisis doesn't just have to be professional. Maybe marriage and parenthood are not as ideal as you had imagined them. Perhaps the reality of a long monogamous relationship seems like a more daunting challenge than it did at the first cupidity of love. Some might feel that they've rushed into a career after school or university mainly to satisfy the wishes of their parents or their bank manager, without ever having given careful thought to what they might have been more suited to and are now, for the first time, seriously contemplating how they want to live their life. They ask themselves how they will attain the fulfilment that they dreamed of when they were younger but were too green to reach for. Do they dare to give it all up and strive for something else? If so – what? How can they be fulfilled and rewarded? Life stretches out ahead – how should it be lived? The world suddenly seems a bigger and harder place than it did from the back seat of the family car. It did for me. I felt dissatisfied and a little empty.

I know now that at the same time as I was experiencing this restlessness – this existential dizziness, if you like – in fact society itself was creating a perfect storm, of which we now all have a steadier view. For this was the world of consumerism and excess before the ensuing financial Gomorrah of the credit crunch. I didn't understand it all fully but, like so many of us, my feelings were partly personal and partly an intuitive reaction to the insistent tug of the encroaching whirlwind. Like ants, we have an infinite capacity to create pointless occupations for ourselves but now this was as extreme as it can have ever been: a world of endless cycles; circles within circles; forms to fill in; committees to compromise; consumer fripperies to manufacture–sell–break–discard–replace; businesses to buy–build–strip–hold–sell – all rotating and counter-rotating within synthetic markets that play pass the parcel with products that don't exist, so that we can lay bets on when the music will stop. And all this activity, this reaching and over-reaching, fans a powerful vortex that spins in an endless gyre, served by myopic hierarchies that face perpetually inward.

I wanted to break away, to endeavour to have my actions match my ideals, to feel a sense of self-worth, even a taste of genuine euphoria. It seemed to me that embracing something of my own choosing whole heartedly and with inspiration would be the only real cure for the restlessness I was experiencing and so I sought a big challenge, something that I thought other people might relate to – partly so that I could feel that what I had done was an achievement, not just inside my head but objectively – because a great undertaking that is not recognised as such externally can also be more easily diminished by yourself.

So, with no prior experience at all and no good reason why anyone would back me, I decided to plan a ski traverse of Antarctica – the coldest, windiest and highest continent on earth. Maybe I hoped to find some nirvana, perhaps I had watched too many movies or maybe I had just gone plain mad, destined to replace one emptiness, one set of endless winds for another. It soon dawned on me that the identity I was experimenting with wasn't a perfect fit and that some very uncomfortable consequences were going to follow when the grim reality of my dream turned out to be a little more than I could handle.

And then Annabel fell pregnant and the mad lunge for the open air didn't seem so sensible after all.

Now, two years after that initial bolt for freedom, I was lying not far from the very remotest point on the planet, off the map, enveloped in whiteness. I couldn't help but consider the radical turn my life had taken. No one can ever tell me now that you can forecast how things will pan out.

I was dimly aware of a thin stream of water trickling across my lips as an ice-cube that was stuck to my nose started to melt and trickle down my beard. I could barely keep my eyes open but I couldn't afford to sleep. The tent canvas creaked, strung taut against the wind. David kept nodding asleep, nearly dropping his rice into his lap. I had to kick him awake to avoid him making a mess in the tent. I wondered what he was dreaming about. Perhaps that he had nearly died yesterday? In this desolate waste land, he probably felt as if he already had. Patrick stared straight ahead, expressionless. His enthusiasm had burned out over the last 30 hours of constant endeavour. Paul, the last of my companions, stirred the pot with an automatic hand. He must have been thinking of his own family waiting for him on the sea ice only a short distance in front of us. He, of all of us, must have understood why I was in such a hurry – after all, I had miles to go and a promise to keep.

CHAPTER 1

Beginnings

I meant to save you from pipe dreams. I know now from my experience, they're the things that really poison and ruin a guy's life and keep him finding any peace . . . Just the old dope of honesty is the best policy – honesty with yourself, I mean. Just stop lying about yourself and kidding yourself about tomorrows.

Eugene O'Neill, The Iceman Cometh

By that morning I had already made my first mistake. Having shaved for the last time, I turned to the pile of clean, shop-folded clothes on my bed. I decided to wear them all in order to save on luggage weight. I picked up the first item: nylon-fronted underpants, windproof at the front, breathable at the back – the perfectly designed garment (except none too flattering). I pulled them on, grateful that they wouldn't be revealed again for the next few months. Long johns and a clinging thermal top followed. Soon they'd take on the tang of adventure and I'd feel like an extra from a low-budget Western. The rest of the layers were piled on top.

The taxi driver and the airport staff must have been in on the joke. I could have sworn that they turned the heating up as they saw me coming. By the time I hit the tarmac to make the short walk to the Russian cargo plane I was sweating profusely. I walked with all the elegance of an astronaut. My brand new, lurid yellow boots creaked and squeaked with each step. It was difficult to bend my arms as my fleece was so covered in logos that it had become as inflexible as a suit of armour. One particularly large corporate logo had been placed with irritating precision on the point of my elbow. The picture wasn't exactly the one I had been hoping to present.

I was about to board the *Valdivia Belle* – its name signed jauntily on the fuselage next to a cartoon, incongruously, of a blonde, mid-western, all-American girl with an impossible smile and tantalisingly easy virtue. Its wings curved elegantly down from the top of the fuselage, which made it look as if it was permanently swooping downwards like a bird of prey. This menacing appearance was enhanced by a hooked nose. Slung under the eyes of the cockpit windows was a small glass viewing chamber that looked like a beak.

The plane had been chartered out of Kazakhstan to fly to Antarctica. Inside was barrel upon barrel of jet fuel. The fact that I was shocked showed that I wasn't entirely accustomed to the risk profile that my new life had assumed. I was about to get onto a roller coaster carrying a cargo of unstable high explosives. On top of them were all manner of expedition bags, rations, skis, sleds and other equipment.

The heads of the other passengers turned as my face appeared at the top of the ladder like a meercat's. I scrambled in through the cabin door in all my regalia. Everyone turned to look at me. In the few seconds that it took me to appraise the group, I noticed an abundance of facial hair, old tattered woollen jerseys, jeans and jutting chins. No logos, no starched fleeces and no yellow boots. All I needed was a hosepipe and a helmet.

'Hey, the firemen have arrived,' someone quipped.

'He could put it out by sweating on it.'

'That's not a person, it's an advert.'

Thrusting back my shoulders and trying to maintain equanimity, I clambered past them.

'Excuse me, sorry, was that your foot? Oh sorry.'

The gear was covered in cargo netting and took up the entire length of the fuselage. There were no bulkheads. There were no orange curtains. There were no plastic overhead lockers. There were not even any seats. There were only three portholes on each side for windows. We had to sit on wooden benches along the sides of the plane. The first mate, a sturdy Slav, wore a dirty white singlet instead of the steward's orange suit and lurid tie, his uniform finished off by a woollen hat rolled up high to his temples like an English navvy. I doubted if he would be offering me any duty free with a wink later in the flight. He didn't put anything else on for the whole trip, despite the plane getting colder as we flew south. I zipped my jacket a little higher under my chin.

It was 1 November. It dawned on me that I wouldn't see natural colour until sometime in mid-January.

We were flying to the site of a small camp that was established for three months of the year every Antarctic summer in the lee of the Patriot Hills; it is used as a base camp for climbers who wish to scale the nearby Mount Vinson, the highest peak on the continent and therefore one of the 'Seven Summits'.

The camp had not been set up yet. The group that had been chuckling at my appearance was made up of seasoned Antarctic regulars being sent out to staff the base. My eyes were drawn to one of them in particular – Boris. He was a bald Chilean with huge hands and a monstrous bushy beard. I stroked my whiskerless cheeks and felt, next to him, like a soft-palmed little whelp. As the plane rocked in the turbulence, his beard flapped up and down like a platypus' bill.

The rest of my team – Patrick, Paul and David – sat in a row talking excitedly. David had been given a children's book at the airport by his brother for a joke – *Oh, The Places You'll Go* by Dr Seuss. He passed it down the line. Somehow its ingenious rhyming was even more exciting than the most stirring literature:

> Congratulations!
> Today is your day.
> You're off to Great Places!
> You're off and away!

It was jaunty and fun but it also went on to remind us that we would have some dark times. I wondered what they would be. What would be in store for us? Would something awful and unforeseen happen? Would one of us die? Would this be one of the epic tragedies of polar history? Or the opposite: too easy – a short walk? It was all unknown, unscripted, like that limitless white landscape ahead of us, an empty page – a writer's nightmare.

The flying time was about five hours, heading almost due south after taking on extra fuel at Ushuaia in Argentina, the most southerly town in the world. It made me realise just how far off the traditional map we were going. In fact, most traditional maps of the world don't even bother including Antarctica. Even if Antarctica *is* marked, it is splayed inelegantly like a spatchcocked chicken along the bottom border of the map in a form that bears no relation to its real shape.

Ancient maps used to mark the borders of the known with furling banners inscribed 'Here be Dragons!' or with drawings of mythical Siamese monsters, half lion, half snake. Beyond these little cartoons the earth was reputed to have tumbled off flat edges in tumultuous waterfalls and the real vaporised into legend and myth.

This situation hadn't changed for me. Antarctica might have been discovered in the interim but it hadn't been discovered by *this* man. As far as I was concerned, it was the land of legend – in fact the only things I really knew about it were the semi-distorted myths of the great explorers. Instead of Hercules, Scott. For Jason and the Argonauts, read Shackleton and the *Nimrod*.

Although I am the antithesis of these heroes, in many ways the story of the wanderer – the person who leaves his home and family to roam in unknown lands in order to prove himself – is the archetype of myth and legend. This blueprint also contains a Darwinian flavour. The young boy leaves to go on Walkabout to come back a man. Having demonstrated his 'fitness', he finds a wife, settles down and has children. His belly slowly expands, the strength in his legs diminishes and the adventure in him is slowly crushed by the weight of responsibility.

I saw this Walkabout as my great test. I was an unripe romantic who had never done anything more extreme than risk being crushed on the Tube or drinking hot wine in the Alps, and who now, untried and unthinking, was on his way to Antarctica to tilt at windmills. As I flew inside this fiery phoenix to the land of ice and snow, it seemed that every nursery rhyme and story I had ever read and every concept of heroism and adventure that had left their mark on an impressionable mind were now being rewritten for me alone.

Antarctica is a mythical place. It is in the thrall of ice, slumbering cryogenically for a future era. Under all that frozen water could be lost civilisations, fossils of ancient creatures, evidence of a lost tropical world. Even though Antarctica has been covered in ice since way before the era of modern man, Oronteus Finaeus drew a map in 1531 based upon even more ancient maps. His map delineates Antarctica's real shape *beneath the ice* with uncanny accuracy.[1] How could he ever have known that? How could anyone of that or previous eras even have known that Antarctica was there? Although some outlying icebergs were discovered by Captain Cook, the actual existence of the continent was not definitely known until first seen by James Clark Ross in 1841. The shape of the underlying land itself, however, wasn't confirmed until satellites took their first sonar readings from space in the 1960s. It is a land that holds compelling mysteries.

As the air in the cabin slowly got colder, people started to change out of their more comfortable clothes into cold-weather kit. I walked stiffly up the plane towards the cockpit, noticing the plane's exposed fuse wires, reinforced steel girders and metal cargo hooks. It looked like something out of a butcher's freezer. It, unlike me, was stripped and ready for action. I crouched down next to the Russian navigator and watched the sea slowly metamorphose into a soup of floating ice-cubes – some as big as small islands – until it died in ice and everything became white.

From so far above, the pristine blanket of snow seemed benign and calm, exuding an ineffable loveliness like a layer of cloud, its jagged folds lost in perspective. Part sea, part land, part sky, all the elements fused into a viscous whiteness, holding no life, no men, no lights, no cities, no petty struggles. Just an illusion of gentleness, patient but implacable; nothing was tiny, everything was large. It was a veil, a hinterland – representing for me the border between hope and fear, the known and the unknown, the physical and the metaphysical.

As we started to descend for landing, I became progressively more nervous. I was about to hurtle down an ice-chute in a 300-ton luge. There are no runways in Antarctica, there are only a few places that an airplane of this size can land and that is on natural blue ice. Where we were headed, tumultuous winds funnelled through a

---

1 Dr Charles Hapgood, *Maps of the Ancient Sea Kings: Evidence of Advanced Civilization in the Ice Age*, quoted in Graham Hancock, *Fingerprints of the Gods*.

mountain pass had blown away all surface drift snow and packed down what was left into a solid, glittering strip. To land, it had to be unusually calm otherwise the aggressive cross winds would destabilise the plane's massive tail fin. The Kazak crew had never been to Antarctica before. This would be their first attempt. I started to tie up my bootlaces just in case I had to move fast. We circled slowly over the shining path only tens of feet above it as the crew tried to survey its contours, before suddenly swooping up and away because something wasn't quite right.

The cabin grew quiet. All of us, even the camp veterans, looked nervous. Only the first mate exuded calm. He sat on his stool, still in his vest, like an imperturbable Buddha.

The idea was to touch down onto the ice and then use alternate reverse thrust to steady the craft since breaking would only induce an uneven skid. The main challenge was to keep the plane straight and not to slew around into the flanking mountains.

The landing was perfect. Better and smoother than a runway. An involuntary cheer went up and the Kazaks took out bottles of gin to celebrate, straight from the neck. I guess it would normally have been vodka but here, in a land that hung like a limpet to the underside of the globe, everything is thrown on its head. The whole back of the plane lowered hydraulically, like the mouth of a giant whale and, Jonah-like, I was disgorged from its belly.

I walked down the ramp out into the bright sunshine, taking care not to slip on the sheet ice. Breaking a bone now would be the very epitome of humiliation. All I could see was whiteness. It was like a bad dream of heaven. I half expected a man with a long beard jangling some keys to be ticking me off a list.

Behind me, the ice was thronged by mountains. The sky was absolutely clear. As it's impossible to land in extreme conditions, every introduction to Antarctica is perfect. The cold hit my face; I drew up my fur hood for protection. It was fresh but not aggressive. It was as if I had opened the door of an industrial freezer, a very beautiful one, cranked down the temperature a little more and then shut myself in for the English winter – I wouldn't be going back inside for nearly three months and, with luck, not until I had finished what I had set out to do: a crossing of the continent of Antarctica.

Very unusually, with no weather delays, we'd arrived exactly on schedule. After putting up our base camp tent, which would stay there until we left Antarctica, it was time to sleep. The clouds had come in and the wind had started to blow more strongly. The sun revolved in a low arc over the mountains, never dipping below the horizon and, despite the clouds starting to fill up the sky, it stayed light.

I tried to work out what I should wear in my sleeping bag. I opted for everything. Suddenly I didn't care what my clothes looked like provided they were warm. It was the first of many of my 'civilised' concerns to become refreshingly redundant out here. Our sleeping bags were rated to -18°C. The temperature in the tent was the same. We hadn't wanted to take heavier bags with us, as we'd have to drag the extra weight. I laid my down jacket over my chest for extra warmth.

The wind flapped the tent violently and noisily. It felt like it was going to lift off. Small particles of frozen breath fell onto my face. Where my sleeping bag touched the flysheet it had frozen and where I had drawn the down hood tightly around my face the nylon surface was crusty with frost. Normally, at home – warm – I slept splayed out on my stomach, now I'd have to make like a mummy for the foreseeable future. Shivering slightly, kept awake by Antarctica's night sun, I replayed the reel of the last few years, before I walked off the map.

CHAPTER 2 | Flaubert's Parrot

My life, which I dream will be so beautiful, so poetic, so vast, so filled with love, will turn out to be like everyone else's — monotonous, sensible, stupid. I'll attend law school, be admitted to the bar, and end up as a respectable district attorney in a small provincial town, such as Yvetot or Dieppe . . . Poor madman, who dreamt of glory, love, laurels, journeys, the Orient.[1]

Gustave Flaubert, Letter to Chevalier

Why the hell was I here? I wasn't an explorer, nor would I ever be one. I was an idealist with a dawning notion that I had just bitten off more than I could chew.

For a few years I had bleated in general terms about being bored with my routine and the lack of excitement in my prospects as a lawyer in a large firm.

'Hey Al, just wondering if you had any capacity? We've got a new instruction.'

'Er, I'm keeping pretty busy with the X flotation, the Y takeover and the Z sale, actually,' I'd mutter as the partner applied some wax to his ears.

'Oh that's great, you can help. Before I brief you fully, I've told the client that you'll be on the next train to Solihull. There are some files in a dank basement I'd like you to review until your skin cries out for vitamin A.'

---

1 Quoted in Alain de Botton, *The Art of Travel*.

I had shaken my fist ineffectually while the pristine idea of Antarctica bubbled and percolated away behind the greasy concerns of the everyday. It's hard to acknowledge your dissatisfaction and then still respect yourself if you don't address it. But I didn't address it straight away: I didn't quite yet have the resolve to let go of the reassuring bannister that I had had to hand all my life.

Having travelled widely, I was also starting to become more cynical about the places I visited. What were the mountains like without pylons? Was the translation of the menu the only compromise? What was the town like before the coaches and trinket shop? How did one travel to Macchu Picchu before the train? Tourism isn't just geographical anymore, it's a tourism of ideas. Now, the guidebooks dictate what you *think* of a place as much as how to get there. I felt that authenticity was in short supply. In this celebrity world, people seemed to undertake adventure more for self-aggrandisement than real romance. I wanted to spend time in a place, *be* there and not just see it through a lens that had been stained by fingerprints. For me, Antarctica lay in a stark contrast to conventional tourism; it possessed mystery and wonder. Behind my choice of Antarctica lay some unreasoned conviction that some corners of the world might possess more magic than others.

A month later, still desiccating in the airless basement, something truly awful occurred, which also contributed to my swerving into another lane of life: a close and greatly talented friend, Alex, was killed on holiday in Menorca aged just 28.

It was an utterly senseless tragedy. I don't know all the details and don't want to, only the bare bones. He was walking along the side of the road with his sister when a car, driven out of control, ploughed into him, missing his sister by millimetres but hoisting Alex up over a high wall like a rag doll and onto some rocky ground beyond. He was in a coma for a week before he died.

It wasn't as if Alex was my best friend. He was just a good friend. He had other, better, friends but I knew him well and liked him enormously. He was one of those people that everyone liked and was probably the most effortlessly gifted person in our year at university: clever, charming and a very accomplished sportsman. He was funny, humble and had the ability to take the piss out of you in a way that made you laugh hard at yourself but without any of the barbs that sometimes accompany mickey-taking. He also had the strength of character and confidence to demonstrate his feelings, compliment someone or tell you when he felt deeply about an issue.

Alex was the first person I knew well to be taken away. Being about my age, it gave me a sharp and painful reminder of my own mortality. He was the sort of person whose sudden eclipse profoundly affected everyone who knew him. It was as if a very bright light had been turned off and we all felt the darkness. Everyone experienced a strange guilt: although we had so much less to offer the world, we were still around and he was gone.

His funeral was a hugely emotional affair, as it always is when someone young and talented, with so much unlived potential, dies before his time. Despite the sadness, we gave thanks for the amazing life he had led. A letter from his aunt was read out from the pulpit by the vicar. The reverence and emotion of the ceremony lent the words a greater power. In it, she asked simply that if anyone had something they truly wanted to achieve, then they should attempt it and dedicate it to Alex's memory – then it would also become his achievement and something good of his would live on.

Then and there, listening through a cloak of tears, I resolved finally to do something that I could be proud of and dedicate it to Alex. Maybe I would have done it anyway if Alex hadn't died, maybe I wouldn't. But he died just when all the amorphous dissatisfaction with society and my life in it were at their most pressing inside of me. Now I couldn't ignore them any longer.

I told Annabel, then my girlfriend, that I was leaving my job to organise an expedition to Antarctica. By some strange alchemy, articulating an idea makes it real. Until the first words are uttered, an idea has no concrete form – other than a vague internal nagging – but once given voice, an idea takes shape and starts to have a life of its own and, like a rolled snowball, becomes difficult to stop.

This massive step wasn't really about Antarctica, though – Antarctica was only a trope, a symbol. I had embarked on a new life that was about doing what you've always wanted to do; about not giving in to the fear of failure that causes most of us to accept a growing pressure in life – especially prevalent in the big cities

– to earn more, work harder and spend more time doing less and less, to give up the talents we have cultivated and substitute them for the spreadsheet and the annual report. I was desperate to haul myself out of my rut and put my face to the wind, to lose myself in endeavour. And in the cold, the snow and the silence of a great immensity to shrug off the restlessness I felt:

> The surface of the earth is soft and impressible by the feet of men; and so with the paths which the mind travels. How worn and dusty, then, must be the highways of the World, how deep the ruts of tradition and conformity! I do not wish to take a cabin passage, but rather to go before the mast and on the deck of the World, for there I could best see the moonlight amid the mountains. I do not wish to go below now![1]

---

1 Henry Thoreau, *Walden.*

CHAPTER 3

A New Life

How dangerous is the acquirement of knowledge and how much happier that man is who believes his native town to be the world, than he who aspires to become greater than his nature will allow.

Mary Shelley, Frankenstein

Caught in a euphoria of resolution, I left my job and took up a part-time teaching role. It soon dawned on me that taking the positive step was one thing but – like walking out of a cloistered library onto a busy road – aware of a brutal world that didn't give a toss, I wasn't sure which way to turn next. It was, frankly, inconceivable that in two years' time I'd be lying somewhere off the common map, wearing everything I possessed and with frost falling on my face.

The time that wasn't spent teaching, I had a space as empty as Antarctica to fill. When you've been used to working all the hours that God sends at someone else's behest, it is very strange suddenly to have to motivate yourself. There's no fear of being fired. There's no danger of having to experience the public shame of packing the contents of your desk into a black plastic bag. Nothing really goes awry if you bleed your time away by watching films, reading and recovering from hangovers. Retribution is far enough in the future not to cast its long shadow. You'll only be found out in a year or two – when all your vaunted goals haven't materialised. At the start, then, there wasn't much pressure to do anything.

The problem is that there is a small insistent voice inside you that accuses you of being lazy. To begin with it's weak and you ignore it.

Then it starts to become more insistent, so your strategy for evading it also evolves: you brush it off by becoming extremely busy but extremely unproductive.

I decided that the expedition would take place the following winter, two years away. I justified this by arguing that I needed to approach companies in good time so that they couldn't use the familiar excuse that they had already allocated their budget. But also, however, with the actual expedition so far away, *I* wouldn't be called to account for my time by friends and family.

Going to the gym was a good way of convincing myself that I was expending positive energy. Doing pull-ups, though, wasn't helping me get to Antarctica. It's a familiar truism: if you can't control your environment then take refuge in controlling your body. Anorexics and dysmorphics are the extreme examples but our prevailing gym culture isn't just about the modern imperative of Beauty. With so much of our future dependent on chance, fate, whimsy and the arbitrary actions of other people, many of us try to manipulate the one area that does, largely, obey us – our bodies. So, to control the chaos into which I was heading, I went to the gym.

Ironically, Scott of the Antarctic, who proved himself in the traces again and again and who drove his party on and on each day – even when the going was at its toughest – also felt that he was, by nature, an idle man. He feared that any form of comfort or the lack of compulsion could bring out that indolent side. In letters on his deathbed, he wrote to his family about the son, Peter, who would survive him: 'Above all, he must guard and you must guard him against indolence. Make him a strenuous man. I had to force myself into being strenuous, as you know – had always an inclination to be idle.'[1]

Many of us either need the framework of compulsion to be productive, or can hide our lack of productivity by fading into the general mass. Now, for me, every temptation was towards inertia. The task was so daunting it seemed hard to know where to start. There was constant refuge in procrastination. Later, on the ice, it would be different: in his *Purgatorio*, Dante describes the slothful as

1 Captain R.F. Scott, *Scott's Last Expedition: The Journals of Captain R.F. Scott.*

purging their guilt after death through endless activity – and this, I knew, was what waited for me in Antarctica.

When the idea of the expedition had first entered my mind, Annabel had introduced me to the boyfriend of one of her close friends, Patrick Woodhead, who had recently skied to the South Pole from Hercules Inlet on the edge of the continent, with one resupply, in a record 46 days. I got in touch and invited him to lunch.

At that moment, circumstance and the universe got in a huddle and started to conspire. Somewhere overhead storm clouds gathered to create the strong pulse that would vivify Frankenstein's monster. The metaphor is apt. In fact Mary Shelley's 1818 horror story actually opens with her narrator, Captain Walton, in pursuit of the Pole:

> This breeze, which has travelled from the regions towards which I am advancing, gives me a foretaste of those icy climes. Inspirited by this wind of promise, my daydreams become fervent and vivid. I try in vain to be persuaded that the pole is the seat of frost and desolation; it ever presents itself to my imagination as the region of beauty and delight. There . . . the sun is for ever visible, its broad disk just skirting the horizon, and diffusing a perpetual splendour.[1]

In the middle of desolate wastes he finds Frankenstein in pursuit of the beast he has created. Walton rescues the hapless creator, numb with cold and near to starvation, and listens to his tale. Walton is Frankenstein's perfect audience. He naturally sympathises with Frankenstein's tenacious commitment to his strange ambition – however outlandish it is – since he himself seeks the Pole for reasons that could easily be attributed to Frankenstein:

> There is something at work in my soul, which I do not understand. I am practically industrious – painstaking; a workman to execute with perseverance and labour: – but besides this, there is a love for the marvellous, a belief in the marvellous, intertwined in all my projects, which hurries me out of the common pathways of men, even to the wild sea and unvisited regions I am about to explore.

---

1 Mary Shelley, *Frankenstein: Or, The Modern Prometheus.*

Of all tales, *Frankenstein* goes much further than the issue of bringing dreams to life, which, of course, the protagonist so tragically does – it is about what follows: what happens if you can't control the appalling situation you have created.

What happens, Shelley asks, if the consequences are bigger than you are? At over eight feet tall, Frankenstein's monster most certainly was bigger. Shelley's dark book is about being deceived by your own fantasies. Frankenstein's hubris caused him to believe he could perform the impossible. He did, but his dream became his nemesis, his fate played out in the ice and the snow. It was a theme that wasn't far from my mind two years later as I lay unsleeping in my wind-rocked tent, about to set off, inadequate, across the continent of Antarctica.

Patrick, when we met for lunch, was the antithesis of Frankenstein's monster. He was 28, of medium height with unkempt, tousled brown hair, a gaunt but chiselled face and piercing blue eyes. Typically, as a trait I would come to know well, he arrived late and breathless.

'Jesus, the Tube! It's hell on earth. I'm sweating like a pig. Have you got anything in your fridge? I'm starving,' he said, rolling his eyes and grinning.

Although it was now a few weeks since he had got back from the South Pole, he was still jaded from the experience. I asked him slyly whether he'd ever consider doing anything like it again.

'Not in a million, trillion years, mate. Having said that, the one thing I really enjoyed was getting these huge kites up – now that was fun, seriously dangerous, but seriously fun.'

Patrick had experimented with using the wind to power him along on that expedition, but for the most part (all but three days of the expedition) the wind had been blowing in his face and hadn't allowed him to use it. But that experience had given him a taste for it.

I opened a big map of Antarctica out on the table for him to show me where he had gone. I started to describe my goals to him. Each time I suggested something, Patrick would offer up a more ambitious alternative.

Together, we started to construct a plan. Hacking Patrick's ideas together with mine, adding a dose of opportunism, a shake of luck and a twist of necessity, and what we were left with was undeniably a monster.

The fact is, Patrick is difficult to say no to. His casualness, as I found many times after that, can be quite deceptive. He has the boundless optimism of the very lucky or the very talented. Totally genuine, he is, however, almost the caricature of the action hero. He drives a fast bike, is utterly nonchalant about the concept of danger, has a touching (and quite inspiring) faith in the inherent goodness of the world and that shut doors are meant to be opened. If a plastic figurine were ever made of Patrick, the Buzz Lightyear button-touch phrase it would repeat would be: 'Trust me, it'll be fine.' It was a phrase I came to be a little wary of.

He makes things sound very easy. He could lure anyone to accompany him on a madcap project and was without equal at making an utterly foolhardy suggestion seem totally plausible. He had climbed unscaled peaks in Kyrgyzstan and Tibet, even been a rhino ranger in Namibia. Never has anyone been able to get friends to work for free so easily, get even the most doughty old secretaries to agree to refer him to their bosses with a coquettish little smile and then persuade the flintiest executives to part with their cash by means of a single perfectly nuanced compliment.

On one occasion, I was skiing in the Alps. Patrick was in town and we were going to celebrate New Year full-on, Patrick-style. The problem was that my hotel had been double booked and Annabel and I were being ejected. I had rung around but there was no room at the inn. I couldn't sleep on Patrick's floor as the landlord had banned me after a loud party earlier in the week. Patrick's solution? He persuaded me, credulous as I am, not only that we could build an igloo, but that that we *should*. Annabel would sleep with his girlfriend, Robyn, and even though we had no sleeping bags he assured her in characteristic fashion: 'Trust me, it'll be fine.'

At four o'clock that morning, abetted by a bottle of whisky and the sounds of the French 'Techno' still beating in our ears, we were kipping on a bed of bracken in our very own ice hotel. Shivering despite many layers, I awoke to find Patrick 'spooning' me affectionately, snoring loudly and a chill wind dusting us with snow through the open door.

'Oy, get the hell off me and mend the door, you moron.'

He awoke, slightly fuddled. 'The door? It wasn't me . . .' he said, before smiling guiltily as he saw his legs sticking out through a hole in the igloo wall.

This was the guy I was going to trust my life to.

CHAPTER 4

Altered Reality

What has brought them to the temple . . . no single answer will cover . . . escape from everyday life, with its painful crudity and hopeless dreariness, from the fetters of one's own shifting desires. A finely tempered nature longs to escape from his noisy cramped surroundings into the silence of the high mountains where the eye ranges freely through the still pure air and fondly traces out the restful contours apparently built for eternity.

Albert Einstein, 1918

That was two years ago. Now, opening half an eye to check it wasn't all imaginary, I saw my gloves suspended from the drying lines swaying above me as the wind rocked the tent. The weather stayed patchy. I wriggled out of my bag, debating whether to pee into a bottle by Dave's head or risk going outside. Gingerly unzipping the tent's inner lining I reached for my boots. About to draw them over my feet, I saw that the insides were choked with ice and thought better of it.

I knelt over my pee bottle. It was hardly the enticing sound of a kettle boiling but it was enough to rouse the giant. He slid his eye blinds on to his forehead and squinted up at me. It took him a second to register what he was looking at.

'Morning, Dave. I'm just making you a cuppa.'

Grimacing, he pulled his eye blinds back down.

David de Rothschild was our third team member. He was tall, bearded, dishevelled and good-looking. He was a good friend of Patrick's sister, Sarah; she happened to mention our plan to him only a few months before we were due to leave and it immediately aroused his interest. He didn't have any major expedition experience. In fact, on learning what he *had* done made me see exactly how he considered this enterprise: he had ridden rodeo bulls in New Zealand, promoted a nightclub called 'Wrong', swum back from Alcatraz and attempted to break the world land-speed record for towing a caravan.

David wouldn't necessarily call himself an intellectual and so he'd chuckle at the idea that I might mention him and Albert Einstein in the same breath, but there are parallels. Einstein maintained that the hardest part of scientific work, thinking up hypotheses, was to him invariably the easiest. The act of writing them down and testing them, he alleged, itself suggested more ideas. David, in the same way, comes up with an infinite number of ideas and the more he dreams up, the more those ideas themselves suggest others. He is a human whirligig of energy and constant motion.

Twenty-six years old, he owns and manages an organic farm in New Zealand, is involved with merchandising for rock bands, breeds horses, writes children's books and founded a Sydney-based local community charity art project trademarked as 'Sculpt the Future', which he plans to launch on an international scale. Those are just his big-ticket occupations. If you could buy stock in a person, you certainly would invest in him. During our expedition, he came up with screenplays, book ideas, inventions, business plans, a project to turn the South Pole into a World Heritage site and an educational scheme based on school kids learning more about the world by following his progress traversing all of the six other continents – an idea inspired by coming to Antarctica. Now he is planning to sail a boat made entirely out of plastic bottles over the Pacific to publicise oceanic pollution. Equally amazing is that he carries out a great proportion of his ideas.

David is an inspiring man and he got involved with our project at just the right time. Initially, I was slightly sceptical about someone joining the team at such a late stage. He wasn't going to contribute financially and, to my mind, only this would have compensated for him not having worked for as long as we had on the project. I was worried he'd be all talk and end up sliding into and then benefiting from something that he hadn't contributed fairly to. That fear was to be unfounded on both counts. More by good luck than good judgement, we had managed to happen upon someone who was also of irrepressible good humour, which was to prove invaluable in the tent as things got tough.

Now, waking up to our first day on the ice, we enthusiastically unpacked our kit. We weren't going to embark on the crossing for three or four days as we still needed to practise some drills and rope-work as a team and also to prepare, divide up and weigh our expedition rations.

Our domed base camp tent was so cold it was hard to stay warm. We sat like four hunched, freezing dragons. A constant plume of thick smoke poured from each of our nostrils. We ripped up the cardboard boxes that had contained our supplies in order to put a small segment under our feet. We hoped thereby, fractionally, to insulate ourselves from the snow underfoot. We all rubbed our hands, twitched our knees and stamped up and down incessantly to keep warm. It was like a Tourette's sufferers' convention.

Twitch, fidget, rub, joke, insult, laugh.

We were all eager to cut our shivering teeth on some Antarctic man-hauling, so we started to get ready for our first dose of exercise. We decided to concentrate on technique, so we left our sleds (known as 'pulks') behind. We wore light, high-performance cross-country skis. Most people nail skins (now artificial fur) to the underside in order to gain purchase on the snow. The skis glide with the grain of the hair and then grip going against it. Although we had both full skins and half-skins in reserve, we started without any, relying for grip instead on a small area of fish-scaling beneath the foot because if we could master it, the lessened resistance would be more efficient when sliding the ski forward.

Cross-country skiing is not particularly challenging on soft, flat ground. This ground, however, was pitted and undulating. The wind had blown the snow into very hard wave-like features (known as 'sastrugi'), so it was difficult to get into a smooth rhythm. The skis tended to skid away on any down slope or uneven ground. My confidence immediately took a bashing. Despite being an experienced downhill skier, this was a different skill and I had only ever done it once on a brief training outing in Norway. There the snow had been soft and the skiing easy. I landed in an ungainly heap going through one twisted patch of sastrugi. I felt uncomfortable and ill at ease. Dave, also unbalanced on the narrow skis, leaned too hard on to his ski-pole and, brittle in the extreme cold, it snapped in half. Minute one – a crucial, indispensable piece of kit broken. To an outsider, this first day must have been laughable – how on earth were these inept novices going to ski across Antarctica without seriously hurting themselves?

As we were preparing the rations, the camp manager Mike entered our tent, bringing with him his own particular brand of idiosyncrasy in the shape of an unflattering orange skullcap with a jagged yellow plume. I half expected him to play the fool and dance a merry jig. Sadly, he wasn't disposed to entertain us.

'Hello, all of you,' he said in a bluff Yorkshire accent. 'I just wanted to welcome you to Patriot Hills and to let you know that we regard this expedition as self-sufficient while you are here, so you can't expect to use any of the camp facilities.' He smiled a tight-lipped smile and walked out of our frosty tent.

'Hi, I'm David, nice to meet you,' David called to his retreating back. 'Did I imagine a funny orange-hatted dude just come in? Anyhow, we're new to the loony commune, so didn't he need to initiate us or something?'

Looking at Dave in his own tight pink hat, I thought he seemed to fit right in.

'Knobhead – he's as nutty as you are,' smiled Pat.

'A raisin short of a fruit loaf,' concurred Dave, pulling a face.

Mike was a burly and blunt Yorkshireman who had spent his life in remote and challenging places. No doubt, he had found himself locked in the sort of love affair with Antarctica in which so many who come here find themselves. Jealous and beautiful, the ice's siren song tends to entrap its visitors.

The skills honed in its unique environment are ill-suited elsewhere and so workers often return. Being paid well to work in a dysfunctional environment allows them to take the summer off, and as the winter comes around again and the money runs out they are summoned back to the ice. And so the cycle goes on. It's not just scientists and camp workers that find this – even explorers like Scott and Shackleton needed Antarctica to create the stories and adventures that they fed off back home. Mike had spent many seasons in Antarctica with the British Antarctic Survey, and Antarctic veterans tend to be an eccentric crew – adapted like a colony of penguins to the bizarre routines of their extraordinary world. You have to love being part of a little enclave with all the rituals, in-jokes and discomfort. In any typical Antarctic camp there is as much alcohol as there are few attractive females. These people become institutionalised in the same way that prison inmates often don't know how to operate in the outside world after incarceration. They lack typical social graces but don't see their own behaviour as anything abnormal. In that way, it's not unlike a late-working city executive who lives at his desk, surrounded by Yes-men, who eventually starts to believe the myth of his own importance. I realised that I was escaping the oddities of city life for another existence that was equally lop-sided.

The camp staff had managed to set up a couple of tents since we had arrived, bigger and stronger than ours, wood-lined and *heated*. While we prowled around the campsite or resecured the guy ropes, we would jealously watch them stumbling out of their room-warm, gas-heated tent making the short walk to the radio tent – which was fitted with another welcoming furnace. The temperature in there was between 30° and 40° warmer than it was in our tent. Then they erected a couple of toilet tents also with wooden floors. We were forbidden to use them, too. We'd have to go in a drifted-up little hutch that we had to clear out with a shovel. It seemed a little strange to forbid us from entering any of these sanctuaries. There were only 20-odd people (in both senses) in a corner of the world with no other humans and yet five of us were kept in the cold.

Keeping us arbitrarily at arm's length seemed another feature of the strange hierarchies and politics of a small community. It was even more unfriendly in this instance given that Paul, our guide and the fourth member of our party, had been to Patriot Hills twice before (even working for the organisation) and Patrick had also stayed there two years previously. Nevertheless, ALE (Antarctic Logistics and Expeditions), the company that ran the camp (and the only one to operate commercially for tourists in Antarctica), contrived to establish an unfriendly and exclusive environment, which contributed to a clear feeling of 'them' and 'us'.

Initially, I didn't really care about that. We weren't looking for comfy sofas and table football – even if they had had them. It was just as well to acclimatise. However, we grew increasingly resentful over the next fortnight as conditions stayed incredibly harsh; we were unable to leave as planned and we found ourselves getting depleted before we had even progressed a yard along our chosen path.

No one owns Antarctica. By virtue of the Antarctic Treaty (which, ominously, formed the basis of the Outer Space Treaty) it has been devoted to peace and science. Under the surface, though, all the Treaty nations are trying to get a grubby foothold in case the ceasefire ever collapses. Hence each Treaty nation essentially has divided up segments of the continent like 'wedges' on a Trivial Pursuit board, making a wagon wheel of territorial claims. At the hub of this wheel is the South Pole where the US has its science station. At the thick end of each wedge, each Treaty nation has its 'scientific' base. In the middle is . . . nothing.

The scientists are notoriously reluctant to fraternise with expeditions. It implies some duty of care if the adventurers get into difficulty. Therefore, unless you can twist governmental arms, the doors of the science stations are generally barred shut and there is no way of getting into Antarctica other than a fleeting visit to the outer perimeters by cruise ship. That is where ALE comes in. They have permission under the Treaty to run a temporary base for tourists, operational for three months of the year, which, of course, is where we were now.

The next day, Dave snuck quietly into the warm staff tea-tent to sniff around – probably because we had been expressly forbidden. Like a big polar bear on the prowl, he was on the hunt for any freebies – a bar of chocolate, a slice of freshly baked bread. Warming his hands by the gas stove for a second, he got too close. His Gore-Tex trousers crumpled and melted, red-hot like burning wallpaper, before he felt the heat on his cold legs.

'Shiiiiiiit!' He jumped back, startled, patting out the smoke.

They were his only pair. Now the trousers that would have to last the next two or three months in all conditions and over all terrains had a gaping hole in the side. David had to spend the rest of the day sewing a piece of spare material, which he had removed from a snow-skirt on his jacket, to his thigh. As he hadn't ever sewn before, we laughed heartily at the wrinkled, skewed patchwork.

'Real slick, ace,' we laughed.

Soon the staff were taking bets as to how long Dave would last once we were underway. Three days was the consensus. Dave bore the brunt of most of this because no one here had ever come across anyone like him. I kept my mistakes a little quieter. Dave would laugh about his to everyone. Most polar adventurers have massive egos, take themselves very seriously, overstate their accomplishments and attempt to fulfil a very hard image. David would clown about, oblivious to what was expected. He made no attempt to disguise his inexperience and no attempt to try to pretend he was other than he was.

At any opportunity he'd try to collar Mike to get him to agree to let us into their steamy tent for any time at all, or even better, a meal. He'd employ any tactic he could – he was a born blagger. One time, as he was goofing around, Mike looked at him askance and called him, light-heartedly, a fool. 'Ah!' said Dave. 'A wise man can play the fool, Mike, but a fool can't play the wise man,' hopping away, leaving him to work out the insult and the implication. David never stopped fooling around but he did, when the going got tough, show huge reserves of strength and endurance.

Anything that could be made into a joke, was. As we were weighing our rations, while I chopped the cheese, Patrick and Dave opened hundreds of sachets of energy drink powder and poured the contents into bigger plastic bags to cut down on packaging weight. Our tent looked for all purposes like some twisted drug factory hidden in a windy, inhospitable ice-field. Dave, in his irrepressible manner, made a game out of it. He competed with Pat as to who could open the most amount of sachets in one go. The loser had to snort some. Soon our eyes were streaming, we were all laughing and the air was thick with apple concentrate.

'Come on, geez, let's have another hit,' he'd say, his blocked-up nose ensuring that the 'mockney' tones he used for effect really did ape Mick Jagger.

CHAPTER 5

Constructing the Creature

Old bureaucrat, my companion here present, no man ever opened an escape route for you, and you are not to blame. You built peace for yourself by blocking up every chink of light as termites do. You rolled yourself into a ball of bourgeois security, your routines, the stifling rituals of your provincial existence, you built your humble rampart against winds, tides and stars. You have no wish to ponder great questions, you had enough trouble suppressing awareness of your human condition . . . Now the clay that formed you has dried and hardened and no man could now awaken in you the dormant musician, the poet or the astronomer who perhaps once dwelt within you.

Antoine de Saint Exupéry, Wind, Sand and Stars

This, of course, was all to come. Two years previously, climbing the very first rung of my treacherous new ladder, it hadn't seemed so inevitable. Patrick's advice had centred around harnessing the Antarctic winds. Not only would that be exciting, he urged, it was incredibly efficient too, and it was possible to go faster and further. If the kiting became a big feature then it would be legitimate to carry more weight. That extra weight would be in the form of more kites of different sizes. Then, the wind could be used almost continually, however strong or weak it was. Patrick had only taken a single-size kite on his last expedition: he had only been able to use it if the wind had blown in a fairly narrow range.

Antarctica's mysterious ice-mass had come to represent the ideal proving ground. The physical tests it offered were obvious and indisputable but it also represented a *tabula rasa* – the clean slate, the great white unknown that would reflect my strengths and weaknesses, plumb my mental depths and help to reveal the man inside – what qualities would cold, loneliness and hardship bring out? But, however keen I was to test myself, it didn't stop me from being afraid.

If I was scared of going to Antarctica, I was doubly scared to go and do something I'd never done before. You don't try and raise hundreds of thousands of pounds on the premise of kite-surfing across the world's biggest expanse of ice if your only relevant experience is having windsurfed (without spectacular results) in the Mediterranean on holiday – and even that was a short interruption from the main purpose of the holiday: sampling the entire cocktail menu and looking at girls in bikinis.

Hauling a sled into the wind was, ironically, what I wanted to do. This was the test. Yes it was slow, yes it was monotonous, yes it was tough, but that was why I wanted to do it. Man-hauling a sled in horrific conditions was the goal itself rather than the destination. Marathons, triathlons and treks all have a similar appeal.

Marathons are no longer the preserve of honed athletes; it has become a virtual rite of passage to do the London marathon. Many people try and drag themselves through a triathlon of sorts – even if under the guise of charitable endeavour. Even the odd desert marathon is now not considered *that* outlandish. There is a refreshing and welcome certainty in attrition-based goals founded on a simple equation of effort in, reward out. The harder you pull, the more you persevere, the further you get and the greater your satisfaction.

Life isn't so simple. It doesn't perfectly reward effort. If you are lucky, creative, over-reaching, of blue-blood or criminally minded, you can cut corners and success can come easier. The noisy customers in airline queues always get satisfied before the quiet ones. Physical challenges, on the other hand, represent a return to the logic of a more ordered universe. The challenges might be arbitrary and pointless but they can be held up as a Holy Grail. Aim for it, put in hard work, achieve it. My goal might have seemed mad but, paradoxically, I thought it would help me keep sane in a world that can be random and unfair.

Now Patrick was suggesting massive modifications to my dogged (and very British) enthusiasm for endurance being a way of assessing success and self-worth. He wanted to make it easier. To me this was as radical as Amundsen, Captain Scott's great rival, deciding to use dogs rather than stepping into the traces himself. Remember that the Norwegians didn't have a history of using dogs. All of Amundsen's were Canadian Eskimo dogs – from Greenland on the other side of the world from him. Using them was a conscious effort and he spent years learning how to do so to improve himself as a polar traveller. Scott had precisely the same opportunity and information but decided against it.

Here was I, a Scott, talking to Pat, a revolutionary Amundsen. My archaic, masochistic preference for man-hauling rather than kiting also sprang from another fear: fear of failure. I could quantify miles and rations. Provided I didn't break down, it was all down to me. Kiting, however, introduced more unknowns. Walking I knew I could do. I had done it all my life. I was good at walking. Kiting? No, I wasn't sure about that. The wind is a capricious agent. What if it gusted into a blizzard, picked me up and hurled me around like a plastic bag? What if it dragged me off into the Great Unknown, powerless to stop it?

In 1996, a Pole called Marek Kamiński, who was racing Sir Ranulph Fiennes across the continent, was evacuated after being knocked unconscious in an accident using a kite and being dragged two kilometres from his sled. In a polar environment, a sled is a life support machine. In it is your food, your tent and your radio. Without them you will die. Marek came to, alone, dazed and confused. Luckily the wind had not covered his tracks and he managed to follow the mazy route his mutinous kite had taken him back to his sled. He was sufficiently shocked to radio there and then to be airlifted out.

Although the Antarctic winds are strong, they are reputed to be consistent. There is nothing to stop them, no trees and no barrier – except the occasional mountain range – for miles upon miles upon miles. They are called katabatic winds – from the Greek *katabatikos* meaning 'going downhill'. Antarctica, unlike the Arctic, is a continent. The ice rests on top of the land instead of floating on the sea. In places that ice is over 4 kilometres thick. This heavy shroud is shaped like the Millenium Dome and is thickest at the centre of the continent, near the South Pole, where it is coldest. The altitude there is 9,300 feet. By contrast, the North Pole is at sea level. The freezing air at this high altitude is sucked down from this cold area of high pressure towards the sea, where the air is warmer and the pressure lower. These temperature and pressure differences cause very strong wind – the strongest in the world.

Because of how it is caused, this wind flows from the South Pole to the coast. If you factor this into planning an expedition, it becomes apparent that walking south from the coast to the Pole means you'll be walking into the teeth of the wind, and going the other way, north, it'll be at your back.

Pat had explained the theory but that still didn't mean I wanted to put it into practice. I wondered if it was a similar fear that stopped the early British explorers from using not only dogs but even skis. Shackleton, on his 1908 *Nimrod* expedition didn't take *either* with him. Scott bemoaned in his diary from the foot of the Beardmore Glacier:

> The snow around us tonight is terribly soft, one sinks to the knee at every step; it would be impossible to drag sledges on foot and very difficult for dogs. Ski are the thing, and here are my tiresome fellow countrymen too prejudiced to have prepared themselves for the event.

These men clearly weren't scared of Antarctica but they did seem reluctant to try out any new mode of transport. What if they slipped, slid and fell constantly, especially given the technical mastery required with the more primitive ski systems? What if the dogs didn't listen to the increasingly strained cries of 'mush' or whatever is the equivalent of 'abracadabra' in the doggy world, and the hapless boss was dragged along on his face to the roars of his men? How would he look then?

Technical skill was also required for kiting. Clearly, sometimes the terrain and the winds would be too dangerous to kite and sometimes there would be no wind at all. Kiting was inherently unpredictable – but when it worked . . . then you could achieve many times the mileage.

In the use of skis and dogs, history had proven Scott and Shackleton wrong and Amundsen right. If anxiety had in any way inspired their judgement, I needed to be cautious of indulging the same sentiment.

'While I was out there,' Pat continued, 'the snow was incredibly hard packed. One man on another expedition walked the entire way to the Pole without even using skis, the ground's *that* hard.'

'So we can walk, rather than ski,' I offered eagerly.

'Er, not exactly, no, it's just that the snow surface is so hard on the route I skied that there may be other ways to travel out there. It was incredibly hard the year before, too. It seems it's always like that, like tarmac. We reckoned you could get a car to drive it. Imagine that!' He continued, breathlessly, 'Then you could get the manufacturer to sponsor the expedition, too! You could bring a film crew, more kit and film the whole thing. It'd be mad!'

The question of the hardness of the terrain had also been vital to Scott and Shackleton in assessing the need for skis and dogs. It was also to become absolutely vital to us. As we discovered later, in fact, the snow surface varies hugely depending on the season and the location. Wherever the wind blows strongly, the drift is shrugged off and the surface tends to be rock hard. In the glacial valleys or high on the polar plateau the snow is much softer. It can vary radically from week to week and year to year, depending on temperature, wind and snowfall. It didn't surprise me that Scott, Shackleton and Amundsen each made different assessments of their requirements.

Hearing Pat, I had to chuckle to myself. Musing over the map with me for a mere matter of moments, he'd come up with several outlandish ideas. I don't think he had even listened to what I had in mind yet. Listening to him, it was almost shameful to say, 'Um, what if I just want to man-haul from the edge of the continent to the South Pole, into the wind?'

As he pored over the chart, however, it started to dawn on me that organising this trip with someone else would be very helpful. There would be someone to divide the labour with. It would be a good way of keeping idleness at bay. With two people, you can acquire a certain momentum. Each of you unconsciously audits and responds to the other's initiatives. If that person were to be Pat then I could see opportunities. With Patrick's footage, photographs, charisma and enthusiasm we had a much better shot at persuading institutions to back us.

Over the last few weeks it had become painfully apparent that I had a number of big hurdles in my way. It had all seemed to be a riddle with no solution: I was a novice; I wanted to go to Antarctica. Anything I desired to do and was capable of doing – just as an author feels anxiety of influence – seemed to have been done by somebody else. To have tried something new and exciting (which was itself a tall order) on my own without any prior expedition experience would have been too great a risk for most sponsors. But if Patrick could front the challenge, showing credibility and a past successful expedition, then they might be interested.

I also didn't have any money. The expedition would only be backed if it could attract publicity. It would only get publicity if it were original – or one of us died horribly. Stopping abruptly at that link in the chain of logic, I started to see why Patrick might be interested in going with me . . .

I never formally asked Patrick to join the expedition but his involvement just became implicit over the ensuing weeks. I also don't think I ever actually agreed to ensure the expedition was planned to make use of the prevailing winds but I suppose it crept in there as a way of luring Patrick onto the project.

The plan, in hindsight, was wildly fantastical, a hideous, over-ambitious traverse of the continent of Antarctica (together, it now seemed, with bells, whistles and a chorus of singing and dancing elephants). We'd start on the sea ice on the rarely visited New Zealand side, in deference to my longing to go the side of Antarctica of the original legends of the golden age of Antarctic exploration: Amundsen, Shackleton and Scott. Other than them, of the then approximately 120 people that had skied from the continental edge to the South Pole, only six approached from the Ross Ice Shelf – and none of them attempted a crossing.

As dogs were banned from Antarctica in 1994, we had no option other than man-hauling. Perfect! We decided to follow in the footsteps of Roald Amundsen, as it was the least-travelled path. There would therefore be a formidable route to negotiate up from the sea ice to the plateau. It would also be into the wind. All the better!

However, once at the South Pole we'd kite north towards Hercules Inlet on the Chilean side. This half of the continent was much flatter, the slope down from the Pole was very gradual and the wind should be behind us all the way. This should mean we could kite the whole way back: Pat was therefore appeased, something for everyone. How the vehicles crept back into the project, though, is a bit more difficult to unravel.

Patrick knew a producer at an independent TV production company that did all of Land Rover's filming for their G4 Challenge – the reincarnation of the Camel Trophy. Naïvely, we thought that this could be the answer to all of our problems. Just for the sake of pitching to Land Rover we decided to add the extra, wild-eyed dimension that Patrick had first suggested: using a vehicle instead of an airplane to resupply us.

Two Land Rovers would drive from Hercules Inlet to the Pole, taking advantage of the very hard snow and gradual incline that Patrick had already experienced. If they could drive through the sand of the Sahara, they could do this.

As we were coming from the other side of the continent, we'd meet them at the South Pole and they could film our entire onward journey by kite. I imagined visions of us racing alongside the Land Rovers in the limitless white yonder, combustion versus 'katabatics', technology versus imagination, power versus finesse. Cameras mounted on the vehicles could capture every cataclysmic fall.

Optimistic and enthused, we started thinking further about this idea. On inspection, this dimension did add commercial appeal. Although it would cost a lot to get the vehicles to Antarctica, having them would mean we no longer needed an expensive resupply flight. They would provide an interesting and original angle for sponsors and the press to latch onto and would also help with communication. One of the big problems with publicity in Antarctica is that there is only marginal satellite coverage with a puny bandwidth. It normally takes hours to download images over a satellite phone. When all you have is a sled and you are pulling it all day, you don't have either the power or the time to send any images back. The Land Rovers, however, could be laden with solar panels to take advantage of the 24-hour sunlight and those inside wouldn't be distracted by either hauling or kite-surfing. We could keep our website (and any papers) up-to-date with any news and developments as they happened. It would be the first expedition to Antarctica where people could virtually be with us, experiencing the highs and lows of the expedition with almost no lag, and the first time that the rigours of a major polar expedition could be properly filmed. It was new and exciting. We'd be travelling in Antarctica in a modern way but still embracing some of the same challenges that our precursors had.

Shackleton, on his *Endurance* expedition – one of the greatest stories of heroic escape in history – had been trying to get to Antarctica in order to attempt a full traverse. He had wanted to ski to the South Pole from one side of the continent and have another team attempt the same feat from the other side. They'd meet at the Pole and then continue back together along the second team's outward route. In essence our plan echoed elements of his.

What we also found out was that Shackleton himself, preferring not to pull a heavy sled, had also brought the first car to the ice in 1908: an Arrol Johnson. He named the Beardmore Glacier after its manufacturer, who was one of his main sponsors. Hence this part of our plan had a noble provenance and so it might be possible to try and fulfil the great man's vision in more ways than one.

Three years later, Scott tried out the same idea on his *Terra Nova* expedition, bringing no less than three cars to the ice. Perhaps we should have been put off by the fact that the fated Scott had tried it. Luckily, we hadn't consulted the oracle of Amundsen yet, or we might have been: 'Today we have had a lot of loose snow . . . for us on skis it was the most magnificent going. How men [on foot] & horses are going to get through in these conditions I cannot understand, not to mention an automobile.'[1]

The inclusion of the Land Rovers was evidence that the expedition had grown organically, like human tissue, from the dream from which it had first germinated. I had never had full control over the

---

1 Roald Amundsen, *The Amundsen Photographs*.

idea and, once released, other elements had arbitrarily intertwined in its creation. I didn't think through the implications fully at this point and, in time, this part of the plan caused me considerable angst.

For Patrick, the added dimension of the vehicles had a further romantic incentive. Something as all-encompassing as an Antarctic expedition can put severe strain on a relationship. Not only is the planning phase fraught, especially towards the end, but the fact that you are away from home for so long adds to the difficulties. Double this if there is any danger involved.

Robyn, Pat's girlfriend, had found it difficult last time he was away, at risk and incommunicado. I can barely imagine what it must have been like for Ruth Mallory when George went on a climbing expedition or for Kathleen, when Scott disappeared into the unknown for over three years. Particularly when, in each case, their husbands became so obsessed with the places with which they would become synonymous that any time back in the bosom of their wives was probably spent either discussing the last trip or planning the next one. And it was, in each case, their return to Everest or Antarctica that led to their deaths. Being left at home with no information and no contact, constantly nagged with worry, is an unenviable position. I've no doubt that Ruth Mallory climbed her own mental Mount Everest and endured trials and traumas at least as great as her husband's.

Patrick announcing that he was going away again on another trip – and back to Antarctica – so soon after fraying the nerves of all his family during his previous expedition would cause further strain. So he was keen to include Robyn in the adventure as an attraction of the bigger project was that she could be part of the Land Rover team and therefore closer to him than had been the case on any of his other expeditions. As he pulled his sled from the edge of the continent he would know that Robyn would be there waiting for him at the South Pole and that would help him trudge his way forward. Robyn, being adventurous and gregarious, jumped at the opportunity.

On the other hand, I knew that Annabel wouldn't be remotely interested. She gets chilly under an arctic duvet in summer, prefers alcohol to orange juice and smoking to going to the gym. Pole dancing is about as near to the South Pole as she wanted to get. My problem was not to bore her to tears about the whole thing. She preferred me to get on with doing whatever made me happy and therefore more fun to be around. In fact, we were both very glib about it. Having had no experience of a stressful separation, we weren't particularly worried about this aspect.

When I finally presented the finished plan to her, it seemed so hair-brained and unlikely that, as an effective antidote to how seriously I was taking the whole thing, we had a good laugh about how absurd it all was. For large periods, she wasn't very optimistic of its success and didn't take it too seriously. What she was more worried about was the effect it would have on my confidence if I spent two years vainly chasing a butterfly and came away with only an empty net. She was protective and anxious for me, which was ironic as, out of all of us, she ended up experiencing the greatest challenge of all.

CHAPTER 6 | There But Still Nowhere

Solvitur ambulando – it is solved by walking.

Bruce Chatwin, The Songlines

Mike, the camp manager, came into our tent again. He didn't have a great track record as a messenger. This was no different.

There were two Twin Otter planes at Patriot Hills, one for taking climbers to Mount Vinson and the other for search and rescue. These sturdy little planes resembled kangaroos; squat with enormous skis for feet. Before we could start our expedition we needed to fly over to the other side of Antarctica. We were flying so far that we needed both of them. They would have to fly in tandem, one carrying fuel and the other taking us and our kit. We'd land halfway, refuel and then bounce on again to the Ross Ice Shelf, where we'd land on the barrier sea ice. The crew would camp with us and then return home via the pit-stop. It promised to be a logistically complex but breathtaking flight.

'Guys, I have to give you some bad news. One of the Twin Otters was damaged landing here at the start of the season. It's had to return to Chile for repairs and won't be back in action for at least two weeks.'

He paused for us to absorb the news. First the weather, now this. Two weeks was very optimistic by any reckoning.

'Does that mean you can't get us out in the field until it comes back?' asked a concerned-looking Paul.

At 49 years old, Paul Landry was a polar veteran. He had led Patrick's previous expedition to the South Pole, they had got on brilliantly and Patrick had been keen from the outset to involve him. He was the world's most experienced polar guide. He had been to the North Pole three times, the South Pole twice, had circumnavigated Nunuvut (originally Baffin Island) by dogsled and lived for more than 20 years north of the Arctic Circle. He was as tough as teak and as grisly as a gnawed bone. He had a face like a crumpled brown paper bag that had been hurriedly resmoothed, etched with character and depth. Furthermore, he was passionate about kiting. He spent months at a time either kite-surfing in the Dominican Republic or on skis at home in Nunuvut.

'No, I don't think so, at least I hope not,' replied Mike. 'We'll need to modify the plan, though. We'll have to fly in the fuel first and then come back and take you, with a hop, in one Otter.'

We all stayed silent, puffing great clouds of exhaled air. The wind jostled the tent, causing ice crystals that had formed on the ceiling to shake down like snowfall. In an ideal world we would have been heading out to the Ross Ice Shelf tomorrow or the day after – but the weather was atrocious.

As he didn't get a further response, sensing a hostile atmosphere, he ducked out of the exit flap. Paul was quick to voice the implications.

'We'll need at least two, maybe three, good weather days to get out of here. Not only that, but the weather has to be simultaneously clear in three places. It's asking a lot. Our schedule will be affected – whatever Mike says.'

'Great, more time shivering here, with fun Mike and the rest of the Mechanics,' sighed Dave. 'Party on.'

We had had incredible good fortune flying into Antarctica on time but it looked as if the luck was wearing thin. We had only brought a week's worth of extra food. At the extortionate rate we were paying for freight that was all we could afford. If the delay extended beyond a week then we'd have to break into expedition rations or beg Mike to uncover the food cache buried beneath the snow. The depot had accreted food every year going back for at least 10. If we had to eat it, we hoped we'd be starting at the top.

Crestfallen, we sat around on our kit bags, talking. Overwhelmed by the prospect of such a long wait, we decided to go out for another training ski. This time we would try hauling loads.

I held everyone up. I sweated profusely from the effort. I became convinced, like any bad workman, that my pulk was the heaviest. My thin under-layer of merino wool was able to 'wick' the moisture away from my body but my fleece, which collected it, froze solid.

Still intent on increasing the efficiency of our styles, we left the skins off the soles of our skis – an even bigger challenge with a sled. With minimal grip, continually pulled back by the load, I slipped and stumbled over the jagged sastrugi. I had to keep telling myself that Pat had perfected the technique over many hundreds of nautical miles and Paul had been born with skis on (which must have been uncomfortable for his mother) – I *should* feel a little inferior. With the heat I was generating from my inefficiency, my goggles misted up and then froze over, making it almost impossible to see anything. I felt beyond hopeless. I was a novice and I was making a novice's mistakes.

Later that evening I struggled to get warm in all my clothes. There was no way of drying the underclothes I had sweated in while skiing. If I got wet, I stayed wet until my body could slowly dry itself. It could only do that out of the cold. The sun stayed largely hidden and the tent failed to radiate. I hadn't been properly warm for days now.

The bad weather truly set in. That night we recorded the temperature *in the tent* at -24°C. The camp meteorologist told us that one cloud was covering the whole of Western Antarctica. He hadn't seen anything like it in his four years here. It was colder that day at Patriot Hills than had been recorded at this time of year in any of the last 15. The wind was picking up, too. Patriot Hills was low-lying; I shuddered to think what the high plateau would be like in these conditions. I dreaded getting there. Outside it was now around -30°C with a blustery gale bringing the wind-chill to below -50°C. My respect and awe of the continent deepened.

Going out to ski again, the total lack of contrast meant I couldn't see the troughs, bumps and hollows and peered down at the ground to try and make out the contours. We skied into the wind to train against the increased resistance and for the experience. After only 15 minutes hauling into its full force we stopped to check that our faces were properly covered up. I lifted my mask while Paul peered at me. After a second or two of intense scrutiny, he calmly took his hand out of his glove and lifted it towards my face. I wasn't sure what this meant.

'What's up?'

'You've got a frozen patch on your cheek; I'm warming it with my finger.'

Shit. The air had clearly worked its way into a chink between the flap of fleece I had sewn onto my goggles and my neck-gaiter.

'Is it bad?' I asked, a little panicked.

'Well, it's frozen, it's turning pink again now but I can't tell how bad it is until we get back in.'

Turning towards camp, the difference in effort without the wind was palpable. I could barely imagine what pulling all day into it would be like. If I had suffered frostbite in the short time that I had been practising, what on earth would happen when I was out facing into the wind all day?

Getting back to the tent, Paul concluded I had suffered mild frostbite – a little worse than frostnip, its precursor. It wasn't too serious. The initial sign of frostbite is the skin turning a waxy, cloudy white. This means that the tissue is frozen, but not yet dead. Advanced frostbite is when the flesh appears black, at which point nothing can be done to restore blood flow. My cheek would scab and heal; I just had to take care to protect that patch in future. I was clearly susceptible to the extreme cold and that started to play on my mind. My worst nightmare became lifting up my goggles after a day's skiing to reveal that I had lost my nose to an ego trip.

Taking my boots off that night I noticed that my feet had been bleeding where I had blistered them. I hadn't even noticed, such was my discomfort in just about every other respect.

What the hell was I doing here? It was a straightforward rather than existential question. I had probably read too much. The romance of an idea is very seductive. Saying you're bored and how you long to plunge into life is one thing, actually plunging in is quite another. If the water is icy cold, you soon start to doubt your wisdom. You find that most writers who have seduced you with their ideas have, for the most part, led squalid, sedentary and impoverished lives occasionally exulted by the beauty of the lofty sentiments they scribble down, but that they have rarely lived the truth of it.

Returning to the frosted tent, there was hardly any difference in temperature from the outside. I wrote my journal, stamping my feet like an African dancer and licking the tip of my pen every few words to keep the pen from freezing dry. Giving up on it, I started chatting.

Dave and Pat admitted to getting numb penises when they skied. It was hard not to smile. With true (and despicable) *schadenfreude*, I felt much better. I wasn't the only one that had suffered! Both had rushed in to check their most important appendages very closely. Getting frostbite on my cheek now looked like a blessing – it could, patently, have been even more serious.

This eventuality had, understandably, been one of Annabel's principal concerns. Partly to ensure that I came back in one piece and partly as it had appealed to her sense of humour, she had cut up an old mink coat of my great-grandmother's and sewed four soft, furry willy-warmers (not all for me) to thrust down our trousers for just such an occasion.

I had brought along a few treats such as these to hide in my sled and to produce at moments of low morale during the expedition to pep everyone up. I was saving these crucial bits of kit until we had scaled the Trans-Antarctic Mountains and hit the high polar plateau, where we would encounter serious cold for the first time, but this now seemed as good a time as any. Pat and Dave would be more than a little pissed off if they had lost chunks of their manhood to frostbite when I had been carrying the perfect prophylactic all along.

It was, however, a little unsettling to see my teammates with excited expressions, a hand down their trousers, eulogising Annabel. Pat immediately sewed his willy-warmer into his long johns. As a statement of hygienic intent this was truly disconcerting: it meant he wasn't going to take those off for the rest of the expedition.

I managed to get hold of Annabel on the satellite phone for the first time since we had arrived in Antarctica. I told her that we were going nowhere fast. Everyone was in the tent and I was reluctant to depress her, so it was difficult to tell her how daunted I was and how mad the whole project now seemed in the considerably cold light of day. Everything was so uncomfortable. I kept to pleasantries; it was such a meaningless conversation. It was just so hard to communicate all my anxiousness in front of the others, through a plastic handset.

In only five days, I felt I had already seen so many different facets of Antarctica. It seemed a protean landscape, changing its expression dramatically with every shift in the weather and the light. One day it was benign and forgiving, its expansive skies would look so bright and alluring that you'd be forgiven for thinking their span took in the vault of heaven. The very next day, the mist could descend claustrophobically around you, so that your world was no bigger than the air inside your goggles or whatever was inside your own head. The whole of Antarctica could just retreat inside you.

In earlier times, any places on the globe that were unexplored were usually just left white. It was to the blank spaces, the white paper, that explorers – like writers – were drawn. They hankered to scribble over that whiteness, to make the unknown known. Antarctica is the very blankest continent on earth but not just physically – it's an emotional white hole, too: it sucks the whole palette of feelings out of you. Over the next few months I was to experience every emotion. It's the place where you discover yourself more than you do any geography. After all, 'Is not our own interior white on the chart?'[1]

Antarctica oscillated violently between rough and smooth. Training, living and waiting in such uncongenial conditions was showing me that I needed to be stoical and patient. I had to keep my head down and my spirit up. Perhaps soon I would be able to see again while skiing, feel my way around the contours instead of stumbling over them and enjoy the force of the sun on my uncovered face.

On day 10, the weather finally cleared for an instant and we received the good news that our fuel cache had been successfully delivered. We were on the verge – all we needed was another respite, just one short hiatus – and we'd be underway. We looked to the skies and prayed to the gods.

---

1 Henry Thoreau, *Walden*.

CHAPTER 7
Family Matters

And immediately I could imagine myself with him gone, gripped by dizzy fear, hurled into the most horrible blackness, into death. I made him promise me he wouldn't leave me. He made that lover's promise twenty times over. It was about as serious as me saying to him 'I understand you'.

Arthur Rimbaud, A Season in Hell

Annabel and I married seven months before I left for Antarctica. At the wedding my father-in-law, Ian – in all probability worried that his daughter was marrying an incorrigible waster – approached Patrick and asked him, in between draughts of chilled wine, what, frankly, were the chances of us pulling off the expedition? About as likely as either of them leaving the party sober, Pat replied, reaching for his glass. Pat didn't tell me what Ian's reaction was but I'm sure he looked around apprehensively at the expensive marquee, while any dreams he had of his daughter marrying well combusted, and reached with a shaky hand for something a little stronger.

Sir Bob Geldof had, apparently, put both the original Band Aid and the Live 8 concerts together by ringing up each celebrity rock star and persuading them to perform for free on the basis that he had already got such-and-such a luminary to commit to the project. It's the domino effect. Businesses, like people, are lemmings for a good idea. If you can get enough swine to jump over a cliff, the rest will follow. We decided to adopt the same tactic. It couldn't be too cynical. There needed to be something to base it on but any time we had an expression of strong interest the relevant corporation would join our suite of sponsors and enter the frame in ensuing conversations with others.

It was slow and unrewarding work and the outlook was murky. Pat disappeared climbing for a month and left me chasing sponsors. After a bender of a weekend, I got a call from Annabel.

'Ali?'

'Yeah?' I could hear her voice quavering slightly. I thought she might still be tussling with the death throes of her hangover. 'What is it, sweetheart? Are you OK?'

'Are you sitting down?'

'Yes.'

My heart started to thump.

'I think I'm . . . well . . . I'm pregnant.'

Pause.

I scraped my chair back from my desk in the staff-room and went running out so I could whoop in the corridor without everyone hearing me.

It was only later, when the initial excitement, surprise and jitters had worn off, that we calculated forward to work out when this small little seedling would be due – sometime in mid-January.

Oh Christ. If the expedition went ahead as planned . . .

The traverse was due to take place during the Antarctic summer when the continent was at its least hostile and the sun shone permanently. The earliest date we could get onto the ice was the start of November but the unpredictable weather of the Antarctic spring meant it was almost impossible to say with any certainty when we would get underway.

Our flight out of Antarctica, back home, had to take place before the winter season got too advanced. It could be no later than 18 January. Our baby's due date was 15 January. Calculating the different permutations was like trying to work out which football results have to go which way, with what scores, on the final day of the season to prevent your team's relegation.

If the baby was a week late, I should, no matter what, get back in time. If I left Antarctica on the 18th, at best it'd take me four days to get home. But if the baby was early or on time, then it would all depend on how the expedition went. Given the kiting element, good wind could mean incredible progress, but an injury or calm weather or a significant delay at the start, the opposite. There was almost no margin for error.

Neither of us knew what to do. With Patrick away, I couldn't consult with him. Perhaps, with this new eventuality I should just leave the ailing expedition to peter out?

We would need energy and determination to turn our fortunes around but everything was sapping my desire. If I pressed on and succeeded in animating my Frankenstein could I, should I, leave Annabel alone? Was it right or fair to undertake a frivolous adventure out of a schoolboy's fantasy comic while real life demanded I get my priorities in order?

I had just committed to the most important relationship of my life. By doing that, I had made the most serious and meaningful decision I would ever make. Putting an Antarctic expedition ahead of the legitimate concerns of my wife and future family was hardly in the spirit of those promises. Annabel needed my help to tackle the unknown that lay ahead.

It is easy to belittle the momentousness of pregnancy because so many people experience it. It is said that a baby is born into our world every three seconds. That should make it one of the tritest occurrences possible, one of the most dangerously common things someone can do. But, instead, of all the incredible things in life, the initiation of it is the most remarkable. For many people, having a baby is *the* most significant moment of their life. For them, if not for the world, it is an epoch-making event. And nothing will ever be the same again. Its commonness doesn't make it routine either. Unlike all other animals, humans can't give birth easily unassisted – this could be one of the most compelling reasons why we are so socialised as a species: we depend upon our community from the outset. Maybe our mate is supposed to be present to help us?

Walking on two feet has caused the structure of the pelvis to change and makes the passage into this world the most dangerous journey any of us will ever attempt. Having another being grow and develop inside her, being afraid that the development wouldn't go smoothly, watching her body contort and change and then confronting the awful uncertainty of the pregnancy's conclusion would be, for Annabel, an emotionally wrenching roller coaster. It would be even worse without any support. If I wasn't there, would she resent me? Would the fact that I missed the birth be brought up whenever any problem occurred in our marriage? She might tell me that I hadn't cared enough to be there, that she came second after my own selfish agenda. Perhaps the baby itself, in future years, might blame a problematic relationship with me on the fact that I hadn't, against the prevailing convention of our generation, decided that he or she was worth meeting face to face? Or perhaps I'd never come back to meet him or her at all.

On the other hand, I had been planning this expedition for a year and a half and felt as if I had diverted the course of my future for it. I had been muttering about undertaking a life-affirming challenge since I had met Annabel. She had supported me in my decision to take it on. If I had to drop the project now, the emotional effort would have been for nothing.

Jacking it in would be a waste of time and energy in a much more comprehensive way than failing to raise the funding. At least in that circumstance I could have comforted myself knowing I had given everything and could have no regrets in respect of my resolve. I could have consoled myself with the fact that it was better to have tried and failed than never to have tried at all. Now I would taunt myself with might-have-beens and if-onlys.

Just as I was worried that Annabel would blame me if I left her unsupported, she was also anxious that if she insisted I stayed then I would forever accuse her of neutering me or that I might always identify our child with the implosion of my dreams.

Much more than marriage, having a baby requires you to come to terms with responsibility and forces you to make compromises. Without children, it is easy to take holidays at almost the drop of a hat, go out late without any ramifications more painful than a hangover – there are no babysitters to pay for or drive home or any bottle-feeding to fill the few remaining hours. You can live in a cheaper flat, sleep in at the weekend, postpone saving money or making investments, avoid thinking about education, life assurance or any of the other manifold consequences of having a family. Without children, frivolity has little downside. Having a baby, however, means making the emotional transition from the selfishness of youth to the reliable solidity of adulthood. Our generation is also having children later, which makes this shift to parenthood after years of self-gratification even harder.

I felt that abandoning this adventure would emphasise the transition even more and leave me feeling as if my one big opportunity to prove myself had slipped through my fingers. I would soon have to start dispensing advice and be an example to a family and yet I didn't feel I really knew anything. I had little pride in the decisions I had taken. I felt that I had just been washed along the stream of life without ever having taken a positive stroke. Wouldn't I be a better father and a husband having got this out of my system, learnt about myself and had a chance to explore this experience fully?

In many ways the dilemma I faced is typical of that confronted by many modern men. We are expected to be sensitive and robust at the same time. Men are required to change nappies, push children incessantly on swings and be adept at baby talk. We need to be open with our feelings, to share decisions and have intuitive emotional intelligence. But then we are also demanded to be men in the old fashioned sense – chivalrous, strong, ambitious, protective and decisive. We are expected to fend for the family *and* hunt and gather.

Now, faced with a stark choice between two sides of a coin, whichever avenue I took, I could only ever be half the modern man. I was faced with a dilemma: I was undeniably excited at the prospect of becoming a dad but the deceptively inconsequential event of the coming together of a few cells had put all the life decisions I had made under intense scrutiny. The uncertainty about everything – not just the outcome of the expedition – made it a more stressful time than it should have been.

For the first time, Annabel must have looked seriously at my prospects – after all, I had taken the decision to explore Antarctica at an earlier time in my life, a time when the stakes weren't so high. What would happen to us now? How would I make ends meet? My decisions had ramifications beyond the confines of my own little world. It wasn't just me who was going to Antarctica now, it was all of us. Each of us would be undertaking a journey; in a very real sense, they were sharing my risk.

There was also Patrick to think about. My dropping out would have been the end of the expedition as surely as if things had been the other way around.

Chasing all of these doubts like mice around my head meant that I fell into a whirr of introspection. The expedition now had to have a greater significance than it had ever really been intended to have. It now needed to be worth leaving Annabel behind for, worth risking my life for, worth missing the birth of our baby for and worth all the financial risks involved. Under the weight of needing to be a justification, it staggered and I started to question the morality of the whole enterprise. In particular, I agonised over the ecological impact.

I had been so energised and inspired by the *idea* of Antarctica. I had considered it imperative to get Patrick on board in order to realise that dream. I had unhesitatingly agreed to alter my original plans to accommodate his more grandiose notions in order to achieve it. Now, in the cold light of day, I started to analyse those plans with more perspective and became increasingly concerned about the Land Rover aspect of the expedition.

I anguished about whether I would be responsible for introducing the blight of the 4 x 4s into a pristine landscape. I feared that their success might open up a land hitherto untouched by the plague of mass tourism. The very lure of the Poles is their inaccessibility. They have the romance of the emptiness of the desert. Wilfred Thesiger completed his journeys through the deserts of Arabia by camel and on foot. He despaired in later years about the effect of the introduction of the car: 'If anyone goes there now looking for the life I led they will not find it . . . Today the desert where I travelled is scarred with the tracks of lorries and littered with discarded junk imported from Europe and America.'[1]

I analysed the issue so many times my brain pounded. Rationally, the Land Rovers were utterly defensible. Their tracks would be blown over by snow in days, there was no wildlife to disturb and auxiliary power would be supplied by solar energy. Having any resupply driven in rather than flown in would use less than a tenth

1 Wilfred Thesiger, *Arabian Sands*.

of the fuel of a plane. Sir Edmund Hilary, the conqueror of Everest, and Sir Vivian Fuchs had used tractors to go to the Pole. Sir Ranulph Fiennes had ridden skidoos. None of them had seen any moral barrier. Was I just being too sensitive?

I had to remind myself that there would only be two vehicles in a continent bigger than the US. How could I worry about two cars when motorways the world over were clogged with them every day? The internal combustion engine has been a fact for over a century. I shouldn't take all the responsibilities for its evils on my shoulders. During the three months of the expedition, we would burn less fuel and consume fewer resources in our vehicles than if we had been using them to do the daily school run. Used responsibly, a vehicle would enable incredible footage of the continent. I was certain that even David Attenborough filmed, without moral tincture, in jungle paradises or snow-laden wildernesses with the support of boats, vehicles or helicopters. I had to keep all of this in perspective. I shouldn't forget the adventure, either. Taking the Land Rovers was a big risk: they might not get anywhere. I should consider it in the spirit of challenge and endeavour not in terms of abstract moral questions.

The problem was that I truly believe that it is only if each person holds true to his notions that significant change can be achieved. It is one of Gandhi's tenets and a credo that I have always wanted to live up to. On our own we can make no impact but if everyone takes just one little step then the result can be a giant leap. It seemed now that the very first time I was being properly tested against my own ideals I was coming up short.

However much I told myself that the Antarctic Treaty existed to control activities within the continent and that if it allowed the vehicles then there should be no issue, I still harboured reservations. These reservations were purely idealistic. To me, Antarctica was a symbol of isolated toil, of hardship and of acerbic beauty, which I wanted to remain faithful to. I didn't want to succeed at the expense of my ideals – my ideals were the very reason I was attempting this crossing. I'd be doing, not talking; living the opinions I had long held, taking life by the scruff of the neck. I'd be doing something for the hell of it and not for commercial gain and, in so doing, shaking my fist at society's obsession with advancement and materialism. Now, set against the backdrop of wider ecological doubts and Annabel's pregnancy, these ideals were becoming besmirched.

It's said that where there's muck there's brass. Most wealth has come from bullying and exploitation somewhere along the line. Melodramatically, even though I wasn't going to make any money from it, it worried me profoundly that selling the expedition on the basis of the Land Rover challenge was allowing me to fulfil an egoistic fantasy at the possible expense of the future purity of the Antarctic continent. Even more melodramatically, Annabel was about to bring life on to earth just as I was helping to destroy a part of it.

In private moments, many explorers must have considered that in entering unknown exotic regions they were bringing progress and change into corners of the world that had been unaltered for millennia. They must have worried that this 'progress' would eventually lead to disease, cultural disintegration and tribal degradation.

They must have thought that if they didn't get to the source of the Nile or cross the Empty Quarter or penetrate high mountains to find the awe-inspiring holy city of Lhasa, then someone else most assuredly would – and probably before the end of the year. In moral terms, in my own humbler way, I also faced this conundrum. Having approached so many people with the idea, I was worried that I had started a process that would now be undertaken by someone else. Most achievers aren't weighed down by over-developed consciences. They go out and act while the academics and the idealists are dithering – but then so do dictators. You can never accomplish anything if the uneven angles of every doubt must always be sanded down. To be a worldly success, it seems, you have to wear blinkers. Or maybe I just needed to redefine my estimation of success.

I never got entirely comfortable with the silencing of the insistent voice of my conscience in this matter. Logic said that what I was doing was fine, but something finer and more spiritual disagreed – after all, 'the heart has its reasons that reason will never understand.'[1]

---

1 Pascal, quoted in the French in William Boyd (1993), *The Blue Afternoon*, London: Penguin Books: 'Le coeur a ses raisons que la raison ne connaît point.'

It showed me that logic, or reason – the very cornerstone of Western thinking – is just self-serving. I am convinced that there is always room in every argument for other less empirical forms of thought, even if they are more difficult to sustain using traditional dialectic: spiritual promptings, ideals, intuition, conscience and dream.

I either had to abandon the trip or press ahead with it as we had conceived it. It was too late to modify the plan to cater for my sensibilities. Besides, Patrick was committed to the undiluted project and the only open funding avenues involved businesses from the dirty world of commerce who were more enthusiastic on the vehicle side of the equation than the ski traverse.

So, while I battled with an overwrought sensibility, a shadowy Ghandi on one shoulder and just about everyone else on the other, Annabel's pregnancy came at a delicate time in terms of my resolve and appetite for the expedition. I discussed the whole issue with her. In many ways she'd have preferred it if I had decided not to persevere – everything would have been much more certain: I could get a job, we could move out of our little garret and I'd be around for the birth. But she was incredibly supportive and understanding, sensing I would have been insufferable if I hadn't gone; she reasoned that *not* going would impact on our relationship more adversely than if I did go. It was important that it was her decision just as much as mine.

In considering whether George Mallory should attempt Everest his third, fatal time, torn between the dramatic lure of the mountains and his sense of love and duty, it was his wife Ruth who told him to go. They had just moved to Cambridge with his family and were enjoying some hard-sought stability. The dilemma must have been agonising for him. Ruth and George had a very modern marriage. They took all their important decisions together. I wanted to do the same.

As he departed, never to return, it is reported that an admirer exclaimed, 'How thrilled you must be to be going out again!' Mallory responded curtly: 'You know I am leaving my wife and young children behind me.'[1]

---

1 Peter Gillman and Leni Gillman, *The Wildest Dream: Mallory – His Life and Conflicting Passions*.

I felt this was my one opportunity. I had to give it my best shot. I thought many times about how Ellen MacArthur had said, before winning the Vendée Globe on *Kingfisher*, that the perseverance required to raise the sponsorship had been one of the biggest challenges she had faced on the entire trip. I was conscious that, in Darwinian terms, obstacles that crop up in the planning of an undertaking that require commitment, energy and the ability to improvise are crucial in order to winnow out those without the sufficient resolve and to prove emotional fitness for whatever lies ahead. I wasn't entirely sure that all the excuses I was coming up with weren't precisely that – excuses.

I remembered sitting in a lecture theatre once at school. There were 400 other pupils there. I had a question to ask but I was scared. The subject moved on. It was no longer relevant. I forced myself to ask it even though it was pointless – just to prove I could do it. I thrust up a faltering hand and everyone looked around at me. It struck me that what I was doing now wasn't entirely different. I had to prove to myself that I could carry this through. It isn't always easy to assess when your doubts are legitimate and when they are just excuses for laziness and non-performance.

Perhaps the Iceman was trying to needle his way into my mind again and urge me to give up my illusions. Eugene O'Neill wrote *The Iceman Cometh* in 1939 on the eve of World War II. It features a band of drink-sodden no-hopers who dream continually of tomorrow. Of course, they are all patently unfit to fulfil their pipe dreams and their delusional bubbles are all eventually punctured. Maybe *I* was just unfit to realise this idea.

I decided to banish negative thoughts from my mind and, with Annabel's consent, continued with the task of impersonating an Antarctic explorer. 'Fake it to make it,' a friend had muttered to me after a few drinks. I clutched on to that driftwood. I was conscious of being a bit of a fraud. I longed to go there and return so that no more questions at meetings or dinner parties would have to be met with hollow responses.

I presented on Antarctica even though I had never been there, until I almost believed that I had. Soon the importance of the expedition came to be as much about not failing, about not committing to a project that I couldn't carry through. It was no longer just about visiting Antarctica and having an adventure but about being credible for the rest of my life and not having every other suggestion laughed at as a mere drunk romantic's pipe dream. With the motivations for the trip warping with time and pressure, the Pole was for me becoming more than ever a Shangri-La – the Promised Land. Getting there was a pilgrimage and the expedition had metamorphosed into a rite of passage.

I had started naïve, single and romantic. Now I was married, and a father-to-be. These years, between 28 and 30, were experienced at the cusp of two distinct phases in life, phases that everyone will have to traverse at some point: between frivolity and responsibility, youth and manhood, adventure and reality. It is a progression that was to be evocatively symbolised by the crossing of the Antarctic continent itself. I would be separated for a time from the poles of my life by a desert of snow and silence. With a child on the way there would be the natural and unavoidable pressure on me to turn away from risk and towards stability. This might be my last and only great adventure.

This decision to re-engage with the project emotionally coincided with some other mixed news that, although very sad, did have a role in the turning fortunes of the expedition: we heard that Paul was splitting up with his wife of 20 years, the polar explorer Matty McNair.

Patrick had had Paul Landry in mind as a guide all along. Experienced polar guides are few and far between. They can be counted on one hand and half of them were too old for this expedition. Paul was the only one who had ever kited. Originally he had been unable to join us. He had been lured away by another, competing expedition, which was being undertaken by a British couple, Conrad and Hilary Dickinson. They would ski the Hercules route and kite back (the latter part of which, of course, was part of our plan). Moreover, the other members of that team consisted of Paul's wife, Matty, and Paul's two children: Eric, 20, and Sarah, 18. If successful, they would become the youngest man and youngest woman to ski unsupported to the South Pole from the edge of the continent. His children had been brought up on the ice and they even instructed kite-surfing.

To ski with them to the South Pole would have been Paul's ultimate fantasy – we couldn't match that.

Just as Patrick had chosen to involve Robyn in some way, Paul had been planning to go south with his whole family. Antarctica is the most inhospitable continent on earth. In the interior it cannot support life. It is the very antithesis of a family holiday. But for Paul's children, snow was more natural than grass. They had been running dog teams before they could run. It might be a family affair – but this was no ordinary family.

Now Paul was splitting up with Matty. It had been a very painful and difficult decision and was agonising for both of them. Paul had been keeping in touch with Patrick and had told him that he was also taking a complete break from work in order to straighten out his head and consider many aspects of his future. Naturally, when we heard the news, it was not appropriate to remind him of our plans – nor indeed was it likely he'd have been in the right frame of mind to accept, even if we had.

As the summer advanced, however, we did slowly start to return to the question of his involvement. After time for thought and reflection, he made himself available to join us, which, of course, we accepted immediately. Matty, Eric and Sarah were still going south – just without him. He would now have both the enticing prospect of spending time with his children in Antarctica – our arrival on the continent should coincide with theirs – but also the awkward one of having to leave them to travel with us. Indeed, in a freak parody of their separation, he and Matty would be walking towards each other for the entire expedition. They were even destined – as it turns out – to meet at the South Pole on the very same day, having started on the opposite sides of the continent.

With Paul back on board things were looking rosier and I started to believe again that it all might come true. Now all we needed was to find the money.

CHAPTER 8

Fly on my Wind

Having weathered my version of Hamlet's existentialist dilemma – to go or not to go? – I threw myself back into the project for a final push. With nothing concrete to show for the last year and a half I was finding it increasingly difficult to field the good-natured enquiries from friends and family about how it was all going. I started wanting to avoid seeing friends and especially old colleagues. Although proud of my choices, I felt ashamed of my results. It all seemed to be such a waste of time. There's only so much time you can spend treading water with a smile on your face.

Slowly, however, our unwieldy tanker did start to turn around and we managed to make some inroads into our funding target. Then David joined the team, adding vigour and enthusiasm like nitrous oxide to a tired engine. The ski team was now a settled, cohesive entity: Patrick, Paul, David and me. It had come about largely by chance but I was very confident that the individuals would mix well – after all, I felt that personality rather than experience was what counted most.

Paul was strong, experienced, quiet but tough. He would guide us on the ground and take the difficult decisions over evacuation, pace and performance. Patrick was the expedition leader – the public front man. This fitted with his previous Antarctic and other expedition experience, his charisma and his prominent role in putting the monster's limbs together. He's quick to see the funny side, reliable and very determined. I thought it likely he would be the strongest physically, despite Paul's accomplishments, as he was 28 compared to Paul's 49 years. I had some vague misgivings that, partly due to that strength, he might be the first to get irritated if one of the team didn't match his exacting standards.

We knew Dave the least. Although very amusing and unorthodox, he had initially kept some of his exuberance under wraps and when the team first got together he was a lot quieter. He, like me, was glad that there was another person on the team who hadn't been there and done it – and wasn't afraid to admit it. We had a good laugh imagining various scenes of inadequacy at crucial moments. He is a massive man and as strong as Atlas but I wasn't sure how he would cope mentally, fearing that a privileged upbringing might have prevented him ever having been properly tested. He lunged excitedly at this challenge that he knew so little about, which gave me misgivings that he had underestimated the gravity of what we were about to attempt.

Even though the expedition had been conceived and nurtured in partnership with Patrick, I was under no illusion that with my lack of extreme experience I would have to be content to be a 'brave' rather than a 'chief' on the ice. Like Dave, I had never been thoroughly tested and so was in the dark as to how I would cope mentally and physically. Like an ostrich, I had buried my head in the sands of organisation as a substitute for really preparing myself mentally for the crossing. Despite my misgivings, I hoped to bring a relatively patient and conciliatory nature to bear on trying to keep the team together and fostering a non-competitive and supportive environment.

With David living in Australia and Paul in Canada it was impossible for all of us to meet. As Patrick and I were both based in London we would discuss progress while training. We'd spend weekends kite-buggying on desolate Norfolk beaches and weekday evenings in Hyde Park hauling tyres around the sand tracks designed for horses. We would get strange looks, talking animatedly as we lugged those dead weights behind us. Occasionally I'd bump into one of my students who, not knowing anything of my plans, would look at me askance as if to say: 'I knew he was odd (aren't all teachers?) but didn't know he was mad as well.'

We had both been eating as much as we could to try and build up some bulk as protection against the cold and to give us a buffer that we could afford to lose, but we were having real difficulty getting the pounds to stick.

A car stopped and hooted us. A very attractive girl wound down the window and asked us where we were going. Pat nudged me, his tongue in his cheek, as if to say, 'Hey, we're looking good, I think we may have pulled, matey.'

'The South Pole,' we simplified in unison, each of us trying to respond eagerly before the other.

'Ah, I see. I had a friend who went to Antarctica. He was about 18 stone before he left. He came back looking a bit like you.' She looked down her nose with a mixture of condescension and amusement before driving off.

'She was talking to you!'

'Oh no – look at you, you runt. It was definitely you.' However, looking at ourselves afresh in our over-tight thermal training tops, pasty gaunt faces and hunched over from tyre-pulling, we had to admit that we didn't look particularly prepossessing.

Later, we encountered the unlikely spectacle of another Sisyphus hauling his load with futile perseverance in the other direction.

'Where are you off to?' he moaned between sweaty gasps, tyres bouncing behind him like tin cans behind a marriage car.

'South,' I replied laconically. 'You?'

'North.'

We nodded and passed on in silent contraflow. In a few months we'd be at other ends of the world and here we were making small talk in the park. Only in London would such a mad scene pass muster for normality. We were like the zombie-lunatics in the *Midnight Express* madhouse, who spend their days walking incessantly clockwise around a pillar for exercise. Soon, with luck, that pillar would be the axis of the earth.

Finally, with only a week to go until we had to confirm the charter arrangements to fly the kit and vehicles into Antarctica, we were given the unofficial go-ahead for title sponsorship. I vividly remember the chief executive giving the go-ahead and walking out to leave the others to the detail. Patrick and I had to continue talking in the same detached, professional way, desperate not to ruin our incredible good fortune by some goofy, over-familiar remark, such as 'I can't believe you actually took us seriously!' – just as Chandler or Joey from *Friends* would have done. We walked steadily out of the building. We looked over our shoulders nervously a few times like amateur criminals trying not to look suspicious until we were comfortably out of sight and earshot and then turned around, hugged each other and jumped up and down, up and down, whooping like semi-deranged idiots.

'Oh my God, oh my God. We're bloody well going, I can't sodding believe it!' we shouted over and over again, or something equally mature and controlled.

The following Monday, dragging tyres was a different story. We pulled with the enthusiasm of long-confined, oat-fed oxen. Suddenly training was crucial. We sweated double to make up for all those cut corners. I flexed with every car that passed, in case the same girl came past, then I could say, 'Hey, we are *actually* going. It's not an elaborate charade, not one great big act anymore.' The burden of pretending to be positive could finally end.

For the first time, I started to worry about injury. I didn't want a 'Blighty' now that we were so close. Every time I got on my motorbike, I had lurid visions of being T-boned and experienced involuntary cinematic flashes of splintered ankles or tangled limbs. I trod warily down every flight of stairs. Like Orpheus looking over his shoulder, I didn't want to wreck my chances at the very last minute.

The team all gathered for a last supper and we wished each other luck, hugging and saying glibly: 'See you at the South Pole.' I saw David's smile fade . . .

'We're going tomorrow?'

'Yes.'

'Shit – I thought it was the day after. Sod it. I've got to go home. I've still got all my ski rations to weigh and pack.'

He disappeared as quickly as water into sand, looking a little queasy.

After everyone had left his flat, Pat and I stayed up drinking a final whisky and unpacking the sponsors' kit, which we still had to distribute.

'I wonder if we really will see the Land Rovers at the Pole,' Pat remarked idly.

'I don't know. It seems too bizarre to say goodbye now and then in two months time ski towards the Pole and just see them standing there waving at us, hooting and cheering. I mean I can't even imagine myself getting there – let alone that.'

'It'd mess with your head, wouldn't it? I can't quite believe that we're going to pull it all together – out of this total chaos,' he added, gesturing to the piles of kit lying in every corner of the room.

It was past midnight now and I knew that neither Annabel nor I would be able to sleep tonight. I jumped on my motorbike and headed home. I folded into the covers with her. We lay together, holding each other for the last time. I felt the baby kick.

'You'll be careful, won't you?'

'Of course I will – I'm much more worried about you.'

'Oh, I'll be fine – we'll be fine.'

'Don't let Mum freak you out. I'm worried that you'll spend so much time helping her that you won't be able to think about yourself. Perhaps you should go and spend some time with your friends instead of her before you go to South Africa.'

My mother was extremely worried about the risks I was taking and the atmosphere at home was characterised by anxiety rather than excitement. It made it hard to see the positives that could come out of a lifetime's adventure and what might also be an affirming and rewarding separation.

Annabel started to cry softly. She snuggled closer to me.

'What really worries me is that you'll change – that when you come back you'll be tired of our life, our routine, babies, houses – you know. I'm so scared of that. Our life will seem boring. I'm afraid you won't want to be with me anymore.'

I held her tightly. She felt so warm.

'That's nonsense, sweetheart. I'll love you more than ever for allowing me to go. I doubt I'll think of anything but you when I'm gone. I think sometimes you have to let go to understand how precious it is to hold someone.'

The following day, the ski team, a rented truck, four pulks, 36 bags and four barrels of kit headed towards Heathrow. As we pulled away from expedition headquarters – Patrick's flat – a car screeched around the corner, skidded to a halt and a glamorous lady in dark glasses jumped out, shouting at us.

'STOOOOOP, for heaven's sake!'

I weighed anchor. The truck jolted to a standstill. She ran up to the window.

'Hi, um, I'm David's mother. Thank God I got to you before you left.'

We looked at each other, worried that something serious had come up.

'David wanted me to try and find him some double strength loo-roll. I've finally managed to locate it. Here it is,' she stuttered, slightly embarrassed, handing over a huge bag filled with puppy-soft toilet-roll.

We laughed hard at his expense but later we were to become, frankly, not a little jealous of his superior product.

After the frantic final preparations, the airport suddenly gave me a calmer time to reflect on what was to come. I focused on being with Annabel. Before I saw her again, I could very well become a father. Would I get back in time? Would everything go OK with her pregnancy? What if there was a problem? I couldn't bear to contemplate it.

Turning around to wave one last time, I saw her sobbing uncontrollably behind me. I passed the barrier, struggling to keep back the tears myself and yet, pathetically, I was too proud to cry openly in front of David and Pat. In a strange moment of clarity and disassociation, I became aware of the music that was playing on the airport system – it was the Red Hot Chili Peppers, 'Zephyr Song':

Fly away on my Zephyr
I feel it more than ever
And in this perfect weather
We'll find a place together
Fly on my wind . . .

I immediately thought of Alex – the Chilis were his favourite band. How poignant that they should be playing right now as I left to try to cross Antarctica in his memory, to raise money for his foundation and while I was so choked up with emotion. How strange, too, that the words should be so bizarrely relevant, hoping, as I was, to harness the Antarctic zephyrs and return as quickly as possible to Annabel and our little baby.

9 | A New Horizon

And I tell you, if you have the desire for knowledge and the power to give it physical expression, go out and explore. If you are a brave man you will do nothing: if you are fearful you may do much, for none but cowards have need to prove their bravery. Some will tell you that you are mad, and nearly all will say 'What's the use?' For we are all a nation of shopkeepers, and no shopkeeper will look at research which does not promise him financial return within a year. And so you will sledge nearly alone, but those with whom you sledge will not be shopkeepers: that is worth a good deal. If you march your winter journeys you will have your reward.

Apsley Cherry-Garrard, The Worst Journey in the World

Even though it was past midnight, I went for a solo ski. For the first time since our arrival in Antarctica, the weather had brightened and the fierce winds had stilled. There was a freshness to the cold. The clear skies were laced with a few solitary clouds that refracted the light pink and lacquered the sky over the Patriot Hills a rose-tinted gold. I wasn't pulling any loads so I didn't sweat and my goggles stayed clear.

My mind could wander and relax, unconstrained by small discomforts. The sun's rays caught on the blue ice and shone back, dappled, on every lily-shaped depression in the ice, like a Monet painting. The sun itself caught on the ice crystals in the air and conjured two sun dots on either side of the bright central orb. The beauty was mesmerising. I sometimes wonder if the soul isn't just a little piece of sun or a compressed fistful of Nature, as we humans seem to expand with such relief when we finally get out under open skies.

I thought about Annabel and how good I was going to be to her. My mind filled with all sorts of positive notions and world-changing resolutions. I couldn't believe where I was. I had well and truly left behind the Scylla and Charybdis of my neon-lit office and flickering screen. It was suddenly all worth it again. I noticed everything around me. The sastrugi were coated in a fine covering of fresh snow, which softened the landscape so that it resembled the sheeny folds of a luxurious dress in a Velasquez painting. Each snow-wave toppled over into a delicate point like the dripping end of a meringue.

We had now been stuck, principally in our tent, for the last 14 days. Apart from rare moments when the weather cleared, it had been cloudy, cold and windy.

Training, however, was only really a momentary distraction from the David de Rothschild show. David continued to amuse us day and night – particularly by winding up Paul. There was something very funny about seeing a young and inexperienced pup baiting and toying with one of the towering figures of polar travel. We couldn't quite believe anyone could be so disrespectful as to poke fun constantly and continually make very lavatorial or juvenile jokes to someone so much older and sterner. It was hilarious in the same way as anything is when you feel as if you really shouldn't be laughing – like hysterics in a church or during a telling-off from a school teacher – but it must have been wearing for Paul.

'Paul's been staying in his own tent all day, avoiding us. Little Paulie's been having a poo in his tent – dirty little Paulie, curling out a big brown one in his porch and not going to the frozen, stinky hutch-loo . . . I know, I heard him . . . Oh yes I did, hmmmm? Paulie, dirty little Paul,' David would say in baby talk, finishing off with a few fart noises and a maddening grin at the 49 year old.

It was impossible not to splutter out our coffee. Paul would just look on with a look of quiet amusement, his weathered, wise, Inuit-like face creased in a look of long sufferance.

The more we fooled around – which was most of the time – to avoid going mad in the subhuman conditions, the more that we must have appeared totally incompetent. Whenever we were not joking, we occupied ourselves keeping warm, fiddling with kit, rubbing hands, holding clothing over the cooker to try and thaw collected ice, or melting snow for coffee. The longer we spent together in one place the more rubbish we talked. With the conditions suddenly improved, we had a brief window – it was what we had been praying for: we were off to great places, off and away. Right now. At last.

The pilot talked in muffled tones over the radio. 'Get ready, guys, and strap yourselves in. We're going for it. We're going to fly across Antarctica.'

My heart beat loudly in my chest. 'Oh my God. This is it . . .' I held on to the armrests so hard my knuckles turned white.

The engine growled loudly, the plane started to shudder and moan, whirring to a high pitch as the pilot increased the engine thrust to free the frozen skis. We rocked violently back and forth until suddenly, released from the captivity of the ice, we shot forward with a burst. Airborne, we climbed in terrifying obscurity. Gusts caused the plane to rise and plunge. I had been looking forward to this flight for so long yet now I could barely make out the plane's wings. After more than an hour I still couldn't see anything. Then, delicately hovering beneath us, I saw the barest outline of the plane's shadow on the snow. Seconds later we emerged with a blinding luminosity like a new birth into clear sunshine. All of a sudden the engines seemed quieter as if the noise could now escape into infinity. All around us it was perfect pristine whiteness and a placid azure sky.

The cache had been laid on a high plateau in the middle of nowhere. The sun was low and it was very cold and windy. Landing briefly to refuel, I could feel the difference of the high altitude instantly. The ground was totally flat with firm but soft snow and barely a single bump for miles and miles. I hoped that the plateau was like this everywhere as kiting on it would be a joy. We were pleased to get back inside the cabin, though – the plateau was a desolate, featureless place. There was no mountain range or even a single feature to break up the horizon and orientate us.

We flew on low over the ice; the vista was superb. The plateau slowly gave way to rows of glorious peaks. We passed the Wisconsin

Range and then the Hays Mountains. Surely only a handful of people could ever have seen them. Another range started to grow up out of the snow until we saw it spreading deep into the distance. Mighty valleys poured down between the ridges as the weight of ice from the plateau slithered onto the sea, covering the water in a cloak of icing many hundreds of feet thick until somewhere far in the distance it calved off into the water in great chunks.

Using our map, we tried to name the huge glaciers that snaked through the mountains like a clutch of icy fingers.

'Is that the Axel Heiberg?' one of us exclaimed.

'Or that one . . .?'

'No it's there.'

Beneath us the sea ice rose and fell in enormous undulations as if the huge depressions in an ocean swell had suddenly frozen. We only appreciated their depth when we skimmed the ground, looking for a suitable place to land. The entire range disappeared from view as we flew into each trough.

We touched down on the barrier sea ice a few miles from land. The nearest peak was an unimposing little knoll with a rocky cap, which looked as if it was right next to us: Mount Betty. We jumped down from the plane, landing in luxurious soft, soft snow – comfortable to sleep on but it wouldn't be much fun to haul our sleds through. There was not a breath of wind.

The sky was cloudless on all sides. The snow had a soft, grainy texture like sand. Compared to the almost constant cold that we had suffered since arriving in Antarctica, it was nearly sea level and a balmy -6°C.

We were now on the New Zealand side. Even though we had flown through the night, it was evening there. We were all too excited to sleep. Within minutes of landing and putting up our tents we were getting ready to ski out to Mount Betty. I'm sure it was part of Paul's plan but we didn't need much persuading. Amundsen had climbed it in 1911 (coincidentally on the same day as us) in order to prospect a way through the mountains as well as to feel some solid rock beneath his feet for the first time since stopping off in Madeira in 1910. He named the peak after his nursemaid, some 20 years his senior, who scholars now suggest might have been something more than just hired help. It wasn't hard to see a Freudian argument in the knoll's comforting curves and rounded summit.

Paul declared it was only half an hour away and shot off. We trotted on after him like a row of eager little warthogs, leaving our pulks behind. We had one water bottle between us but half an hour turned into one, one into two, and so on. The horizon rose and fell so that we regularly lost the plane and even the mountain itself. The fact that Paul, despite his experience, had underestimated the distance really underlined how vast the scale was. From now on, we invariably found that sight was deceptive.

We were all hot and tired when we reached the base of the rock – we had been going non-stop, at quite a lick, for nearly three hours. Amundsen had been pulled by dogs for the hundreds of miles from the sea itself, and the excursion to Mount Betty was also the first time that he had had to run on skis.

Scrambling up the last bit of scree, we heard Paul exhale dramatically. There in front of us, perched on top of a small promontory was a small pile of rocks built by Roald Amundsen himself and still standing 94 years later – the only tangible remnant in Antarctica of his great journey. Paul sat beneath it and looked out, as Amundsen must have done before him, over a myriad of imposing peaks. It was a magical moment. The plane was only the size of a fly on this great icy sea, lost in between two giant swells, with the pilots oblivious to the fact that they would have been swamped had time itself not frozen.

Paul was a disciple of both Peary and Amundsen – and, of the two, Amundsen foremost. He had already driven dogs along Peary's route to the North Pole and now he was on Amundsen's trail. A landscape's ability to move us isn't purely dependent on its beauty. The effect of a place is enhanced when it has an historical or emotional significance. It is almost impossible to look at a battlefield or the site of a momentous meeting dispassionately. We could only begin to appreciate what this was like for Paul. We were witnessing a transcendent moment in his life: a second in which the elusive, airy quality of dream metamorphosed into something real before his eyes. He had lived nearly his whole life in the ice, driving dogs and hauling sleds. Now, finally, he was fulfilling a lifetime's fantasy by treading in his mentor's footsteps in a place where so few had ever stood before him.

From Mount Betty, Amundsen thought he spied a route through the range. He wanted to go the most direct route south and this meant skiing over the shoulder of some smaller mountains to the north. By taking this short cut he eventually dissected the Axel Heiberg Glacier some way along it, as there was a very formidable cataract of ice at the foot of the glacier. He had, without knowing it, cut off two sides of a triangle.

We, on the other hand, were going to skirt along the edge of the sea ice and join that glacier where it flowed off the continent. Then we would drag our sleds west along the glacier floor, up towards this icefall. From there we would be able to look up the northern slope to the point where Amundsen had descended from on high.

We were so hot when we arrived back five hours later that we stripped off and rolled in the snow. After a fortnight of bitter, bitter cold, bathing in the snow with nothing on except my (still very unflattering) underpants was an incredible release. Invigorated psychologically by our climb and by finally starting our journey we helped the pilots pack up their tents and load up the plane. With excitement and a touch of anxiety, we waved them off. The Twin Otter circled a few times and then headed off into the blue sky before melting away.

It was a strange feeling. We were now very much alone and I had only the vaguest idea of what we would encounter.

I clicked into my skis to set off across Antarctica.

It was a depressing revelation. I heaved and jerked at my harness several times before I could get my pulk to shift. Our trail-blazer had dogs to do his pulling for him. Tugging ineffectually at the trace with all my might made me sympathise with those poor beasts.

It was murderously hard. I've never known physical work like it. The expectant excitement that comes with any beginning departed immediately (taking with it my confidence). After the first hour and a half, it was my turn to break trail. I heaved until I thought my back might break. I cursed and swore and groaned and pulled. I tortured myself with the thought that the others were growing more and more impatient behind me at my slow place. It was plod, step, heave, plod – infinitesimally slow. My heart thundered. I genuinely wondered if my back, which was aching terribly, was going to hold out doing this for the next couple of months, all day, every day. The landscape was mesmerisingly beautiful but that was scant consolation when I spent all the time looking at my ski-tips.

If it had been windy or cold it would have been even more insufferable. In fact, we had the opposite conditions. Even in only my merino wool under-layer, with my trouser side-zips fully venting and without a hat, sweat poured off me, trickling down my nose onto my skis and causing my sunglasses to slip down with the moisture. It can't have been much different for Scott and Amundsen, who both comment in their diaries about sweating profusely in the valleys from the hard work.

In soft snow, skis are a huge advantage. Scott's party skied although they were not as proficient as the Norwegians. Birdie Bowers, however, left his skis at the top of the Beardmore Glacier when he was selected to join the original summit party as an unplanned fifth member of Scott's team. He trekked the whole way to the South Pole from there – and back – without skis, while pulling in time with four men who had them. He was unbelievably brave and strong never to have complained about the extra strain. We could only manage five hours of pulling on the first day but were reluctant to play ourselves out after the exertions of the previous night, the difficulty of the terrain and our collective blisters. We covered a paltry 4.9 nautical miles.

One of the hardest aspects of a polar trip is comparing your performance with that of your teammates. Dave, at 100 kilograms, weighed almost as much as his pulk and, mathematically, had more leverage. He also packed more weight down onto his skis, which made the skins grip more. This meant he didn't waste as much energy sliding backwards. Nothing can be more frustrating than losing purchase and slipping back on the spot as if you are on a gym treadmill, without moving the pulk at all. He made it look easy. Paul, being the most experienced, managed to ski efficiently enough not to have the same grip problem, even though he was the lightest. Pat confessed that night in the tent to feeling as if his lower back was going to come out of his backside. I couldn't have put it better.

I have never had such a gruelling, soul-destroying day. It was difficult to escape from the repetitive accusation my own mind made against itself – you spent two years of your life for *this*. You bloody idiot. While I strained in the harness, every instinct I possessed hovered above my flesh, poor carrion that it was, and criticised me – mocked my strength, mocked my decisions and with every wing beat seemed to squawk: 'Two more months, two more months!' I was the divided self, both Frankenstein and his miserable monster chasing each other forlornly across the polar wastes looking for retribution.

One moment particularly grated. It was my turn to lead for a second time. I was struggling to move my sled at all. I was worn out, the snow was very heavy and we were travelling up a slight incline. The only way I could move at all was to herringbone my skis and then jerk two or three times with my pelvis to get my sledge to budge. I couldn't slide my skis forward as the sled would stop and I would have to commence the whole sorry charade again. I struggled on, breaking trail, panting, splay-footed for nearly 10 minutes.

Eventually Paul said behind me: 'Don't bother if you have to herringbone, Al. It's not worth the effort that it's costing you. You'll burn yourself out.'

'It's OK, I'm fine, I just hit a sticky patch of snow.'

I just couldn't manage it with straight skis and half skins. I kept sliding on the spot in a parody of Michael Jackson's moonwalk without moving the sled at all. Eventually, silently, David swung out from behind my tracks and took over breaking trail. He managed. I skied behind him, still struggling to move but at least not having to plough the course. I felt abject.

Looking back at the naïve enthusiasm I had for the project, I found that much of the beauty of the dream had vanished. The reality of a hard expedition doesn't ever stack up faithfully to the enticing images you have envisioned. It's not that the images are contorted, it's just that they are precisely that – images. Each one only lasts a second. In anticipation, your mind parades a sequence of equally alluring ones before you. But on the ice you need to endure many hours before the slide projector shifts – and the transition is painfully slow.

That night we discussed some of Paul's other expeditions. I was quieter than normal. He described one in which a client just hadn't been up to the particular challenge. He had lied about his training and constantly held the team up. It made me never want to let Paul down. I wanted to prove myself to him, to show him I wasn't just another incompetent 'client'. It was the first day of the traverse and I had already experienced the worst feeling of a polar expedition: not being up to something relative to the group. I knew that the armchair critic – which was usually where I found myself – would have just muttered 'work harder, go on, dig deeper, keep up.'

It's fine to have dreams. All of us have read stories of derring-do and want to emulate the hero. Sometimes, you just have to understand that you are simply not up to it. If you can't accomplish something because you are not strong enough there is little that your own encouragement (or anyone else's) will achieve. Up to a certain level it's a case of will power and laziness but when you are operating at the very limits of your strength, when you are fitter than you have ever been in your life and you are finding it hard, after a while you realise there isn't an extra gear. It's not as if I'm a small guy either, I have done all sorts of endurance races and trained obsessively for this challenge. I needed to try to abandon pride and work within my capabilities. An expedition can only go at the pace of its weakest man. But for that man it's not a comfortable place.

All day we aimed for the mountains that stood at the entrance to the glacier valley and all day they got no closer. I had to keep my spirits up and try not to compare myself to the others. For all I knew it was just as bad for them.

The following day we put full skins on our skis. Paul had never been forced to do that in six previous polar expeditions. Again I found leading especially hard. I peered at my skis and concentrated the entire focus of my being on keeping moving. I would have preferred to go fast (that being a relative term), pant at a standstill for 20 seconds and then press on and so on. That anaerobic style isn't the most efficient method or the way that the rest of the team was operating. It would lead to inevitable breakdown. A body just cannot handle days and days of repetitive sprinting. The front man had to act as the metronome. If he concentrated on direction and steady progress, then the others could afford to let their thoughts evaporate. I found the slow plod pure tedium. It was almost as if each stride was a fresh start, requiring me to jerk the sled out of a rooted inertia.

I noticed that even Paul slowed down that afternoon, not always keeping up with either Pat or Dave (who outstripped all of us). I took a pathetic pride (it was something paltry to clutch onto) in the fact that I was the only one not to have stopped once for his entire 45-minute lead. I felt that I had used everything I had just to break the trail for that one session without faltering. I tried not to contemplate the next eight hours. Thankfully a break came next and I could cool down (rapidly) and eat some salami and cheese to get my strength back.

Hesitantly, I ventured a suggestion.

'Leading for 45 minutes seems a bit much – better on flatter ground. I've got to be honest, I'm going to find it hard to keep this up. Maybe we could switch the lead a bit more through the valley, every half an hour – you know, keep us fresh?' I tried to sound casual. I looked up slowly from my snacks, taking silence for contempt.

'It's a great idea,' Paul responded, saving my pride.

'Totally up for it – after all, I haven't led yet!' Pat added with a grin.

'Let's do it, then, but after your lead, Patrick,' countered Paul, trying to maintain his authoritative manner but betraying just the smallest hint of his amusement at seeing Pat's face fall.

Towards the end of the day, to save us some miles, instead of continuing to haul parallel to the mountain range until we hit the mouth of the glacier, we decided to go up over a spur and drop down into the valley a little further along it. We aimed for a saddle between two hills. To attain it, we needed to pull our sleds up the steepest slope we had negotiated so far, the back-lift of a particularly big undulation in the sea ice.

We found it impossible to haul our sleds up this slope on our own, so we experimented with tying two traces to each sled and pulling in tandem. It was instantly more manageable. It was also more fun to have the companionship and the rhythm of someone alongside you to share the ups and downs. This was how Scott's men pulled every yard – together. Pulling on your own – the modern trend – even if you are only a few yards from the other, means you are as separate as two bubbles.

The tips of the mountains we were approaching were hidden from view by the steepness of the gradient. As we mounted the crest, suddenly we saw for the first time the inspiring vista of the Axel Heiberg Glacier, a massive, wide, flat motorway thronged by mountains extending in file towards the perfect pyramid of Mount Don Pedro. At the foot of that mountain we would find the legendary icefall, which was still obscured from view.

Looking out over the glacier, I took in the frothy crescent of crevasses that collected at its diaspora, where it fanned out into the sea ice of the Ross Ice Shelf. From there I scanned across the sweeping summits of the limitless mountains, each one a different shape, each more beautiful than the next.

After only two days of heavy hauling, we woke up to an array of new-found aches and niggles. We only had the glorious view to sweeten the prospect of a further eight hours of pressure on our lower backs, the rubbing of open blisters and the certainty of painful toil. I dreaded getting out of my warm sleeping bag, dressing and clearing enough debris to make room for Paul, who slept in his own tent, to squeeze in to join us for breakfast.

It was another excruciating first two hours. I led last. I couldn't have moved slower and *still* moved. I grunted and groaned like a stuck pig, knowing the others would be listening to their mini-discs and unable to hear me. I shouted the odd muffled obscenity to the air. First I tucked my woolly hat into my gaiters and then rolled up my shirt-sleeves. Sweat collected in my sunglasses, welled and then slid down my nose, teetering for a moment before adding a crystal of frozen moisture to the billions beneath me.

As we grunted up a steeper gradient, I tried to focus on my music, *Hôtel Costes: La Suite* by Stéphane Pompougnac, to keep me from stopping. The words seemed prophetic: 'You better keep moving boy, or you'll get left behind.' Mercifully, Paul stopped towards the end of his shift and got us together.

'This is ridiculous. We're going to burn ourselves out. I suggest we relay the pulks, two per pulk, like we did on the spur last night. Everyone happy with the decision?'

I could barely whimper my assent. I had been longing for that moment. Paul had a wonderful way of leading. His experience, skill, age and personal reserve gave his statements an air of authority. Once he had spoken he was content to let his point drift into silence. He would just quietly nod, staring at us with implacable, piercing blue eyes. He never followed his words up with a hasty qualifier to show that he wasn't absolutely confident. However, despite his authoritativeness, he encouraged consensus and discussion. We always felt that we had contributed to the decision and yet, subtly, that decision usually just happened to be what Paul had been suggesting all along. Where he had a clear preference, he communicated it; where he didn't, he also let us know. I felt very confident in him.

Luckily, making our way down to the glacier floor, we had to keep halting to check the topography in order to work out the safest route to avoid possible crevasses, giving me the opportunity for a breather. We had to try and skirt around hillocks without ascending or descending in order to expend minimum effort. The terrain ahead looked benign and flat but the scale was so grand that up close every tiny ripple was a challenge. I was a tortoise trying to get to the end of the garden and finding that even the blades of grass were hard going.

As we progressed up the glacier towards the icefall, even though the gradient was negligible, we resorted increasingly – and finally permanently – to the solution that we had found at the end of the second day. The scale was so deceptive that each day we thought that we were going to arrive at the base of the falls and yet each day we came up short. I felt like a Lilliputian in the land of the gods and half expected some Gulliver, more fitting to the scale of the country, to come tramping down the flanks of the mountains.

Two men pulling one pulk worked well. Having to return, demoralisingly, along our self-same tracks to tow the second set up the very incline we had just gained, however, was like a nightmare from *Groundhog Day*. For every mile gained we travelled three. It was scant consolation that both Shackleton and Scott had been forced to adopt the same tactic. After eight hours we had achieved another miserly four nautical miles.

The fourth day was Patrick's birthday. We celebrated with an indulgent cube of fudge each. A better present awaited us, though: on our daily scheduled communication with Patriot Hills we learnt that the Land Rover team was flying towards Antarctica. It was a huge relief – and must have been for them, too. They had been waiting in Punta Arenas for the weather that had kept us hemmed in at Patriot to clear. With the intelligence came a new anxiety. We all prayed that the Land Rovers would drive successfully out of the plane. From now on we all fantasised eagerly about their progress.

CHAPTER 10

The Icefall

Come on! Marching, carrying heavy loads, the desert, boredom and anger!
Arthur Rimbaud, A Season in Hell

Crawling into the tent each night was unadulterated bliss. With the hot sun on the canvas it became warm inside. Just as in a sandy desert a day's journey becomes a scorching march towards the longed-for cool breeze of evening, so in the Antarctic it is the same in reverse. It was wonderful to rest my limbs in the irradiated air and rehydrate with hot chocolate and tea. My blisters were quite bad now, my hips and Achilles tendons sore from the pulling, but overall I felt in good shape.

I was getting a text message from Annabel every day, which I read at breakfast when we turned on the satellite phone for our daily report to base camp at Patriot Hills. The morning text messages had become a bit of a ritual. We'd pass around the phone so that each person could read theirs privately rather than have it read out aloud. The baby was getting very big already. I hoped this didn't mean it would come early. Our progress up the glacier was much slower than we had anticipated. It was obvious that unless we could make up distance on the plateau with some exceptional and unexpected kiting, we were going to arrive at the South Pole behind time.

After five days we finally arrived at the foot of the icefall. As I skied, I considered whether I had a favourite mule to pull alongside. David's stride was so massive that it was hard to step in time. Like an efficient rowing pair, the better your timing, the more efficient and faster your progress. Compensating for that, he chuntered away animatedly, seeming not to notice the exertion, and transported me away from the tedium of the slog. Whereas he swished his tail and pricked up his ears, looking this way and that and whickering contentedly, my ears were pinned back against my head, haunches straining. Pat was nearer my height and with him I found it easier to swing in rhythm. With Paul as the lead pony, I felt the pressure to pull more than my fair share, perhaps to prove my competence and strength to him, which made the session a more stressful one. Travelling in pairs, although much slower, was a veritable pleasure compared to pulling the same load on your own. Surrounded by a novel and complete beauty, I finally started to enjoy the hard work, the act of supreme exertion that hadn't yet crossed over into mind-sapping pain.

This was the feeling I had been searching for. To pant up a slope is to feel alive: to feel your heart beating strongly, your lungs expanding with vivifying air and your soul grow big in the largeness that surrounds you. At the same time your body feels small and fragile – only as strong as the arterial walls that pulsate with the blood pumping from your loudly beating heart – and you become aware of your supremely physical self, gloriously vital but above all mortal, all tissue, bone and sinew.

The Axel Heiberg Glacier tumbles off the high polar plateau at around 8,500 feet. A drop of 5,500 occurs in only a few nautical miles. The glacier that Scott and Shackleton trudged up, the Beardmore, climbs to the same height over more than 100 miles. Up ahead lay a twisted, jumbled heap of crevasses and crushed ice.

Amundsen had ascended the icefall and progressed up and onwards through the entire upper reaches of the glacier in only four days. In the same amount of time, we were still at the bottom of it. The slight upwards gradient of the glacier had been leading us gently and inexorably to this pile of twisted ice. It looked absolutely impassable. If we struggled so much now, where it was comparatively flat, how could we possibly climb the tumbling cataract in front of us?

We studied the glacier to try to pick out the route that Amundsen had taken. On one side was Mount Don Pedro, named after an

Argentine that fitted out and supplied Amundsen's boat. It was a perfect pyramid and a starkly beautiful pillar to the falls. On the other was Mount Nansen, a huge, flat cake with a layer of serac icing. Between these two mountains hung the falls, like an ice-curtain. On the left side the cliff was almost sheer. The right side, however, slumped away, as if part of it had collapsed. There it made a more gradual slope, up which, threading between vast crevasses, it could be possible to ascend – but only as far as the first terrace. Past that, the way looked blocked: a sheer cliff of jagged tumbling ice, falling thousands of feet.

Although I had been practising my knots in the tent during our wait at Patriot Hills, I was not an experienced climber and I had never trekked through glacial valleys roped up. Indeed, demonstrating that I knew the drill to Paul in Pat's flat on the eve of the expedition I had managed to tie myself up like Houdini without being able to perform the escape part . . . he hadn't been greatly impressed. I think he even considered leaving me there, trussed up, while the others went to the airport.

I tried not to think about what awaited us or what would happen if we couldn't move our loads through the falls. Each way looked equally challenging to me but eventually Paul suggested we should tackle the middle section, as any route under the shadow of the mountains would leave us vulnerable to bergschrunds (a gap or crevasse at the junction where the ice abutted the rock) and avalanches from the overhanging seracs. Ahead I could see huge cubes of ice; perfect squares jumbled one on top of the other like the ice equivalent of the Giant's Causeway.

Amundsen was fortunate to have approached the glacier from the particular point he did. Had he progressed up it from where we were he would never have been able to see the route through the mayhem along the shoulder of Don Pedro. We couldn't even see it from the middle of the icefall and certainly not now, at the foot of it. You needed to be adjacent, high and north to spot it. Amundsen came down into the valley, as luck would have it, from probably the only place that the one route through the maze is possible to discern. Otherwise, perhaps he would have abandoned the Axel Heiberg altogether.

If so, with his dogs he might have been able to seek out another route. We, on the other hand, were travelling so slowly and laboriously that if we couldn't climb it, it would mean the failure of our expedition. It was this route or nothing. No team had ever hauled loads up it without dogs. Amundsen's success, with the benefit of hindsight, seems so inevitable – but it wouldn't have seemed so to him: a totally untravelled road ahead.

Being on skis helped us to spread our weight and not sink too deeply into the powder snow but it was like climbing in clown boots. Mountaineers negotiate crevasses by sending one roped climber in advance. If the front man falls, his companion has to throw himself onto the snow. As the first man swings in the crevasse, the other, holding his weight, needs to instigate a complicated procedure to haul him out. We decided to employ a modified technique. Instead of having a pair of climbers at either end of a long rope, we doubled the load. We fastened both the front men and their pulk to a rope which in turn was tied to both the men following behind. It broke the golden rule of travelling in crevasse country – which is to spread your weight. Two people side by side on the same ground, only a few feet in front of a heavy load, is not ideal. If a snow bridge collapsed the entire front party would be hurled into the void and rely entirely on the second party to hold them *and* their sled. But there was no other way for us to be able to pull the huge loads. We needed two men per sled. Would the rope hold such a weight?

We split into two groups. As Patrick and Paul were the most experienced climbers it seemed sensible to divide them up in case one party had to rescue the other. Paul picked David. It was like a donkey and an ox being tied to the same yoke. It looked quite comical. Their strides couldn't have been more different. Dave's enormous strength would be useful in breaking trail through the deep snow although I looked at his massive frame and the heavy pulk at their heels with dismay: fat chance of holding them. We'd better just be careful.

Pat and I laughed as they grunted slowly off, tied together. 'Eee-aw,' we chorused. 'Pull mules!' We considered waiting to see if we could just get towed along.

The gradient was the steepest we had yet tackled. As we sweated, tugged and grunted our snail's pace up it, we could see livid blue scars on either side of us. Snow bridges as wide as dual carriageways covered them. They seemed very stable but because of their size it was hard to tell what was bridge and what was solid snow. The crevasses were so chaotic that they probably extended in a complicated network beneath us. From a distance, finding a path through the criss-crossing striations looked inconceivable. Up close, however, the scale came to our rescue. Gaps which looked tiny from afar were easily big enough for us to sneak through. I couldn't help but worry, though, what hid beneath this honeycombed surface.

Every so often the snow decompressed underfoot with a different, more hollow ring. This was likely to be trapped air reverberating in the fluffy powder but it was unsettling.

To minimise the jolt of any fall we needed to keep the rope taut between us. This was easier said than done when climbing up a twisting path of different gradients and contours. If the front party were on a flatter section their progress would be quicker than the toiling second group. We were so used to pulling with all our might and not looking behind as we strained in our harnesses that, should the second party have to stop or slow down, invariably the front party would just drag them over or into the very obstacle they were trying to skirt around. Frequently lost from view beneath a ridge, we would holler for them to stop.

We made barely two nautical miles in nine hours.

Every time we laboriously gained a false summit, we would untie our traces and, free from our load for a blissful few moments, ski down the depressingly short distance to collect the second pair of pulks. In so doing, each time, we enacted the myth of Sisyphus, who has become an existential icon. In the classical myth, Sisyphus is doomed by the gods ceaselessly to roll a rock to the top of a mountain. Just as he reaches the very pinnacle, the stone would roll back down to the bottom of its own accord.

There are conflicting reports on Sisyphus' crime. In one version, which struck a chord, he is punished for testing his wife, but in essence his crime was loving life too much. He escaped from the underworld and refused to come back, preferring to feel the sun on his body, to touch the warm stones and let the soft sea massage his feet. He was eventually snatched back and given, according to the French writer Camus, 'that unspeakable penalty in which the whole being is exerted towards accomplishing nothing'.[1]

The story struck a note with me not just because of the futility of the current task but because in a wider sense it suggests that the pleasure comes at a price. Application and pain are the flip sides of enjoyment and accomplishment – just as there is no sun without shadow. I have always felt it is hard to enjoy anything if you haven't worked for it. It was easy for me to imagine Sisyphus, his hands clotted with earth and his face screwed up, locked in the tyranny of effort. Every fibre of his being is subject to his punishment until the moment when he releases the stone and watches it hurtle back down to the depths of the underworld. Then, for a blessed period of freedom, he turns slowly back down the mountain, light as a feather and superior to his wretched fate. In just the same way, we would ski lightly down the glacier, free to contemplate its beauty.

That night we camped at the lip of huge crevasse on the only moderately flat ground we could find, halfway up a formidable slope, with another gash in front of us. Suddenly the reliable calm and hot weather deserted us. For the next two days the clouds set in – and brought with them a colder tent. Snow started to fall in swathes. It might as well have rained treacle as every layer would make the task harder. With the blanket of cloud around we could see nothing. Unable to avoid the crevasses if we couldn't see anything, we were confined to our tent.

We used the enforced rest to repair some kit. The crucial bar on Patrick's boot (onto which his skis fastened) was working loose again. Paul wrapped a scarf around his nose and mouth to protect himself from the fumes and, hunched over his little stove like a crack addict from a Tarantino movie, he melted the toughened rubber of the sole to try and mould it over the area of weakness. This period of rest gave our various niggles a breather to heal. My blisters were particularly bad. The ends of my toes were bleeding and my heels

---

1 Albert Camus, 'The Myth of Sisyphus'.

were raw. Getting into my sleeping bag was agony, as even touching the delicate nylon was painful.

We spent much of the time playing cards. Even Paul, who loathes cards, was so bored he decided to join in. Paul is something of an enigma. For much of the time he was aloof but sometimes he thawed completely. As he dealt, he confided to us that his children sometimes told him that he was too serious. There is something precise and Nordic about his personality. His attention to detail, his directness and his methodical approach all revealed his more ordered side. Yet, in the mood, especially with David's constant banter, he giggled, with his tongue between his teeth and his weather-wrinkled face creased up in genuine gnome-like amusement. Liberal in attitude, he was a very interesting companion on almost any subject. A mix of contradictions, levity and seriousness intertwined throughout his personality like matching spirals of DNA. He has a pony tail but he doesn't like to look scruffy and unshaven; he eschews a desk-bound life yet he is accomplished at planning and has terrific attention to detail; he had a separate tent from us and yet it was clear that he hugely enjoyed the meaningful interactions of a team expedition and has never wanted go on adventures alone; he loves to kite-surf – an enlightened, young and frivolous pastime – and yet he'd engage in it to the verge of obsessiveness, kiting for hour upon hour, way after most people would have got tired or bored.

Passing the time talking, reading, updating our diaries or joking around meant that the only time we went outside was for a pee or to check the weather. Normally having a pee into snow is mildly fascinating in a childish sort of way. You can watch the snow melt rapidly beneath you or write silly words. When you are camped on a snow bridge, however, it's a different story. A deep hole formed beneath me. I suddenly realised that we had all being peeing in a circle around the tent. Mid-flow, I suddenly panicked, imagining an ignominious end like something worthy of Homer from *The Simpsons* where the tent would disappear into the void in a puff of yellow snow – like a car tax-disc being punched from out of its perforations. My only achievement in life would have been to appear as a footnote to the Darwin Awards (a prize given to those that have died so stupidly that their departure only leaves the collective gene-pool stronger).

I found being locked in the tent again so soon after leaving Patriot Hills incredibly frustrating. The glacier that had been so mesmerisingly beautiful a day earlier had morphed overnight, its brilliant whites and deep blues, sharp angles, fine lines and glorious expansiveness had been swapped for a claustrophobic murky uniformity, a blunt covering of snow and a pervasive greyness. The tight confines of our tent were echoed by this horizon-shrinking cloud all around us, which prevented us from travelling onwards.

CHAPTER
11 | The Layer Cake

We were still stuck the following morning. The Land Rovers, however, had had more luck. They landed safely at Patriot Hills and mercifully drove off the Ilyushin without a hitch. They must have looked incredible in the open hull of that stripped-down plane, all loaded with gear.

For a number of months before we had left for Antarctica, we had been considering the appropriate make up of individuals for the team that would accompany the Land Rovers and drive them to the Pole. Since we hadn't been able to offer anything concrete until the sponsorship had come through, and it had only been confirmed a matter of days before departure, it was hard to find people who wanted to be involved, could suddenly be away for three months and who were prepared to take the risk on a project that might turn out to be a chimera.

The leader, in a complicated hierarchy, would have to be under Paul's ultimate direction but would need to be sufficiently experienced to make the day-to-day calls for that team. We selected Steve Jones. He had completed two last-degree expeditions to the North Pole, been a member of the British Greenland Expedition, helped Rosie Stancer with her logistics on a solo trek from Hercules

Inlet to the South Pole and had a lot of experience with Land Rovers, even driving a Camel Trophy Discovery.

This confidence and experience was dramatically illustrated to us early on the morning of the official press launch of the expedition in the prestigious Royal Automobile Club in Pall Mall. Most of the members seem to spend their day sleeping over a glass of warm sherry with a freshly ironed newspaper on their laps to catch the crumbs, awaiting their maker's summons. Steve must have made them think that the call had come early as he thundered one of the Land Rovers aggressively, with inches to spare above and to either side, into the foyer and up the main stairs – a 45-degree angle – to park it under the cupola alongside a replica of Shackleton's 1908 Arrol Johnson.

'I say,' exclaimed one member, spitting out a mouthful of kipper, 'this is the Royal Automobile Club but a chap can't come into the clubhouse like that!'

'Whatever do you mean?' announced another. 'He *is* wearing a jacket and tie.'

I had also been discussing the expedition with the father of a close friend, Steve Cotton. Although, he hadn't had specific expedition experience, he was a very tough man. Formerly a Great Britain rower, he had then proved his durability working on an oil rig in the North Sea. He was incredibly practical and good humoured. Unflappable, with lots of common sense and organisational capability, he had the mechanical skills of someone who had had a hands-on love of cars, especially Land Rovers, for many years. As soon as we confirmed that the expedition was funded, Steve Cotton immediately dropped everything to help coordinate the work that Land Rover was doing on the vehicles and sourced, with Chris Jacobs, any other parts that were needed.

We had had a long and difficult search for a cameraman. Initially, we were focused on tying up a deal with a television production company, which, despite many meetings and a number of hopeful leads, we finally realised was a vain aspiration. They were looking to double the budget – no doubt intending to bring a couple of Winnebagos and hordes of unnecessary extras. I could imagine it: 'The Pole is lovely but it's a bit flat. Let's shoot it with some mountains. One bit of snow is much like another – right? Alastair, you don't look tired enough. Grimace. Lovely. Put some ice on your beard . . . just rub your face in some snow or something. Perfect.'

It is very difficult to get concrete decisions from television executives, and warm words and procrastination didn't help when we were pressed and going to the cold, so eventually we turned instead to sourcing experienced but enterprising individuals and making the film ourselves. As part of this process we were referred to Conor.

Conor Hipwell had been working on the team of another Antarctic expedition being organised by the family of Tom Crean – Scott and then Shackleton's heroic companion – which had failed to get funding. Its failure meant he had an unscratched itch. He had been dreaming of Antarctica incessantly, had already been considering cold-weather filming strategy and was super-keen to get involved. Furthermore, he taught a film course at Trinity College, Dublin and so, even without actual proof, it seemed very reasonable to take a punt on his skills. With the two Steves, Patrick's girlfriend Robyn and now Conor, the team were four.

Lastly, we included a good stills photographer. Rather like Paul had been our only realistic option as a guide, Martin Hartley was the only photographer we would ever have been happy with. Martin is the Frank Hurley of our generation. Amazingly gifted, he had been to a host of the coldest places conceivable and was incredibly modest and amiable despite it all. Indeed, we were so impressed by him that he joined the ski team early and flew with us to Patriot Hills, ostensibly to record our flight across the continent to the Ross Ice Shelf. During the claustrophobic, tent-bound start he had been nothing but the very best company.

This team was strong and the roles, to some extent, interchangeable. Although Martin and Conor were present primarily to record the event, they were ready to assist Robyn and the two Steves in digging, pushing, camping or anything else that was required.

The Land Rover team had been put together at incredible speed. Martin and Conor had never even seen the vehicles, which had been shipped before they finally signed up. Only Martin had ever been to Antarctica and, not having been intimately involved during the planning, they courageously took a leap of faith in our assessment of the conditions and in the equipment we had provided for them.

I was amazed at the camaraderie and the dauntlessness of this team. They hadn't known each other before. Only the two Steves had credible 4 x 4 experience – which they supplemented with training days at Land Rover. Their adventure would, in many ways, be the most unpredictable and would require huge reserves of ingenuity and patience.

In the case of Martin and Steve Cotton, their other halves had had to get suddenly and rapidly used to the idea that they would be separated from them for months, including Christmas. Jo, Steve's wife, particularly found it difficult to come to terms with the fact that her placid husband of 30 years was suddenly, in his early fifties, embarking on a wild adventure that was bringing out qualities in his personality that she had either half forgotten or didn't know were there. She once confessed to Annabel, who became very close to her throughout the process, that it vigorously renewed her love for him. This discovery of a different side to her husband caused her to feel a little more uncertain of what she had taken for granted and this mixed with a new admiration for him. When Annabel told me this, I remember feeling so pleased that the expedition *as an idea* – the goals and spirit of what we were attempting – could have such a positive emotional impact on the people and families that made up the whole team. Of course, I hoped that the same would prove true for my relationship.

Now that they had arrived, we were excited and optimistic about their progress and looked forward to the incredible footage they would take of our wild return by kite.

Our bubble didn't take long to burst. On their very first day in Antarctica they got stuck four times just going down the runway to get fuel. The problem was that the whole camp had got drifted up during the last 18 days of bad weather. Maybe it was just a case of waiting until the harsh winds blew away the drift snow and started to pack down the surface again, but our timetable was already looking bleak. We agreed with them that all of us should put back our schedules a week, so we would aim to reach the South Pole on Christmas Day. After that, however, we had no further rations. This way they would have more time for testing or to reconoitre the first 100 miles without heavy loads.

Their initial trials didn't go well. But other than offer advice, stuck in a cloud on a precarious lip of the icefall and hundreds of miles from anyone, there wasn't much we could do.

We agreed that the worst scenario from a PR point of view was getting the Land Rovers stuck. This would also have huge cost implications. Obviously, the team would be evacuated but it would be catastrophic for us as we had to have a resupply at the South Pole. At best, the marooned supplies could be (expensively) picked up by a Twin Otter *en route* to the Pole.

Depressingly, I overheard Robyn telling Patrick confidentially over the satellite phone – it was a small tent after all – that she didn't rate their chances as more than 1 in 50. It was a total about-turn from our original expectations. None of us could believe their dismal progress. It seemed as if they had thrown in the towel already. I was reluctant to admit that the project might be too arduous and assumed unfairly – clutching at the only straw available – that every avenue, every effort had not yet been made.

They were in a difficult position. With Mike, the camp manager, out of Antarctica no one had been anywhere more than 30 miles outside the Patriot Hills camp, except in a plane, and so couldn't give any reliable advice on the conditions further afield. Instead they were sceptical and negative, which just reduced the confidence of the team.

Paul and Patrick were still convinced that the project could succeed. Paul, particularly, aside from knowing the terrain intimately, had seen all sorts of 4 x 4s succeed in the Arctic, and thought that they should be trying out different options: with and without weight, relaying their loads, with and without trailers. They *were* trying all of those different ideas but from where we were we couldn't see all the hard work and the inevitable draining frustration that was occurring on the other side of the continent.

We understood all too well that the snow was atrocious around Patriot Hills and probably would be abominable for the next 100 miles. However, further into the season, perhaps in as little as a few weeks, the surface – with renewed sun and wind – would inevitably harden again. Further out it would be rock hard for long stretches. We saw an analogy with what we were going through and wanted them to put in a parallel effort. If we had thought that the same gloopy snow we were encountering would continue all the way to the Pole we might well have chucked it in. Yet we hoped that the plateau was flatter and harder and that our mileage would increase there. So far we had made a derisory 20 nautical miles, all westwards – not a single mile towards the Pole.

All expeditions have moments of tremulous uncertainty – 'tipping points' – as indeed do so many aspects of life. I felt that this was such a moment for us. The Land Rover team was confronting its own reality. It was impossible for us to tell them that things were different when we could see nothing. However much we wanted to will them to get to the Pole, it was more likely with the equipment we had given them that the task really was just a pipe dream. When should you push on and when should you quit an impossible task with dignity? It was the million-dollar question and one that had arisen so many times now in various guises. How would they know? How would we? These were impossible questions since the answer doesn't always lie in the individual and the die is often already cast.

This situation was doubly hard on Patrick. He was desperate for the experience to be rewarding for Robyn personally, especially after her long emotional involvement in the expedition. He was eager that her participation shouldn't be tinged with shame. Each day he had to call her to talk dispassionately about the expedition, their progress, or advice, the schedule and the weather, and each day all he probably wanted to do was to tell her that he loved her and missed being with her. Any couple that works together has to cope with additional stresses on their relationship. But overcoming that pressure here, on top of all these other ones, must have been difficult for both of them.

In addition to the effect on our sponsors and the financial burden we now bore, Patrick and I also felt responsible and guilty for getting this eager, enterprising team out to Antarctica to take a leap of faith based on what now seemed be a fool's errand. Sitting in the tent in that miserable cloud-covered day gave us plenty of opportunity for reflection, worry, anger, guilt and hope.

By the third day the mist that had hovered like an albatross above our tent started to lift, letting us back into the labyrinth, and at breakfast we heard that the Land Rovers had accomplished 10 nautical miles in testing the previous night and the team seemed much more upbeat about their chances. Perhaps our fears had been premature. It helped to brighten what was always a low point in my day. Not only did I have the prospect of heavy toil, but breakfast was always my worst meal. I had to force down a stack of dry muesli mixed with an unappetising combination of melted snow and powdered milk. It seemed to take hours to ruminate, getting drier and more tasteless with each mouthful. We were like a stable of mules with droopy ears and downcast eyes, our heads mournfully stuck in the oat trough before being yoked for a day at the plough. It also probably explained why the others were so eager to leave the tent for a day's skiing – anything was better than watching me eat.

The visibility was partial but we elected to leave. Almost immediately, David nearly fell into a corner of the mouth of the crevasse behind the campsite while trying to head straight up. There were some stunning, deep blue crevasses on all sides of us. Lips of curled-over snow partially covered the openings, like waves toppling over into surf.

It was much more difficult than we imagined trying to decide the line that Amundsen had taken. On the right the rock striations of Mount Nansen formed a chocolate and cream tiramisu that we christened the 'Layer Cake'. In the centre, a vertical tumble of drapery cascaded down in massive slabs into a graveyard of obelisks. The hewn blocks made Stonehenge look as though it was composed of tiny dominos. The slabs were piled haphazardly one on top of the other. The ground, which itself was further broken up by gashes and scars, resembled a quarry of monumental proportions. To the left, the sides of Don Pedro collapsed into this mayhem in luxurious folds.

After a brief glimpse of the available options, the cloud descended again. The blue crevasses we had marvelled at seconds ago were swallowed up by the mist – where they now lay in wait for us. Paul told us later that continuing in these conditions had been touch and go. We should have stopped, but after two days in the tent all of us were over-sensitive about progress – at almost any cost. We were also divided about route. Patrick and I favoured hitting the steeper slope in front of us towards a ridge whose outline we could dimly make out through the gloom – which meant cutting across the elbow of the longer path that Paul was suggesting.

Our view prevailed. Paul and David bravely continued to break trail but the slope soon got too steep for us. Finally, leaning exhaustedly on our poles, none of us could budge an iota further. We had to find another solution.

Between us we had two ropes. We decided to climb the hill, dig in an ice picket and set up a pulley system by joining the two ropes together. We would attach one end of the rope to a skier, who would ski aggressively *down* the hill and thereby lever the pulks up.

It wasn't as easy as it sounds. The rope was dynamic, which meant if you fell down a crevasse it would stretch a little, like a bungee, to absorb the force of your fall. Using it as a tow rope meant the skier would jerk like a drunken puppet on his harness, flopping forward and back, without actually moving the sled. Also, the one pulley we had was not set up for these forces. It burnt out from the friction in a matter of seconds. The rope smoked and the pulley twisted out of shape with heat – despite the low ambient temperature. But it was the only way we could think of cresting the ridge. Eventually, using two skiers on the downhill section (and another poor bastard, trudging knee deep in powder, pushing the pulk from behind) we succeeded in getting the pulks up the hill.

After one and a half hours we had made 200 feet of elevation and had tackled the steepest part of the gradient but didn't have the appetite or the energy to repeat the manoeuvre, so we started to traverse in order to gain the summit of this immediate slope by zig-zagging. The snow was deep enough to rise above even the sides of the sleds so there was little danger of them slewing down the face. We pitched camp when the clouds totally closed in again, after another excruciating and long day. In ten hours we had travelled just over one mile.

The blisters on my feet were bleeding again, as were my shins. This became normality. Initially they hurt, and then the work and the concentration anaesthetised the pain. Then, for some reason, towards the end of a day of battery, the dull ache returned and intensified towards the end of the session until the tent just came to represent a blissful release from my boots.

As we climbed higher, we realised that we should have followed Paul's advice and crossed back further on ourselves to avoid a succession of lavish wounds in the glacier but it made exciting and beautiful travelling. The route was now directly uphill, our steepest two-man ascent to date without resorting to pulleys. Patrick and I led it – it finished us off before the day had even started and made us appreciate the efforts that David and Paul had made so far. The only way to progress was to count under my breath to 100 while walking, before stopping to catch air. Each number represented one step. To get the sled started we also had to count – if we mistimed it, we couldn't budge the load at all. We prayed that the route out lay on a strip between two great scars. But unfortunately hope distorted our judgement – the second chasm was impossible to cross and we had to turn back.

There was now a brisk head wind blowing down Silence Valley which we caught as we started to emerge from the protection of the icefall. We could now see the full prospect of Mount Nansen from the other side of the valley. Another vast glacier flowed down from the summit and calved off the top of the Layer Cake, accounting for the giant fronds that hung over the edge. During the day, four huge avalanches poured down the cliff. We watched the spectacle in awe from the safety of the other side of the icefall, appreciating the delayed stereophonics of the falling snow.

I still vividly remember the grandeur of watching those thousands of tons streaming uncontrolled down Nansen's sides. T.S. Eliot spoke of 'epiphanic moments', instants of magical intensity that make life worthwhile. Undoubtedly, sitting on my pulk in that valley so rarely seen by human eye, I was experiencing such a moment myself. I wondered if I'd invoke this memory to inspire me at times in the future when life was difficult and I needed to draw strength from the memory of an uplifting experience. I closed my eyes and made an enormous effort to hold every detail inside me.

We believed we had gained enough elevation to start moving around the back of the cliff but again found the scale had deceived us. What we had thought was only a gentle undulation turned out to be another mighty hill between two even bigger crevasses. Paul and I skied off without our sleds to survey the ground. I felt like Magwitch relieved of his ball and chain; I looked down expecting to see arrows on my Gore-Tex and a team of Alsatians following my scent. Paul skied a rope-length ahead of me while I kept the line taught in case he fell in. I revised the magic mantra of the rescue drill in my mind over and over again: 'Don't fall in, you bastard!'

We headed into the most disturbed area to see if we could snake through the trouble. All around us was twisted wreckage. We skied right along the top edge of the falls. To my right huge blocks balanced on the edge waiting to teeter over. Paul skied down one long tongue which lolled out to nowhere and stood poised for a moment at the end of the causeway looking over a Victoria Falls of ice, like Gandalf above the abyss. Seeing the shards close up at their most confused, rather than taking the usual wide berth, was truly impressive and gave me a deep respect for the power of this ice-river. We pitched camp between another two large crevasses, one of them so huge its emptiness cut back and extended far beneath us.

From this lonely little spot, so far from any human beings, we called the Land Rover team. It was our twelfth night, but it wasn't as merry as that original festival.

'This is Patrick. Hi, Steve. We're all fine.' Pat gave our position. 'It's slow, uncertain progress but we're almost out of the icefall with only Silence Valley between us and the plateau. What about you all? Are the conditions any better?'

We were huddled together, each in a different corner of the tent with our knees bunched up against our chests. We all watched Pat's face intently to try to pick up his reaction to the growl of the receiver. He nodded slowly. Would it be good news? Was it getting any easier?

No. It seemed that the vehicles were foundering and spirits flagging.

'OK. Are you sure about that? Are you confident you've tried everything? What does the weather report look like? Mm. Yeah. I see.' Pat kept probing for hope. 'Is there any prospect it'll harden significantly over the next few days? Uh. Uh. Have your tried everything? What about altering the loads? Yup – their position over the axle? You've tried that, I see. Look, Steve, you know best. All we can say is that we're gutted that it hasn't worked out. It's just very disappointing for everyone. Look, I'll talk things through with the guys and we'll come back to you tomorrow with some more concrete ideas of where we go from here.' Pat was looking at each of us as he spoke, shaking his head slowly. He shrugged his shoulders once with a slight grimace, arching his eyebrows: the South Pole as we had planned it was unattainable – they were pulling out.

It's hard to describe the sense of deflation in our camp. So much of our work for the last two years had just slid abruptly away from us, our expectations of a dramatic reunion at the Pole had been punctured and we sympathised keenly with the disappointment of the people we had lured into the project. Added to this we no longer could rely on a resupply at the Pole. Even if we made it that far on our rations, without further food being dropped we couldn't continue: we'd have to call in a plane to evacuate us. It looked as if even the plans to kite back were disappearing into thin air.

We had based part of our plans on attempting to fulfil, in spirit, Shackleton's legacy. Coincidentally, the *Endurance* expedition had also been divided into two teams, each approaching the heart of the continent from different sides. It is rarely mentioned now that Shackleton had a second team arriving at the Ross Sea in the *Aurora* to lay supply depots for his expected traverse. Three men lost their lives in that attempt, even though Shackleton has become immortal for not losing a single of his men in trying circumstances over on the other side of the continent. Although one team has been lauded, the other has been conveniently forgotten by posterity. I wondered whether, if our traverse ended up being notionally successful, events would slowly fold over this failure and it would also be quietly deleted from the hard-drive of the expedition.

12 | Down and Out

Why should we be in such desperate haste to succeed and in such desperate enterprises? If a man does not keep pace with his companions, perhaps it is because he hears a different drummer. Let him step to the music which he hears, however measured or far away.

Henry Thoreau, Walden

Where did we go from here? We weren't sure. The blame lay with Patrick and me, in the planning and the preparation, but in many ways we couldn't have done any more. With funding coming through while we were already on the plane to Antarctica we had done all that we could in a very short space of time. It was a miracle, under the circumstances that the Land Rovers had even got to Antarctica at all. Having said that, although I couldn't admit it to anyone in the tent, I felt in subtle ways that my reservations with this aspect of the trip were coming back to haunt me. If I had been less ambivalent then maybe I would have put more energy into its organisation. I felt an acute guilt as well as unarticulated relief, which I struggled to even acknowledge.

The next day, when we reported in, we were told how some of the other expeditions were faring. The three Australian housewives – dubbed 'The Ice Maidens' by the press – attempting the South Pole without a resupply or a guide hadn't fared very well. They had taken advice as to the best procedures to follow but it looked, from where we were sitting, to have been very strange advice indeed. Instead of sleds they were hauling kayaks despite the fact they were hauling at altitude with no sea ice or leads (both common in the Arctic but unknown here). For energy, they poured oil on their cereal. I found breakfast hard at the best of times; nothing would have induced me out of my sleeping bag every day if the only thing to look forward to was the prospect of a bowl of muesli and vegetable oil. Two months of that: pure torture. I would have preferred to lick the metal edge of our ice axe at -30°C. They seemed to be taking masochism and misery to a new level.

These two parts of their regime had filtered over to us. We presumed it was the tip of the iceberg in terms of eccentric planning. Having made only a handful of nautical miles in their first few days, they abandoned their plans only a short distance from Patriot Hills. It seemed such a pity to have spent so long planning and publicising their expedition but we recognised the irony of criticising them, though, given the failure of our Land Rovers. Of course, they must have been gutted and ashamed and we all felt for them. Antarctica can be miserable – more miserable than the romantic illusion fostered by the stories of the golden age and an over-stimulated imagination. Three others on separate expeditions had also been evacuated – one with frostbite, two others with torn Achilles tendons. One of the expeditions had also lost their tent in high winds. Now these evacuees must have been wondering why on earth they had endured this purgatory.

Undertaking challenges like this, however, isn't that unusual. Many of us are choosing increasingly extreme holidays in which we snort a sharp line of another life: dog-sledding in Lapland; sky diving in Cape Town; swimming with dolphins in the Brazilian pampas; or trekking in the Yosemite. Occasionally, some go further – climbing in the Himalayas, perhaps even Everest itself – but it's not necessary to be a career adventurer or professional climber anymore.

Ease of air travel means more and more places are accessible. You can voyage to the source of the Nile on a package holiday. It's not only possible to enjoy the same awesome spectacle of the Victoria Falls as Livingstone but you can white-water raft down the Zambezi, too, just for kicks. The Inca Trail, covered over by forest and jungle and forgotten for years, formerly a route to a lost city of exiles hidden from the marauding Spaniards for generations, is now a well-trodden hiking trail. This is not to belittle these wonders, it is only to argue that the world and our horizons are now smaller. The concept of exploration has changed forever.

If people want to test themselves, to get off the beaten track, they have to resort to more and more extreme measures. To cater for this market, Sir Richard Branson is investing millions in an airline that travels to space and back. Antarctica is, admittedly, still on earth but only just. The interior, due to both inaccessibility and cost, by comparison to almost every other bit of land on earth is virtually un-trodden. It is the one place that is, to most of us, a closed book – but nevertheless one whose pages are now being increasingly thumbed.

With so much travel possible, with so many different training possibilities allowing us to sample different professions in one lifetime, we are now able to experiment with different incarnations of ourselves. This is true in both business and travel. The nursery rhyme: tinker – tailor – soldier – sailor is due for an overhaul. Today it is soldier (part-time sailor) – MBA – banker – holiday-maker. If we really want to, we can visit any place and be anyone we want to be. Like Younghusband, we can drink yak tea with the Tibetans; like Cook, we can step off a ship in Tahiti and be garlanded by flowers. It is all within our grasp. Part of me, regrettable and odious as it is to admit it, must have wanted to try on Shackleton's hat for a while, just to see if it fitted.

Our generation is the first real generation of choice. Anyone, from any background, can – with determination, some talent and a little luck – pursue any career. You no longer have to plough the same furrow as your father (or the other men of your community). Sons of miners don't go to the coal-face but to the computer, sons of immigrants aren't shop-owners but doctors or investment bankers. And women no longer have to stay at home. It is, I accept, very hard to argue that too much choice is in any way a misfortune. Poor lucky little bastards that can do anything they want to . . . the problem is that having too much choice can, itself, create angst. (Don't tell me there aren't lots of women at home who feel real anxiety about not wanting to have a career – and vice versa.) Now there aren't just two alternative paths dividing in a forest – the one less travelled and the trampled road – so much as a veritable Spaghetti Junction. The generation of choice feels an anxiety of direction. Somehow, just pursuing a career is seldom enough. We need to feel that we are both different and making a difference.

The first question we are asked on meeting a stranger is: 'What do you do?' There follows an involuntary impression and a judgement, positive or negative, of our choices. Many of us feel the need to be interesting, if only to maintain our sense of self, of not being categorised, tagged, stamped and discarded. Conventional careers are seen, for the most part, as unthreatening and dull. To validate that choice, many in our generation feel compelled to try to become either exceptional or exceptionally rich. Set against this pressure is the increasing cost of life. To opt into something 'different' or 'interesting' can often require a huge sacrifice of potential earnings and can mean that the experiences – even the education – that you want to be able to give your children may need to be sacrificed so you can live your life the way you want to live it. Our variety of choices can lead us into a Catch 22. Now, with a child on the way, I wondered if I could afford the indulgence of my romantic and unrealistic fantasies.

As the cities become more competitive, as the need to earn and save for future security becomes more onerous, so we are forced to fit our fantasies into a smaller space. Lust for adventure has to be crammed into two hectic weeks of holiday a year. The lemon is squeezed until the pips cry for mercy. Many of us feel that we live an Ikea existence – that we are, to some extent, clones of the other. We live in similar terraced houses. Sitting room in the front, kitchen and living area at the back. A tiny garden. Two or three bedrooms upstairs – depending on whether you've got round to enhancing the value of your property with an extension. According to the playwright David Hare, the epitaph of our generation shall be: 'They left no loft unconverted.'[1]

To get away from this rut, we feel compelled to dangle every so often by a thin cord above a raging torrent – literally or metaphorically.

---

1 David Hare (2002), *The Breath of Life*, London: Faber & Faber.

Some argue that this tendency to challenge ourselves artificially is because our generation has not experienced a war or a major privation. Ironically, on the eve of the Great War, Shackleton himself saw this as a reason some would chose exploration: 'Why seek the Pole? War in the old days made men. We have not the same stirring times to live in and must look for other outlets for our energy and for the restless spirit.'[1]

Friends described George Mallory in 1924, about to leave to attempt Everest a third time, as taking his decision to return with foreboding, explaining that what he had to face this time was 'more like war than an adventure'.[2] The threat of terrorism from Al Qaeda or other jihadists apart, the wars we have encountered have been well removed from us. The concept of survival is almost totally divorced from making our daily bread, trapping or hunting our meat, sleeping somewhere warm and moving somewhere safe. Survival, now, is about not getting fired and keeping up with our mortgage repayments.

Had we needed to grapple with the bare essentials of conflict or finding prey, perhaps many of us would not have such a strong itch – scratched or just tolerated – for adventure. Rudimentary psychologising could suggest that we are being increasingly alienated from our original selves. The challenges of modern society have moved us so quickly from the demands we were evolved to meet that evolution has not quite caught up. This developmental lacuna has caused many of us to yearn for something more basic.

Those of us that came to Antarctica that season were being offered a chance to simplify. We would be able to think for months on end about only the 'bare necessities' of life: food, warmth, travel and shelter. I wanted to feel alive in a life that is no longer about survival. I could become Mowgli. Nothing extrinsic would need to enter. I could reacquaint myself with my alienated, primitive self and forget about filling in utility forms or paying councils for services they don't perform.

1 Sir Ranulph Fiennes, *Mind Over Matter: The Epic Crossing of the Antarctic Continent.*
2 Peter Gillman (ed.), *Everest: The Best Writing and Pictures from Seventy Years of Human Endeavour.*

I would also be forced to indulge in the bizarre luxury of being in my own mind. We are all so very scared of boredom – we don't know how to handle it anymore. We've invented a myriad of distractions from having to be alone with ourselves: the television, the radio, the BlackBerry and the mobile phone with its handheld games. Now I was forced into my own company – driven by *ennui*, you could say – to go and experience being bored.

For the first time in my life I felt as if I was taking a positive step off the conveyer belt that had produced me, the conveyer belt that was based on exams, institutions, professional excellence and conformity. An escapist has to have somewhere to escape to. Indulging romance, adventure and fantasy is all very well in a dream, but is it really feasible to live a whole life on those sentiments? Maybe that's why so many of us resort to drink or drugs. Antarctica was only an expedition and, like a dream, sooner or later it would have to end and I would need to return – whether a relative success or a failure. And what then?

I wondered how dipping my toe into this alternative life would affect me. Would it change the curve of my life? What would I do when I returned? Would I turn my back on risk, sated with it? Or would I seek it out, adrenalised and addicted? We all need to take chances in our lives; risk is essential in order to keep growing and learning. It helps us to keep our judgements fresh and our prejudices dulled. Moving out of our comfort zones can help us see how thin the line is between success and failure and help us empathise with those who have made different choices. Whether or not I slipped back into the sticky web of bureaucracy in which we live, one day I hoped to be able to leverage this experience, to be able to savour the same sensation of excitement and uncertainty again, to feel – as I did now – that I was active in shaping my own destiny, even if the call of responsibility was about to make those avenues less clear.

CHAPTER 13 | Silence Valley

I left the woods for as good a reason as I went there. Perhaps it seemed to me that I had several more lives to live and could not spend any more time for that one.

Henry Thoreau, Walden

Despite the depressing news about the Land Rover team, we had a good day, climbing higher before hauling slowly behind the jagged icefall, weaving between the last big crevasses and entering the quiet haven of Silence Valley.

The valley is in reality just the upper reaches of the glacier as it flowed down off the plateau towards the falls. It is sheltered by the ongoing hulk of Mount Nansen, Don Pedro and another domed peak catchily named Mount Olé Englestadt. Whereas Shackleton, the first man to pass through the Trans-Antarctic Mountains, had called his peaks by magical names such as the Cloudmaker, Amundsen clearly didn't possess his whimsy.

The snow was still very soft and although we tried to pull solo on this flatter section we just weren't strong enough. It took us a further two days to traverse the valley. The temperature also started to dip, sinking to -25°C, our coldest since Patriot Hills. The plateau was beckoning. Underneath the soft snow we could tentatively feel a hard crust. In all probability, if we hadn't had the recent snowfall, the pulling might have been quite pleasant here.

The route out of the valley was only partially discernable but it seemed that there was only one more daunting slope before we gained the plateau itself. However, climbing that final section represented our most challenging obstacle so far. The Axel Heiberg waved us farewell with a sting in her tail. Pat and I started our loathsome counting routine to get us through the worst stages. Again the slope grew too steep and again we had to resort to hoisting our pulks up the slope by using pulleys, this time contrived from an ice axe and a karabiner. At the very threshold of the plateau, in the final upper stages of the glacier, we encountered further folds of snow as the plateau squeezed into this channel through the mountains.

Pulling with Pat had become second nature. We stepped in time and swung the sled along. On the flatter sections, we talked as we toiled. He told me what a relief it was to be able to share the stress of the expedition with someone and discuss the situation with the Land Rovers, the prospect of not seeing Robyn at the Pole and how she would take the setback.

Dave was starting to feel the effects of the hard work up the glacier. Perhaps we had overused his prodigious strength leading? The many hard climbs had put a lot of strain on his knee, which was swollen and painful. Instead of fortifying himself at breaks he was spending the entire period stretching on the snow or on his pulk trying to perform physiotherapy on himself. He was a little quieter in the tent. With his knee in this much pain, and no hope of a let-up, he must have been realising that the next two months were going to be tough.

As we edged over the crest of the glacier the terrain started to harden into windblown waves. Our sled clattered over the sleeping policeman. It slewed sideways, yanking us off balance.

'C'mon you bitch!' I hollered at the sled.

'She loves it when you talk dirty,' Pat countered.

Insulting our pulks was our favourite pastime. We hated them, even though they held all our worldly belongings and were the key to our survival. Mine, which we pulled second, always felt especially heavy.

'It's because you've got so many bloody photographs of your wife and so many stupid plasters for your feet, you great girl.'

'No, it's because I, at least, am carrying my fair share of the kit.'

The going was difficult and slippery to manage. It was our first taste of plateau hauling and evidently scintillating progress wasn't going to be a given. We were finally on the plateau now, although we could see further undulations spreading forever onwards like shock waves. We all felt excited at the thought of taking our own sleds, not having to cover the ground twice and finally starting to make inroads into our mileage deficit. However, we soon discovered that this was pure fantasy. The uphill progress was still too hard. We hauled in the relative sunshine two abreast and then, as the next hill levelled out, went back to soloing, oscillating between the two. Psychologically, it meant all of us knew that pulling our own sleds was right at the limit of what was possible and we constantly expected we might receive the instruction to join teams again.

As I led, due to a mixture of the effort and the altitude, blood dripped steadily from my nose.

'Thanks for rolling out the red carpet, Al,' said Dave, merrily, at our next break.

We climbed still higher and ended the day 100 feet above the level of the Pole. Even though at least half of the day had been spent toiling individually and not in pairs, we had only made four nautical miles. We insisted Paul check the GPS. It was crushing. How could we ever extend this? We now needed to make three times that distance each day.

During our last session, the temperature suddenly plummeted. From sweating in my fleece, I suddenly had to don my windproof jacket. The wind started to pick up; it was our first really stiff breeze for the last fortnight.

Amundsen had been following the shortest route to the Pole. From the apex of the glacier, he had travelled due south but had encountered severe disturbance at the top of another glacier by hugging too close to the mountains. He christened this area the Devil's Ballroom. We had no need to tackle these dangers gratuitously now that we were on the plateau so we aimed to steer west of this zone.

Pat stopped abruptly, his nose in the air, like a dog sniffing the wind.

'Guys, can you feel that?' he asked excitedly.

'Feel what?'

I could hardly hear him above the wind.

'The wind.'

'Yeah, it's sodding cold. And?'

'It's from the south-east. It means we can kite!' He looked quickly at Paul for confirmation but Paul was already unpacking his sled, rummaging around for his kite.

None of us could believe it. What a stroke of luck! No sooner had we emerged from the mountains than we had encountered wind – not just any wind but one that blew counter to the prevailing direction. Perhaps we really would make up our time! We put kiting to the vote. Nobody seriously thought that anyone would refuse the chance.

Privately, I was a little reluctant. I had sweated a lot on the hauling and my fleece was still damp. The temperature had just fallen dramatically, we had been out all day and were dog-tired. Basically, I was scared. It would also be my first time kiting with a pulk – and these pulks were very heavy – which at least meant, I hoped, that they would stop us being lifted into the air. We hadn't been expecting much usable wind on this side of the continent so we only had one kite each. We also only had our thin, light cross-country skis with free-heel bindings, which would be very precarious over rough ground, and to save on weight we had left behind all our protection and our special kite-surfing harnesses (deciding to make do with our climbing gear instead).

The wind started to swirl. It increased as we unfolded our kites and sipped the dregs of our water bottles – now composed of crushed ice. I unscrewed the skins from under my skis. Clicking back into them they felt light and skittish without the grip.

I quickly swapped my damp fleece for my down jacket. I didn't have time to put anything extra on my legs. I knew that kiting would be lower on effort and could involve a lot of waiting if any of us had an accident. It would be easy to get cold. This was going to be a baptism of . . . well, ice.

I jerked my kite into the air with my heart in my mouth, lurching forward in the grip of power and somehow staying upright as I tried to clear the first obstacles. The first half hour I progressed gingerly and conservatively, feeling my way into the power, swooping the sail down the edge of the wind-window and feeling the force begin to take hold of me. I tried to avoid hitting bumps other than straight on so that my precarious bindings wouldn't be tested. Slowly my confidence grew. The wind increased as the visibility decreased. Blown snow swirled around.

Dave was not finding the experience easy. He was falling regularly. He clearly felt his knee desperately and the pressure on it was agony. A big man, he also felt very unbalanced on our thin skis with only the tips of his toes connected. It was like asking a novice to do ballet in a blizzard. Each time he fell we had to wait for him to pick himself up and untangle his kite. There was a huge risk of breaking an ankle or a wrist, or further wrenching his knee on the uneven surface. After an hour or two we entered a field of simply enormous sastrugi. The half-formed waves stood up to four feet tall. We had to edge away or ski rapidly towards our kites to weave around these tumuli. They had steep, sharp edges where the wind and driving spindrift had undercut them. Our kite lines would undoubtedly snag on the overhang if we fell.

I was way overpowered and travelling at serious speed. Each time I thumped over a ridge of ice there was a time lag, like waiting for the sound of thunder, before my pulk hit the same bump and jerked me roughly in the belly. I had to be careful to prevent it smashing into an obstacle that I had narrowly avoided as it fishtailed behind me. If my sled got snagged, I would be pulled one way by a ton of wind and the other by an immovable object. Considering both pieces of kit were tied separately to me, it would be like tearing paper.

Our sleds had been specially designed to be stable enough for kiting yet narrow enough to minimise drag. Reassuringly, mine rode the frozen waves like a motorboat, its hull slamming into the snow behind me. Thwack. Thwack. Thwack.

Dave was in all sorts of trouble. I looked back to see him vainly trying to avoid an enormous bank of hard ice. He scudded into it with a thud before being catapulted into the air. His 100-kilogram pulk launched skywards after him, crashing to earth before rocketing with vicious purpose into his shoulder. A split-second later his kite hit the ground with a shuddering crash. As he lay at his most vulnerable it just hoisted him and his sled back into the air in a dangerous cartwheel. The kite crunched back down to earth. I was certain the fibre would split with the impact. Filled again by the inexhaustible air, it dragged him along face down on his belly, pulling his jacket up around his armpits and filling every chink with snow.

Pat staked his own kite to the snow with a ski and ran over to help. Together they tried to get the kite under control and flip it the right way up. Instead it bounced menacingly on its back like an upturned crab. No sooner had they flicked it over than the wind whisked it into the air again – lifting Pat, Dave and his pulk up into the air before smashing all of them to earth.

Getting up slowly and wiping the snow from his face, Pat signalled to all of us to regroup. I gave Dave a hug. We were finding the conditions, exacerbated by tiredness and our lack of the proper kit, incredibly difficult. When I let go of him, he had tears in his eyes and it wasn't only the pain in his knee.

'You poor sod. That looked brutal. You're showing a shit load of guts.'

I really felt for him. I was struggling, too, and it could easily have been me. I empathised with anyone that felt, even a fraction, feelings of inadequacy relative to the team and the huge challenge we faced.

Paul suggested that Dave water-ski on his pulk-trace behind Pat. Paul would pull both his own and David's sled. I would kite at the back as, now towing the least weight, I would be overpowered and would lose them in the cloud if I got too far in front. I hoped they'd look around every so often in case I fell. As we zig-zagged through the gloaming, I didn't know how we'd find each other if we got separated. We could see the sun glowing dimly through the spindrift. We aimed west of it, digging our edges in as far as we could. The load was too heavy for Pat to tow Dave for long and they couldn't make enough ground upwind – Dave was forced to get his kite out again.

The wind was still rising and was now seriously dangerous. Catching an edge on some overhanging sastrugi, I dumped my kite into the snow. The lines snagged taught on a ledge of ice. Half reined in, it spun around and around like a demented whirligig. The visibility had sunk to zero and we called it a day. It was nearly midnight. We had made a further seven nautical miles – making more than 11 for the day. It was our best total so far but not gained without some bruises. We had genuine difficulty getting our tent up and kites packed away in the howling wind. By the time we finally wriggled inside, it was gusting to over 30 knots. It was the start of what was to become a very dangerous blizzard.

Sitting in the tent that night we were all worn out. I was elated at our progress and it made me much more confident for the future if we got any other favourable winds. Dave, on the other hand, was pretty down. His knee was agony and he felt as if he had held us up. It had hurt all day hauling and instead of resting it he had just given it another five hours' battering. He sat quietly – the first time on the trip, awake, that he had not talked for a five-minute stretch. He was clearly imagining the interminable haul to the Pole that lay ahead.

Paul never avoided the tough questions. As if David hadn't had enough punishment for one day, he went straight for the jugular.

'The knee seems pretty bad. Is it?'

'It's all right,' Dave evaded, 'You know, if I stretch it a lot, pop some pain-smarties. It should be OK.'

'Can you cope? We should know the situation.'

'I dunno, it's hard to tell. I'm hoping this flatter ground will work different muscles and give it a rest but you never know. I'm a bit worried, though, yeah.'

'It's fine for us to go slower and take more rests but then we'll need to be out longer. We've got no choice but to make the miles. We're seriously pressed to make the Pole by Christmas.'

'And if it doesn't get better?' Pat asked.

'Then we have to evacuate Dave.'

I didn't even want to look at Dave.

'Evacuation' was the very worst word that could be mentioned on a polar trip. I prayed to God I would never have to hear it. For two years I had dreaded that word. Being flown out when the rest of your team were continuing represented, for me, a particularly graphic kind of inadequacy.

1 Alastair

2 Paul

3 Patrick

4 David

5 Our first taste of man-hauling at Patriot Hills

6 Patrick and Alastair hauling up the Axel Heiburg glacier

7   Looking out over Independence Hills in the Heritage Range

8   Patrick and Alastair crossing a snow bridge on the Axel Heiberg

9   A parhelic circle above Silence Valley

10   Taking a break on the high polar plateau

11 Heading due south

12 Over sastrugi

13   Emerging from a blizzard

14   Patrick being pursued by a battered pulk

15   At the axis of the world

16   A euphoric team

17 Alastair meets his baby

David's evacuation would in all probability lead to our own. If we called in a plane we would have to wait for it to arrive. That delay, which could be many days, would be disastrous for our timetable.

Typical of his magnanimity, David was even more reluctant for our expedition to end than his own: 'If it comes to it, just leave me in Paul's tent with a phone,' he said quietly.

CHAPTER 14

The Sword of Damocles

'Very well, Damocles,' replied the ruler, 'since my life strikes you as so attractive, would you care to have a taste of it yourself and see what my way of living is really like?' Damocles agreed with pleasure.

So Dionysius had him installed on a golden couch covered with a superb woven coverlet embroidered with beautiful designs, and beside the couch was placed an array of sideboards loaded with gold and silver plate . . . There were perfumes and garlands and incense, and the tables were heaped up with a most elaborate feast. Damocles thought himself a truly fortunate person.

But in the middle of all this splendour, directly above the neck of the happy man, Dionysius arranged that a gleaming sword should be suspended from the ceiling, to which it was attached by a horsehair. And so Damocles had no eye for his lovely waiters or for the artistic plate. Indeed, he did not even feel like reaching out his hand towards the food. Presently the garlands, of their own accord, just slipped from his head. In the end he begged the tyrant to let him go, declaring that his desire to be happy had evaporated.'

Cicero, On the Good Life[1]

Left alone in these conditions, Dave would have felt the most complete sense of isolation possible. I doubt there can be a greater solitude than the wastes of Antarctica. Life would have depended entirely on his supply of gas and the battery power in his satellite phone. Unable to walk properly, his utter impotence would have been psychologically wretched but yet that still wouldn't have

---

1 Book V of 'Discussions at Tusculum', translated by Michael Grant.

been as oppressive as the sense of having been left behind – of not mattering.

We would never have abandoned an injured teammate, of course, even if the rescue plane knew where he was. We would never have forgiven ourselves if something had happened but the thought was touching and it showed how desperate he was not to let the rest of us down.

As usual now, while we melted snow for tea, David padded across to Paul's tent to stretch his battered leg, before rejoining us when the water had boiled.

'Guys, the strangest thing just happened.'

Paul looked up from stirring the cooking pot.

'I was calling my brother on the sat-phone. He wasn't in – anyway it beeped straight through to voicemail. I was going to leave a message and was about to talk but I—I . . . just found no words came. I couldn't help crying. I couldn't stop. It was so sudden and strange – so I hung up. Then I felt shit that Anthony'd hear my voice and think something awful had happened. So I figured I had to ring back. I called again. It went through to voicemail . . . and the same thing happened. Jesus. I just couldn't stop crying. I was telling him I was fine, not to worry, that I loved him in this incoherent slobber. I don't know what he's going to think.'

As David told us what had happened, I realised that even the most buoyant, outwardly exuberant of guys, such as Dave, can get caught up in the stress and strain we were under. Every small niggle was magnified over a day of hard grind, each tiny discomfort was enhanced by the snow, the wind and the isolation. There was no one close to hug you so that even something as vicarious as a recorded voice was meaningful contact.

We debated whether to take a rest day. The wind was still howling and Dave's knee could do with some respite. It was hard for everyone to articulate their emotions as each of us wanted to be sensitive to Dave's condition but it also didn't sound like an ailment that would get better overnight. Eventually, after everyone had said that they were either torn or indifferent, I suggested – evading Dave's eyes as I did so – that, on balance, we should go out and make some miles. We were all conscious of how far we were falling behind and I was desperate to make even nominal progress. I was dreading going out in these conditions but that made me more sensitive: I felt I might be staying put out of fear rather than kindness. I needed to force myself out into the wind to prove that my comfort wasn't the real reason.

Everyone agreed with the decision. David stoically started to get ready straightaway, showing no sign of irritation. It was difficult to tell whether, inside, he was cursing me or worrying about how he would cope. None of us wanted the others to think that they were in any way a limiting factor.

We dug out the tent and packed it away. The fly sheet flapped noisily in the wind that seemed to penetrate every chink of our clothing. As I opened my pulk to pack in my kit, more blown snow gusted in, filling it up and weighing it down further. We were extremely cold by the time we got into our harnesses.

The trick of breaking camp, particularly in the wind, is to do it quickly enough not to get cold. Taking down the tent and untying the guy ropes was impossible wearing anything but the thinnest gloves. Our hands would get so cold that during the first few hundred metres after a break or a campsite, it was not uncommon to see one of us stop and windmill his hands frantically, trying to push blood back into lifeless fingers, before hunching forward on his trace and heaving his sled so as not to be left behind.

You get cold quickly breaking camp because going out for a day's hauling means you need to dress for doing exercise. If you put too much on you'll sweat as your heart rate climbs. If you stop for a moment or start to slow down then the moisture freezes, achieving its biological function many times more efficiently than it is supposed to. Encased in a straitjacket of ice, it's then impossible to get warm. Paul's favourite mantra was – 'You sweat, you die.' Although delivered humorously, it was deadly serious.

I never quite got the knack of regulating my temperature. You can't just keep stopping to make adjustments as it's infuriating to keep breaking the steady rhythm of the people behind you. If you're at the back it's hard work to keep catching up (indeed the acting of hurrying to make up the ground again makes you sweat further). If the wind is blowing then you can't unzip or vent as your clothing soon becomes clogged with spindrift. So the only solution is to dress absolutely right for the day. I found the surfaces and the wind – and therefore the speed and effort – were difficult to predict. My only certainties were that it would be cold and there would be snow: not exactly rocket science.

The very worst thing about overheating wasn't the logical next stage (getting cold) – it was the effect on my goggles. I found that if I got even slightly too hot the heat from my head would penetrate my goggles. They would mist over. The cold air would freeze the fug into an impenetrable ice-curtain and I would be blind for the day. It is difficult to overstate how uncomfortable that was. I would then try and scratch clear patches through the ice crystals. Putting my goggles inside my jacket could melt the ice but as soon as I drew them out again, they would refreeze instantly. It is a beautiful, if barren, landscape. Without sight you are robbed of one of the only privileges of the journey, your world shrinks and your focus is internalised: mainly onto your discomfort. If I took my goggles off then I faced the risk of snow-blindness.

All this sounds like the confessions of a whingeing novice but much of Antarctica is about experience. The less you know about yourself the more uncomfortable you are. It was revealing for me that everything seemed to boil down to self-awareness – not just mentally but physically, too. The more you know about your own body and how it copes in various conditions the more you can try to work within yourself. How can you tell when you are just tired and when you're at breaking point? Is your Achilles tendon just painful or is it tearing irreparably? Are your extremities numb or are they getting seriously frostbitten? Who knows? I certainly didn't.

Part of my motivation for coming was to help define my physical boundaries, to test myself. But in Antarctica you don't have any major physical revelations other than your own weakness. It is impossible to push the envelope in the same way as on a 24-hour adventure race. If you get injured, you're screwed. You need to maximise your comfort instead of the reverse. Less is more. You have to take any precautions you can against the conditions. In fact, the process is actually counter-macho. Paul (who also has the happy advantage of being susceptible to nothing except kryptonite) is so successful partly because he is the most systematic with his procedures; he has taken the time to develop and tailor his kit and pays the most attention to all the small things that will enable his body and his equipment to be preserved. We imagine 'hard' guys as disdainful of plasters and able to handle any conditions in a loin cloth, equipped with only a Snickers and a sub-machine gun but that's just not the reality.

Having got frostbite on my cheek at Patriot Hills (without noticing), I had lost all my confidence. I had no idea of my thresholds anymore. I covered my chin with my neck-gaiter, sealed my face with my goggles and nose guard and pulled my dog-fur hood snugly around my head. We set off with the wind blowing diagonally into our faces.

My toes were numb. Numbness wasn't that unusual but they stayed numb, like blocks of wood, all day. It would prove to be a pivotal day for me – and ironically it had been my decision, ultimately, to go out.

Paul admitted, during a snatched break hunched up against the wind, that his toes were right on the edge – it made me even more uncomfortable. If Paul's were borderline, with his resilience to the cold . . . then surely mine were too? But with feet, what can you do? Short of running up and down on the spot (which isn't exactly desirable after hours of hard slog) it is impractical to get them out of your boots and warm them under your armpits – even if I had done any yoga before I set off, that particular posture would have been a little challenging. So I just dragged on, trying not to think of them.

These severe conditions were much more what I had imagined Antarctica to be like, rather than the Axel Heiberg, which, although vaster, was more Alpine in character. Spindrift blew across my skis all day, like dry ice. It became disorientating at times, as if the whole world was moving beneath my feet. The altitude caused me to pant roughly as I hauled. Soon my nose guard was covered in ice. A long stalactite hung off it like an elephant's trunk. My beard froze to my neck-gaiter.

I really felt the pace, even though it was laboriously slow. Dave limped at the back. He can't have been enjoying it either. The wind was such that we couldn't see beyond a few yards so he didn't have much option – he had to keep up. For the first time on the trip, I noticed Paul really feeling it now that we were up high – dropping back a little when Patrick led and struggling to breathe even when eating his snacks on our short breaks.

I ate a lot less than I had on the glacier as my cheese, which I brought into the tent at night to defrost, was frozen solid and impossible even to gnaw. I got too cold to bother to eat properly. I couldn't listen to music either, as it was too complicated to organise it with all my headgear and I was paranoid that fumbling around my face to ensure an earpiece stayed in would cause me to leave a part uncovered and get frostbite. I felt the pulling and the cold in equal measure. Pat showed his resilience by stopping to film a few parts of the day – I could no more have brought myself to hold a camera with a naked finger on that day than ski with my penis out.

After a day's exertion we had made a miserly 5.5 nautical miles – less than half of what we needed. Partly due to our late start (itself caused by getting into camp so late the previous night) and partly as the wind had now increased to over 30 knots, we pitched camp. It flapped and rattled loudly as we concentrated hard to put it up without a mistake in the driving snow.

Despite the relief of getting into it and out of the roar of the wind, I found myself curiously without an appetite. I had just done a work-out the equivalent of a marathon on a gym step machine and yet I didn't feel the slightest hunger. I pushed the rehydrated food around my plate; normally I would have devoured it with gusto. I couldn't have altitude sickness, could I? We had climbed so slowly – and we weren't *that* high.

I had forgotten that at the South Pole the air pressure is lower than the equivalent altitude elsewhere on earth. Due to the elliptical shape of the planet, which makes the sky lower at the ends of the earth, the physiological effect of altitude is enhanced. The highest point of the plateau, 11,000 feet, which we were due to reach over the next fortnight, is therefore roughly equivalent to the altitude at which pilots start to use supplementary oxygen. With roughly 40 per cent less oxygen per breath, your breathing rate has to increase markedly, even at rest. The body function is streamlined to preserve vital organs. The stomach is not a necessity, so it ceases to digest food.

As I sipped my hot drink after dinner, I was hit by a wave of nausea. David was unzipping the tent to go out into the wind to have a pee.

'Dave . . .' I muttered with the quiet voice of urgent panic, 'Look out!' I dived past him, vomiting as I lunged, spraying the inside of our tent with couscous, vegetable protein substitute and stomach lining – our tent that we had to live in together, cheek by jowl, for the next couple of months.

Lying on my stomach in the snow, I retched and retched until my belly was empty. My uncovered hands, moist from clawing chunks of sick away from my mouth, froze in seconds. Snow blew in my face and the storm raged about me.

'Oh God, ugghh – I'm so, so sorry. It's the worst thing. I can't believe it – to puke in the frigging tent . . . it's unforgivable. I'm so, so sorry.'

'Aw, look what you've gawn and done! You've really gawn and done it now!' exclaimed Dave with a broad grin, aping an Aussie accent and pointing dramatically to the tiniest chunk of vomit sitting on his leg and ignoring the carnage around him. Miraculously it had otherwise missed him. 'You've gawn and bloody vomited on my trousers, you flaming mongrel!'

Pat reluctantly reached for his loo-roll. He only had two rolls for the journey. He used the remainder of his first roll mopping up my mess. Vomit froze onto me. Usually our tent was quite cosy – now, with the sun obscured by cloud and billowing snow, the inside wasn't much warmer than the outside. Feeling remorseful, guilty and sick at the same time, I skulked back inside. The tent stunk. Luckily, as it froze, the smell diminished. I apologised repeatedly. I felt I had let them and myself down.

Pat looked disconsolately at his empty loo-roll. His mind must have fleetingly drifted to the uncomfortable possibility of having to wipe his frozen buttocks with a bare hand and a large snow block. Doing what I had done could have broken bonds but everybody was incredibly sympathetic.

'You've bloody used up all my bog-roll. I can't believe it. I've got to ration my wipes now. Anyway, talking of wiping – you must feel like shit.'

'It's the altitude. You'll probably find you're off your food for a day but you'll feel better in a day or so.'

'Great!' Piped Dave with a large grin 'It means that Al's shortbread is up for grabs . . .' He looked around to see if anyone else was going to challenge him for my ration.

'Mmm, nice thinking Danger . . . Maybe he won't feel up to all his snacks tomorrow. I'll have his flapjacks and you can have his dried fruit.'

'Dried fruit? Bollocks, I'll have dibs on his Galaxy bars.'

It was the classic British response to a difficult situation. Make light of it. Make the wounded one feel that it couldn't be too bad, after all, or no one would be callous enough to actually take delight in eating at my expense – would they?

Paul melted some more snow in the pot to help clean up the tent and to make me a cup of tea to ease the stomach.

After a silence, the inevitable topic of our progress surfaced. We were now into our third week since being dropped at the Ross Ice Shelf. Our best distance hauling (other than the kiting) on the whole expedition had still been the 6.1 miles that we had accomplished on our second day. With our remaining rations we had to make an average of nearly double that. We were far behind schedule.

Paul spoke. As usual he was relatively curt and to the point. Although a gentle man, he isn't very British in his manner. He might feel sympathetic but that won't be revealed in his demeanour. As I had seen with Dave, he isn't one to skirt around an issue.

'I'm worried about our schedule again. After the exertions of the last month, I don't think we are a strong team.'

He said it with his characteristic, slightly nasal, Canadian twang – it seemed even harsher because of it. He paused afterwards, almost for us to acknowledge and then dwell on our weakness.

'We've got very little in reserve. Although the South Pole is attainable, it is going to be very hard. We are on a knife-edge.'

He nodded, looking slowly around at each of us as we ate our soup.

All my pre-expedition fears were transpiring. As I crawled into my sleeping bag, I looked around the tent. It was damp. Lots of fine, wet snow had blown in. The fabric flapped, shuddered and groaned violently all night, bringing the very fragility of our existence home to bear. This flimsy lining, being persecuted by the wind, was all that separated us from the storm.

The howling rose to a higher pitch, increasing to over 45 knots – roughly 80 kilometres an hour. It beat the tent remorselessly. Nature is ruthless and implacable; there was nothing we could do except sit tight and hope everything would hold together. The chances of travel the next day were now non-existent. Blizzards in the Antarctic normally lasted around three or four days. If this one did, our schedule would be put under even more pressure.

Snow fell from the roof onto my face. Everyone was asleep. I felt so very alone. I thought of home and of Annabel.

She had written me a series of cards to take with me on the trip. On the envelopes were instructions as to when I should open them. I opened the first during the flight into Antarctica. The second was intended for the top of the Axel Heiberg. Although technically we had got there yesterday evening I had decided, using it as a motivation to keep myself trudging on, that I would only open it when we completed the 85th degree – still 19 nautical miles away. In our condition and circumstances that was probably more than a week away. I was sufficiently unhappy to decide that I needed to open it now. I dug into my stuff-sack and pulled it out, studying it for a while before slowly ripping open the envelope taking care not to tear the lipstick kiss on the back. I pulled the card slowly out of it, wanting to dwell on the moment now that it was finally here. I had all night.

On the card was a quote from Winston Churchill: 'Never, never, never give up.' It couldn't have been more prescient. Inside, referring to getting to the top of the glacier, it read: 'Congratulations! God knows what or how you must be feeling but I know the worst is now over and you have already achieved so much! Hopefully it will be a little more fun now and not so gruelling.'

God, it didn't feel fun now. If the plateau stays like this, I thought, I'm not sure if I will make it.

It continued: 'Thinking of you and giving your very sore, bruised, tired little feet big kisses to make them stronger for the journey ahead. Love you!' She signed it over a further lipstick kiss saying 'Kisses for the toes and the soul!'

I missed her more than ever. What she could never have known – I didn't even know it yet – is that when I next inspected those toes that she had sent so much attention to, I would find them badly frostbitten.

The next day travel was impossible. The weather was very dangerous. We were only a short distance from where Amundsen had camped at the top of the Axel Heiberg Glacier. There, the animals that had laboured so impressively up the steep sides of the mountains were rewarded with the knife. Twenty-four of his 42 dogs were slaughtered and the 18 fittest spared. Amundsen calculated that the rest of the way to the Pole should, on Shackleton's evidence, now be largely flat and he wouldn't need so many. He'd feed the butchered animals to his men and to those dogs that remained so as to fortify them. He could then cache some meat for the return journey.

As they toiled up the glacier Amundsen confessed that

> . . . the thought of the fresh dog cutlets that awaited us when we got to the top made our mouths water. In the course of time we had so habituated ourselves to the terrible idea of the approaching slaughter that this event did not appear to us so horrible as it might have been.[1]

However, when the day did arrive, the cold reality was a more difficult proposition: each man was given the task of killing the dogs from his own team. This ensured the most humane outcome as each man, with the bond he had established over the last month, could be trusted to deliver retribution as kindly as possible. It must have been a wrenching experience but Amundsen himself didn't take part in it.

The episode tells us a lot about him – a mixture of aloofness, pragmatism, humanity and steeliness. He describes the scene vividly. I can almost imagine the white snow turning blood red as each dog

---

1 Roald Amundesn, *The South Pole*.

was slaughtered and the ghoulish mayhem as the surviving dogs, resembling primeval wolves with their dappled fur and preternaturally bright eyes, ravenously tore out the glistening entrails of their fallen comrades.

Amundsen started to pump the primus stove to a high pressure:

> I was hoping thereby to produce enough noise to deaden the shots that I knew would soon be heard – twenty-four of our brave companions and faithful helpers were marked out for death. It was hard – but it had to be so. We had agreed to shrink from nothing in order to reach our goal. Each man was to kill his own dogs to the number that had been fixed.
>
> The pemmican was cooked remarkably quickly that evening, and I believe that I was unusually industrious in stirring it. There went the first shot – I am not a nervous man, but I must admit that I gave a start. Shot now followed upon shot – they had an uncanny sound over the great plain. A trusty servant lost his life each time. It was long before the first man reported that he had finished; they were all to open their dogs, and to take out the entrails to prevent the meat from being contaminated.[1]

His camp has been given the sobriquet the 'Butcher's Shop'. There the weather also set in and he and his men were forced to hunker down at that unpleasant slaughterhouse for a further four days.

Now, in nearly the same place, lying like a cold-cut in my sleeping bag, I was locked in a similar blizzard. I hoped it wouldn't last as long. It did.

During the night, drift snow had blown into through the outer shell of the tent and blocked up the entire entrance. Our boots, lying in a pile on the snow (there was never enough room to bring them in) were totally buried. David drew a face and a pair of eyes on the drift-snow-pile and made a snowman.

'Look what Paul's built in the night to block us in!' he laughed.

'No, Amundsen's dogs have been digging for Al's sick.'

Our bodies were in a pretty settled routine now, and even though I had shown scant respect for my dinner last night, I still needed to make my daily ablutions at around the same time as the others. We'd

---

1 Roald Amundesn, *The South Pole*.

have to knock down the snowman to get out. All of us shuddered at the thought of taking down our trousers in what was now a wind-chill of -78°C.

'You go first . . .'

'No, you go first . . .' we all joked childishly. We weren't being very macho about this.

The best technique employed was to dig a small hole. The shovel would then be speared into the ground to clutch onto to prevent you from being blown over backwards onto your leavings. You had to face the wind so that your bum was in the lee. You tried to keep your head cocked to prevent your nose from getting frostbitten – which was frighteningly quick to happen in these conditions.

I used to hold onto the shovel with one hand and use the other to try to shield my private parts from the gusts and the blown snow. I would then reach hurriedly for my ration of loo-paper. I had to take off a glove to do this (for obvious reasons). If snow was being blown around, then very fine spindrift would land on my uncovered hand, melt onto my warm skin and freeze.

This particular experience had all these complications magnified many times. The trauma was unthinkable. The wind roared incessantly, rocking me as I squatted. I watched my crap freezing as soon as it hit the ground.

After I had been, David went out. Barely a few seconds later we heard him running back to the tent against the gale. He couldn't have finished already.

'All done!' He shouted triumphantly. He unzipped the outer fly-sheet and pressed his nose against the inner cloth but made no effort to come in.

'What are you doing, Danger?' Pat asked.

'It's called a porch-wipe,' he shouted, half-laughing, against the wind. 'Desperate times call for desperate measures! There's no way that I'm wiping my arse out there in this. Jesus!'

We all laughed. We could see his whole face pressed up against the tent, creased in a mixture of amusement and discomfort – not only at the cold but because of the contorted posture demanded by the task at hand. Five minutes later and we were laughing at Pat's face slobbering on the tent canvas exactly where Dave's had been.

If I hadn't tried to be so stoical by doing it all out in the blizzard, to show I could manage it, I would have had a more 'comfortable' time. That was typical of me, whereas David didn't mind what we thought – especially not about something so absurd. He would, quite rightly, prove himself when and where it counted. This was Dave's character all over. He was happy to try anything new and didn't mind looking like an idiot – which meant he seldom did. For him and Pat, any excuse to make a joke out of something was accepted with open arms. It made what might have been very hard, so very much easier.

The rest day would probably do us lots of good, provided that the enforced inertia didn't run over that period. Almost by definition, rest days taken due to bad weather are seldom enjoyable since the sun is obscured by cloud, making the tent freezing cold.

To make matters worse we found a slight rip in the fly sheet, which was responsible for letting in the spindrift. Even though the tear was small, having one at all in these conditions was unsettling as we weren't sure how it would take the stress. There was so much snow swirling about that it seemed to drop in from the roof continually. Our belongings got damper and damper.

Paul ventured over from his tent to cook some food. He looked completely unimpressed at our sodden, frozen and crusty belongings and tried to sweep away a pile of snow that had gathered on the tent floor where he usually sat.

'This is bloody ridiculous.'

To pass the time we played Indian poker – a very simple variation of the classic game. We would each put a card on our forehead, turn out a trump from the pack and then bet against each other without knowing what we had. Money had no currency here, so, to Paul's consternation, we bet for peanuts. Literally. And, boy, did it hurt to lose. Food was precious. Our initial stake was one peanut or to be precise half of one – as that was how they usually came. You can't imagine the haggling and arguments we undertook to determine the relative values of macadamia (worth three peanuts), brazil (five), cashew (two) or dry roasted (two – inflated in value due to the salty coating). And when chocolate started to enter the equation it became a different story. I once paid out 40 winning peanuts for a largish square of white chocolate. It hardly sounds like big bucks but it was the only substance that had any value. We had recklessly played for dares while in Patriot Hills but now that was almost inconceivable – the stakes were too high.

All day I had been worrying whether I should declare the state of my toes. It seemed that the blisters I had sustained on the glacier had frozen at some point over the last few days, or even in the cold tent. They didn't look too good.

Paul studied my second toe for a while in silence. Only two days before I had sat listening to Dave being threatened with evacuation if his knee didn't get better. I knew what was coming.

Paul was as cool and aloof as Amundsen. I felt as if he was holding a pistol in his hands. I was a weak dog and he would dispatch me with one word. I twitched before him.

'You see this line,' Paul said, as he traced his finger across my toe where the pink colour gave way to a brown blister. 'There's a clear line of demarcation. That's a classic symptom of deep frostbite.'

He seemed to be talking with almost the dispassionate air of a doctor looking at an interesting test case. Further up the toe the blister went darker and turned finally, at the tip, to black. I just sat there unblinking, looking at him, trying not to show any emotion, waiting for the shot that would end my expedition.

'Er, I think most of that's just blister, I've had it for a while,' I evaded.

'Yeah, I think it looks better than it was on the glacier,' added Dave to encourage me.

Pat asked Paul what the outlook was.

Paul paused.

'Well, I guess we need to wait and see if it gets infected. If it does then we have to treat it with antibiotics. If that doesn't work, then we'll have to . . .' he paused 'think about getting Al out.'

The last resonant word sounded like 'oot' with Paul's accent.

I said nothing. I tried to conceal my emotions from the others and look calm. This was the very moment I had dreaded from the outset. Even a bad accident was preferable as it wouldn't relate to my own strength and capability. Please tell me this was not happening. Please, please tell me it wasn't.

Altitude sickness and then frostbite, stuck in a blizzard that didn't look like clearing any time soon. Could things get any worse?

Part of my toe looked dead. The one relief with the onset of frostbite is that now it didn't hurt. It had been agonising on the glacier. If it was dead, then surely it would infect. If it infected there were two worries – contaminating the blood that flows to the toe (if the blood flow wasn't already impaired) or the infection spreading down my toe. To me, given its colour, feeling and daily swaddling in unwashed socks, infection was inevitable. It was a question of 'when' not 'if'.

Over the ensuing days, I had to check my toe each evening after travel. I dreaded that moment all day. For nearly eight hours of interminable, back-breaking work, I imagined my toe suppurating quietly in my boot. Every night, I feared that infection would be revealed. The sword swung above my head by a slender thread.

Damocles wanted his taste of another life. Soon he found that the precariousness of its reality was not to his liking. I was certain I would not have opted for what I was currently experiencing, if I had known – I mean really known – the abject uncertainty I was feeling right then.

Each day that we progressed I grew more bitter. If my toe betrayed me now, I used to think, evacuation would have been so unfair. Whether it became infected or it didn't seemed to me to be the responsibility of some unknown and capricious agent. I was keeping up with the others, I was managing, and yet, even after I had climbed the glacier and as I battled through the winds of the plateau, I feared that when the South Pole was in touching distance, as things got easier, I would still be denied my prize and have to return home to be judged a humiliating and shameful failure. I despised that toe. I resolved many times that I would, if push came to shove, cut it off with my Leatherman.

In some cultures, particularly the US, failure is almost celebrated because it means that you've striven. It doesn't have the same stigma as in the UK. To be an adventurer or an entrepreneur, failure is a constant possibility. In fact it is often unavoidable. Conditions over which you have no control can intervene. Kit that has been tried and tested can break or the body which was given to you may just not be strong enough. You shouldn't be ashamed of that. Learning from mistakes is often the best way of arriving at success. But I *was* scared of failure. Maybe because I had never really failed, maybe because I'd never really tried anything. It occurred to me that we measure success by an arbitrary yardstick. Wealth and recognition are the blades that carve the notches when perhaps it should be character and love.

Some adventurers embrace risk for the sheer adrenalin with barely a backward glance or an introspective moment, but most are driven by the concept of 'legacy' – the footprint they make in the world, the way others think of them. They might not enjoy every second but they want to have *done* something incredible. But this obsession means they're in danger of missing out on real life. They're too busy going out doing things they don't enjoy to impress people who don't care. And of course, if things go wrong, life is exactly what they'll miss out on.

On the second day of the storm, 1 December, I realised we had been in Antarctica one month. It dawned on me that we had arrived in Antarctica on precisely the same day that Scott had left his base.

I hoped that that wasn't a bad omen.

CHAPTER 15

Difficult Decisions

Your pain is the breaking of the shell that encloses your understanding.
Kahlil Gibran, The Prophet

The failure of the Land Rovers was having complicated reper-
cussions. Each day we would call into Patriot Hills and try to haggle
with them to fly in our resupply to the Pole. This was far from
simple. Matty McNair's expedition, like us, also needed a resupply.
As a way of part-financing our expedition, we had offered to drive
theirs in for a fee.

Paul was responsible for making the final call on matters of safety
and evacuation. Clearly, as guide, his interests lay in ensuring
the resupply was in place as soon as possible. Patrick and I on
the other hand bore the financial risk. The expedition budget was
already exhausted and we needed to pay Matty back as well as
find further funds, so it was imperative for us to find the best price.
How could I tell Annabel the sums that we'd need to borrow? The
negotiations continued for nearly two weeks. They coincided with
and contributed to our most stressful and difficult period on the
expedition, emotionally and physically.

Should we abandon the expedition now?

We had to contemplate this. No sponsor would agree to pay
additional sums – and we were reluctant to approach them after
they had just swallowed the bitter-tasting PR pill of the Land Rover
team's decision. We either had to give up or Patrick and I had to
come up with the credit. From a tent in a blizzard in Antarctica,

in probably the remotest place on the whole planet, it wasn't that easy. It had taken two hard years *in London* to get even what we had. Our only option was to use the money owed to the tax man and borrow the rest. We'd have to worry about paying our substantial VAT bill when we returned. Hardly flush after part-time teaching for two years, this would represent the bitterest of homecomings. Of course, ironically, if either Dave or I were evacuated we would have squandered the money. Was all this worth being destitute for? I looked at my blackening toe and at the fine, damp snow filling up our cramped tent.

That evening, Paul talked further about Amundsen. He explained how, after the four storm days that he had experienced at the Butcher's Shop, he had jettisoned some weight. Paul emphasised our position. He wanted to gauge if we had any moral issues about burying excess gear in order to lighten our pulks. He made his case out.

We had discussed a similar issue earlier in relation to whether or not we should dump rubbish into crevasses on the Axel Heiberg. Paul is one of the most environmentally conscious people I have met. His passion and enthusiasm for the polar ice caps is unrivalled. He has made his life visiting, protecting and taking others to see their wonders. His view was very defensible and predicated on safe environmental practice.

His argument was that taking rubbish out to burn inefficiently and improperly in Chile, which had inadequate and unsophisticated waste management systems, or to bury it in squalid landfill sites had a more negative impact. This wasn't even mentioning the huge cost of flying it out of Antarctica in terms of cargo space, weight and fuel. If we were to bury the paltry amount of garbage we had (most of the packaging had been removed prior to leaving to save on weight) he didn't see that throwing it into a crevasse would make any difference to the environment. It would be enveloped in snow, crushed to smithereens and eventually deposited, in a tiny coffin-like cube, into the sea in a few million years hence.

It did make sense but somehow, debating it on the Axel Heiberg and looking out at the pristine beauty of the valley we couldn't bring ourselves to do it. It was similar to the debate I had had with myself over the morality of bringing the Land Rovers to Antarctica, however defensible that had been logically.

Now, in relation to kit, the argument seemed different. We had a pressing need and, somehow, with the environment so hostile and ugly, the little bell in our heads just didn't chime so loudly. So, we resolved to leave our rope, ice axes, books, Pat's broken boot, some clips, harnesses, karabiners and other now-redundant climbing gear. We would put it all in a duffle bag, sealed like a time capsule, and bury it in the snow.

It did make sense – any lessened weight would help us cover the daily required mileage that was now escalating steadily. I got the impression that Paul felt a lariat connecting him to Amundsen – the parallels with Amundsen's experience were uncanny and this was just one further connection. We had climbed Mount Betty on the same day that Amundsen had and had found his cairn. We had camped where he had camped on the icefall. We were stuck at the Butcher's Shop in the same blizzard, for the same amount of time and now we were burying the mountaineering equipment that we had used to climb up the glacier – just as Amundsen had also buried both his climbing kit and his dogs in the exact same place.

Amundsen has been chided in some quarters for his hard-nosed approach to polar travel, sacrificing his dogs so brutally on the hard anvil of his ambition. He was no stranger to moral controversy. Maybe leaving this equipment was, subliminally, Paul's own statement of partisanship and solidarity for his revered mentor's approach. But it had to be done. Polar travel was about making hard decisions.

The next day the weather was undiminished. It was another anxious day of enforced camp in awful conditions. The wind still harried and blustered against our tent. On the first day we had built a barrier around it with our pulks to shelter it from the worst of the blast; now we had to go back and dig out the buried sleds and remove some of the worst of the drift, which was leaning heavily and dangerously onto its sides, in order to relieve the tension on the canvas.

On the morning of the fourth day, the wind was still strong but had lessened a little. We had to leave now. Three days huddled together without moving, following weeks of arduous endeavour had caused a lot of stiffness – besides, we had almost bet away all our peanuts.

As I stuck my head out of the flaps to survey the scene, I noticed the snow had drifted around the tent to leave a clear slipstream for more than 50 yards, which was stained with piss and frozen crap, as most of us had gone there to try to get some protection.

Before leaving, sparing a thought for Amundsen, we buried the duffle bag in the hole we had dug for our drinking water and hastened out into the swirling snow. Paul marked the cache by driving an ice axe into the snow, just as Amundsen had thrust a ski into the ice. I realised again that this was more than a practical gesture, it was an act of homage to his polar hero.

> The fourteen dogs' carcasses that were left were piled up into a heap . . . The spare sets of dog-harness, some Alpine ropes, and all our crampons for ice work, which we now thought would not be required were left behind. The last thing to be done was planting a broken ski upright by the side of the depot.[1]

We were leaving when, to be honest, it was marginal: the winds were still raging; there was almost zero visibility. Amundsen had a similar dilemma. He comments glowingly on his men's courage in going out into the gale. They had been camped for one day longer than us, although we had travelled on the first day of the blizzard:

> 'It's the devil's own weather here at the Butcher's,' said one, 'it looks to me as if it would never get any better. This is the fifth day, and it's blowing worse than ever'. We all agreed. 'There's nothing so bad as lying weather-bound like this', continued another, it takes more out of you than going from morning to night'. Personally, I was of the same opinion. One day may be pleasant enough, but two, three, four and now it seemed five days – no it was awful. 'Shall we try it?' No sooner was the proposal submitted than it was accepted unanimously and with acclamation. When I think of my four friends of the southern journey, it is the memory of that morning that comes first to my mind. All the qualities that I most admire in a man were clearly shown at that juncture: courage and dauntlessness, without

---

1 This and following quotation from Roald Amundsen, *The South Pole*.

boasting or big words. Amid joking and chaff, everything was packed, and then – out into the blizzard.

It took us about an hour to break camp. Our pulks were full of drift snow (and therefore heavier) and we had to dig them out again. We then worked to free our tents from the drift. Paul ripped his tent's snow skirt with the shovel, as he struggled to free it from the heavy accretion of snow. We were delayed half an hour while he brought it into our tent, lit the stove to dry the rip and to warm up the tape.

When we finally left, the conditions were truly awful. My goggles misted and froze instantly, so I saw even less. For survival, it was necessary to keep up – people really don't look back when they pull, especially in these conditions.

I vividly remember leading (which, in a white out, you do with a metal girdle tied around your waist that holds a compass out in front to peer at through the gloom). Paul stopped to tell me that, judging from the direction of the wind, he felt I was on the wrong bearing. It was only then that we noticed that Pat wasn't with us. His hands had got dangerously cold and he had stopped to warm them. In a fraction of a second he was lost to view. We waited. Half a minute later, Pat materialised out of the spindrift. First you could see the dimmest outline, then a shadow, which slowly took the shape of a man, and finally it metamorphosed into Pat's distinctive skiing style. Thank God. With us about to change angle and our tracks being instantly covered in spindrift, he would have lost us.

Leading in a white out is an extraordinary sensation. You literally head off into absolute obscurity. You can see *nothing*. There is no difference between air and ground. You don't know if you are skiing uphill or downhill, left or right. With my misted-up goggles I had to hunch over to peer at the snow. That way I could just make out the sastrugi. I tried to decipher the wind-lines etched on them to confirm that I was at the right angle to the prevailing wind. If I was lucky I could see snow blowing over my ski-tips to confirm the angle.

Up above us, frustratingly, was blue sky, but there was so much wind-blown spindrift that it was like being in a cloud. I struggled to keep my temperature right as it was impossible to vent in those conditions, otherwise all my clothes would be instantly clogged with snow. The first five to six hours were unutterably miserable, and then, during the last session, blue sky appeared and we could suddenly make out three of the last of the vast peaks of the Trans-Antarctic Mountains, named after Amundsen's men; Bjaaland, Wisting and Hassel. It was a miraculous moment. It was our first proper glimpse of the plateau. The white plain extended on and on before us, fringed by these glorious and imposing mountains. These ghosts of Amundsen's southern party seemed to watch us toiling slowly over the frozen chop of the ice-sea like sentinels from a past era.

The sky was lit crimson with striated clouds. The snow reflected all the colours of the spectrum with the same dappled variety of water in an impressionist painting. Snow is water, after all, and just as the sea is seldom only blue so the snow is rarely just white. We had been here long enough that we were becoming accustomed to see in it the whole spectrum of change and wonder that we would have previously seen in sand, grass, rock and tree.

The wind died abruptly, so we decided to strike camp so that we could get our tent up safely. We had made 9.1 nautical miles. It was under what we needed and every step had been hard fought. I was shattered from the effort. I knew that making more than 14 nautical miles per day, which was now our target, was going to be challenging. If only the weather and my toe held. We took the opportunity to empty our pulks of drift snow and take out our kites to untangle the lines that had knotted so drastically in that extravagant few hours of sailing at the top of the glacier four days ago.

I celebrated the good weather with my first change of underwear in Antarctica, 32 days since I had arrived. The wind got up again soon, but the tent was like a new place after those miserable storm days.

I hoped that with this glorious open desert in front of us, things were looking up. I suddenly felt freer in spirit and, unlike the last few days, was filled with wonderment at where I was and what was in store.

CHAPTER 16

It's All in the Mind

Direct your eye right inward, and you'll find A thousand regions of the mind Yet undiscovered . . .

Henry Thoreau, Walden

At some point during that unbearable day I had managed to get frostbite on my ear. My ear, of all places! An ear that heard nothing all day, other than the sounds of the winds blowing inside my empty head on the way from one part of the earth to another. How could that have happened? It had been covered up by a hat and my hood.

I complained that it was a little sore and asked David to look at it. 'Is it OK? It feels a little odd. It can't be frostbite as it was all covered up,' I said with faux-confidence.

David inspected it closely and then started laughing, 'Looks like a swollen cabbage.'

Pat saw an opportunity for humour: 'Look ear, Van Gogh, you're going to be hideous when you get back. One ear, no toe and a ginger beard!'

Paul chimed in: 'Al, perhaps you could keep an ear out for the wind tonight?'

They all guffawed loudly.

Having established an opportunity for a gag, they all ran with the general theme of bad puns on ears for the next five minutes until everyone was beside themselves with mirth. I couldn't help laughing too. The problem was that each time I tried to say, 'No, seriously, is it bad?' I would just start the hilarity again.

The wind continued throughout the next day blowing strongly into our faces but we had reasonable visibility. I spent all day locked in my own little world, thinking about what absences constituted this strange nothingness. I was strangely emotional.

I can remember crying four times in my adult life. The first was when I crashed a car, aged 18, when working with horses in Australia and I called my father, ashamed, to tell him what had happened. Everyone around me had been accusatory and unsympathetic. Dad had just asked me if I was OK. He was the first person to ask that question. He wanted to know if anyone else had been hurt; the hadn't. He said brightly, 'Who cares, then? I crashed three cars by your age – it isn't the car that's important.' Having him tell me that, from the other side of the world, caused me to feel a surge of homesick emotion that meant I had to say a hurried farewell.

More recently, I cried after talking to the mother of one of my best friends who had been having a battle with serious depression. I cried at my grandfather's funeral, more than anything else at seeing my Dad so emotional, and I cried at Alex's – at the sheer tragedy and waste of it all. And each time I had tried desperately to control it.

So it was very strange to me that today, for no particular reason, I cried twice. I wasn't crying due to the physical pain. It seemed to be welling up uncontrollably within me and coming out in floods behind my goggles. There was no one to see this and due to the wind no one could hear it. I could sob freely. It was comforting being so gloriously unrestrained. My tears froze on my eyelids. Sometimes my eyelashes stuck together when I blinked and I had to flutter them rapidly to free them. In Dante's 'Inferno' the very worst circle of hell, the ninth, is composed of ice. There the very eyes of the damned are sealed by tears:

> Their very weeping there won't let them weep,
> And grief that finds a barrier in their eyes
> Turns inward to increase their agony;
> Because their first tears freeze in a cluster,
> And, like a crystal visor, fill up all
> The hollow that is underneath the eyebrow.[1]

---

1 Dante Alighieri, 'Inferno', Canto XXXIII.

I felt that at home so many men, uncomfortable with expressing feeling even to intimate friends, exemplified a prevailing emotional desertification, a drying-up of tears. Now, in the privacy of this desert that reflected our feelings so remorselessly, we could pour out what we had long stored up. I was almost ashamed to admit this catharsis in the tent but I was also curious whether the others had been more emotional than normal, half expecting the others to seize on another good opportunity for a gag. However, David in particular concurred. He also admitted to experiencing a liberation of feeling. He especially indulged in the ability to contemplate any subject. He raked over the past, the wonderful moments as well as the tortuous break-ups. This, he said, was one of the only true luxuries of the trip. The beauty was in being conscious, of having the lucidity to escape and travel inside ourselves or somewhere else entirely.

Absorbed mentally during these periods, David was transported so as almost not to notice the terrain he laboured over. It was as if all of us were skiing through a private psychological landscape. The contorted sastrugi, the hidden crevasses and the ceaseless undulations were only really physical manifestations of our internal topography.

The weird otherness of the landscape contributed to a strange ethereal sense. The wind formed the snow into shapes that could have adorned a surrealist painting: there were huge cubes deposited seemingly at random in an otherwise flat surface: daggers; blunt, asymmetrical anvils; or waves frozen in the act of breaking.

As I skied, I couldn't help worrying about my face. We were out in the wind all day. What was happening to it? I seemed unable to go out without sustaining some damage. Getting into the tent at night, I would peel off my goggles to begin a nightly frostbite audit. My nose was scabby, as were my cheeks under the bristles. It didn't seem to be anything serious but the constant accretion of minor damage was unsettling and made me fear what would happen if I got my protection just a little wrong or if the conditions deteriorated further. We were still climbing, after all. I genuinely felt I would be a monster when I returned. Annabel sent me a short text saying that she was on cloud nine after talking to me the morning that we left storm camp. That meant so much. I hoped that she would still love me when I got back, whatever I looked like. Rather than seeing myself as a Frankenstein, held in the grip of a terrible obsession, I was now, if anything, nearer to embodying his hideous creature.

This, our second day out of storm camp, we made a hard-won 10.9 nautical miles. We had 22 days of food and our pulks would only get lighter. Dave was still feeling his knee, preferring to stay at the back rather than alternate places in the file. We watched him limp painfully into each break. He told us that it was getting better on the flatter ground without the strain of the steep gradients.

The following day the wind was worse. We could almost lean against it. Peeling off my hood for my daily check-up, I had suffered further frostnip on my face. I was relieved in a selfish way that Patrick had got a small nip, too. It showed that the conditions were hard for all of us.

Paul wanted to inspect my toe. I was reluctant to show him. What happened if, as I peeled off my damp socks, it had obviously become infected? Part of me wanted to just hide it, like Captain Oates had hidden his foot. If it was infected I would have at least got to the South Pole before I would have to deal with the consequences. I felt as if I was getting exam results and my parents were insisting that I open the envelope in front of them. I always preferred taking it into a quiet corner so that I could marshal myself against their disappointment.

I started taking as many precautions as I could to minimise my chances of sustaining damage. In the four 10-minute daily breaks I would take precious minutes putting on my down jacket over my Gore-Tex to try and keep my core temperature up and therefore protect my toes. I started to wear an extra under-sock and now I kept my boots in the tent, even though there was barely room, so I wouldn't have to chip the ice out of the insides in the morning.

Now, as I peeled off my damp sock for Paul, my foot looked white and shrivelled as if I'd just got out of the bath, except for my toe which was brown, green and black. It didn't look any different – thank God. Paul discussed evacuation again openly if it deteriorated. The sword swayed in the breeze of his words.

I shuddered at the thought of the next few weeks going out to crap, taking down the tent, hauling into the wind, putting up the tent, examining my damage. Again and again and again. I suppose it was the polar equivalent of rush-hour traffic, cowed shoulders, office cubical, crying baby and hysterical wife, ad infinitum. It was difficult to see where the balance lay. Where was the vaunted literary romance? Had I swapped apples for oranges, six for half a dozen?

It seemed to me that either escaping or at home, you'll still face the possibility of danger, boredom, unpredictability and routine in all avenues of life. And wherever you go, of course, you yourself will still be there. I think all I was seeking was happiness. I thought by escaping I'd both have the time to ponder what it is I wanted out of life, as well as, paradoxically, getting something out of it at the same time.

I pulled on, always aiming for the horizon, but, unlike any other horizon in the world, this one never changed. There were no milestones with which to measure my success. I simply never noticed each time I laboriously gained the point that I had aimed at a few hours previously. My goal just hung perennially in front of me, like a succession of identical futures.

As I hauled that day I had another cry. My mind kept returning to the same worn themes, thinking in grooved lines like watching a collection of old movies with a hangover. It required minimum effort and was oddly soothing. I wore my thoughts like a pair of old slippers.

Sometimes you just need something to kick it into a new sphere. Often I just thought about what I was going to think about. I tried desperately to daydream about other topics but it was virtually impossible unless I was comfortable. Any small increase in pace was tortuous and made me curse the leader repetitively in the most foul-mouthed terms. When the going became unbearable I'd start, mind-numbingly, to count my paces in order to feel a sense of time passing. At 500 I'd start again. It was the only mental activity I could manage. It meant it was impossible to escape to another plane. At that point I was firmly in the present, the goal of all Buddhists, but it didn't feel very Zen.

I had been eager to come to Antarctica to experience the mental challenge. The attraction had two main aspects: trying to sub-limate the physical challenges I encountered into mental ones and experiencing how my mind would cope with the lack of extrinsic stimulation.

Antarctica is a vast desert. For much of it, it is unchanging in all but subtle respects. Snow, ice, wind. Wind, ice, snow. Ice, wind, snow. It is so featureless that it, most perfectly of all topoi, exemplifies the Romantic notion of the pathetic fallacy: that your landscape reflects back to you your own mental state. Whether it is beautiful or ugly, harsh or comfortable, is totally dependent on you. You can travel for hours and be uninterrupted by any stimuli other than your own thoughts. Our society is awash with colour, noises and information. Our brain accepts everything passively. It is not often that we look at dazzling nothingness for days and weeks on end. How elastic is our lazy modern mind under such conditions?

Not very elastic, it seemed. I kept returning to the unavoidable conclusion that my mind itself also seemed to be a desert. I needed a sun-lounger, a cocktail and a palm tree to come up with my most incisive thoughts. Now my mind just seemed to want to shut down whenever it could. It was surplus to requirements. It was hard for me to dwell on anything other than pain or, when expending intense physical energy, to have enough extra to spare on vigorous mental activity, dreaming up exciting novel plots or new business ideas. For me, thought became a distraction just to whisk me away from where I was. It wasn't indulged for its own sake. A trance was the most envious of all states. Sometimes I would try to bring one on by staring and half closing my eyes.

David had disc upon disc of trance music and must, to some extent, have empathised. There is little doubt that running in parallel with our increasingly prevalent tendency to want to test and adrenalise ourselves, we also seek to slow down and concentrate the small time we do have to de-stress. It is no wonder that yoga, in all its different forms, has become so popular.

The irony of meditation, however, is that by practising it you seek not to free your mind to think but rather to enjoy the state of just being. Days, hours, minutes pass by in a blessed oblivion of *in*activity in which you have almost totally shut down. The paradox of Antarctica was that I sought to achieve that same calmness by the opposite means: the sweet oblivion of activity. One of the reasons that many people like to jog is to acquire a void. The body moves mechanically and automatically beneath you and the mind is freed to muse on any subject you set before it. It's a relaxing way to think, as thinking is secondary. Antarctica seemed to offer the same disassociation between mind and body. There I hoped I could meditate and explore, with the time lacking to me in London, on life and love and fill the white page around me with words – but in reality the page stayed blank or I just scribbled down the same thoughts, like the dysfunctional caretaker from *The Shining*.

Having hours to think produced two conflicting results the desire and the opportunity to ponder, imagine different scenarios, indulge the natural creativity of the mind versus the contrary impulse to shut down the mind entirely and just 'be'.

I started to reach the conclusion that stimuli of all sorts were generative of thoughts, and a barren landscape helped to induce Zen. I shouldn't beat myself up about failing to attain sophisticated imaginary heights. I should just let the natural state of being here take over. I was increasingly finding that what I had expected to be the case before coming to Antarctica was rarely so and that the only way to peace was acceptance.

My mind wasn't the only feature that had shut down. Initially I had enjoyed the occasional lurid sexual fantasy as an antidote to the monotony of hauling. They were easy to indulge and made the time go quickly but I found them becoming rarer and rarer as the expedition progressed. By now, and for the rest of the trip, I barely had another erotic thought. The cause seemed obvious – aside from sharing a tent with two smelly, pale and hirsute men, my body was consuming all its energy keeping warm and pulling my sled.

That wasn't the only reason, though: the pared-down asceticism led inevitably to chastity in the same way as a hermit or a monk leads a life of discipline and solitude. More than that (and something I had never appreciated that I would even notice or find significant): for the first time in my life I was spending months in a landscape devoid of advertising. The image, enthroned elsewhere, had no power here. The canvas was blank in all directions. Sex is the cornerstone of our society. Barely a single advert, television programme or magazine image doesn't use it either overtly or subliminally to carry its message. Here our minds were spared the aggressive bombardment of sex. There was not a single casual reminder.

The advertising industry specialises in making us feel inadequate. It presents us with images of our ideal self and then, in the gap between where we are and where we want to be, it positions its products. Consumerism fills our empty spaces and we buy to feel better about ourselves. Antarctica, where everything is empty, is the perfect place to come to terms with the hollowness inside, to just be or, perhaps occasionally, to conjure visions that are genuine – wholly generated from within – and free of perversion from the crooked fingers of marketing.

CHAPTER 17

Uncontactable

Why do some human beings desire with such urgency to do such things: regardless of the consequences, voluntarily, conscripted by no-one but themselves? No-one knows. There is a strong urge to conquer the dreadful forces of nature and perhaps to get consciousness of ourselves, of life and the shadowy workings of our human minds. Physical capacity is only the limit. I have tried to tell how, and when and where. But why? That is a mystery.

Apsley Cherry-Garrard, The Worst Journey in the World

Our target, with constant under achievement, just continued to rise so we added an extra half an hour to our daily schedule and for the first time managed to hit the desired 14 nautical miles. Aside from the extra time, our increased distance was due to the ground getting harder and our sleds running better. However, where it got harder, it got more disturbed. We were clearly in an area of high winds, which were solidifying the snow into mile upon mile of daunting sastrugi.

We crossed these bulwarks at an angle of 45 degrees, hauling our pulks up over the lip and then sliding one ski at a time down the other side. For a split-second the harness pressure on our stomachs would cease as the pulk hurtled down behind us before jerking us in the guts as the trace snapped taut. You could hear each man exhale as he took the hit a step away from the buttress. Sometimes the wind moulded the sastrugi into long ramps, like improbable catwalks which we would sashay down to an audience of wind and snow.

Each morning we'd phone Patriot Hills and try to resume our negotiations for the elusive resupply. It was like dealing with a faceless corporation: if you want a vital resupply flown into the South Pole, please press 1, please give your credit card number followed by the hash key on your touchtone phone, now. The operators insisted that Yorkshire Mike was uncontactable – *he* was uncontactable! As the only possible source of our resupply, they had us by the balls. It was a great negotiating tactic. Business is business. Pat and I watched our solvency disappear as fast as a chunk of Cadbury's down David's throat. One of the attractions of the expedition had been to escape the mundane reality of finance, bills, direct debits and demands for payment. Just for a few months I thought I wouldn't need to fret over a red balance. So it was wretched to have this delusion popped so comprehensively by waking up each day to the same charade.

When I got into the tent again, I found that the winds that had set the snow had also frostnipped my face again. After getting a few laughs for the latest scaly patch, I endured the now-customary communal inspection of my terrorist toe. I took a certain pleasure in the fact that my feet hadn't been washed for nearly two months now, so at least the others couldn't have been enjoying the experience either. Even if my toe didn't get infected now, Paul still expressed deep worry as to how I would cope kiting when I would have to endure long periods of waiting. Once you've been frostbitten you become much more susceptible. After all, the damage had potentially been caused during the only stretch of kiting we'd had so far.

Since the glacier we had had no further issues with crevasses. I hadn't seen one and had become quite blasé, thinking that that stage of the trip was now over. Complacency is provocative. The very next day we hit a big crevasse field. The day had so far been much better, with a drop in the wind and gorgeous open-hearted sunshine. The ground had been so hard that David, to vary the repetitive motion of skiing, had started towing his sled on foot. I was forced to follow suit when a binding broke. Without the skis to spread his weight, David's front foot broke through the crust and he sank in to his knee. He stepped back hurriedly. We all drew level. Dave started prodding the snow with his pole. The ground fell away with each stab to reveal a vast hidden crevasse. Through the hole he had made we could see blue ice and then darkness. We hurriedly put our skis back on. It had been impossible to tell – the surface had looked no different to normal. I wondered if it had been like this beneath us all along.

'Go on, Davy, lead the way, mate! Show us where they are, go on, that's the lad.'

'No sodding way. I'm the heaviest. I don't want to die yet,' he retorted. 'I'm staying right here. You go.'

'You go.'

'No, you go.'

It was good macho stuff.

Paul, exasperated, volunteered to lead. No one contradicted him. We all smiled happily at each other. 'Phew!'

As we scanned the ground ahead now that we had all been shaken out of our plodding reveries, we could see tiny criss-crossing fault lines mapping out a net of subterranean crevasses. We had ditched our only ropes at the Butcher's Shop.

Paul prodded each snow-stripe that he crossed gingerly with his pole to test the strength of the bridge before stepping onto it with his sled. It was impossible to refrain from assessing automatically where the best place in the file was – Second? Last? Maybe the bridge would have been weakened by successive passages across? We were a trail of little ducklings scurrying across behind mother. Some were only narrow fissures a foot across, others 10 or 15 feet wide. The time flew. It was exhilarating. I couldn't help smiling under my mask.

Getting to the tent that night, we had made 12.9 nautical miles – under budget again – and further bad news was to greet us. Martin, our photographer, whom we had all come to like so much during our compressed fortnight at Patriot Hills, had injured himself at Patriot Hills. Dosed on morphine Martin had to wait to be evacuated – with atrocious bad luck, the weather at Patriot Hills had set in again.

We were getting closer to finalising a deal with ALE. Offering no reduction in price, they offered to throw in a free flight to the Pole for one of the Land Rover team to accompany the resupply. It was going to have been Martin. With Martin out of the picture, Pat was angling for Robyn to fly out instead. He was desperate for her to get something positive and concrete out of her experience in Antarctica.

He felt that coming to the Pole could be a way of salvaging the experience for her. This new development created a different set of logistical issues. If the resupply was scheduled to coincide with our arrival at the Pole so that Robyn could meet Patrick there, this would leave the margin for error far too tight. This became the next breakfast question to resolve.

I decided to bite my tongue for the sake of the team dynamic. We were working brilliantly together and getting on despite the punishing nature of the journey, the stressful negotiations, the various physical uncertainties and our pressing timetable. I viewed our principal issue with the resupply to be cost. The second was about getting it in quickly so that it was waiting for us when we arrived. As I was shouldering half the financial burden, I felt Pat owed it to me to try and achieve the best possible deal. Wanting to get Robyn to the South Pole could push against that obligation. I was eager for him to be more robust in trading off her flight in return for a cheaper resupply. I made the point once and then decided to hold my counsel. In many ways I sympathised with his position. Deep down I knew that ALE just wanted to get as much money as possible. Once this was achieved, taking an extra passenger was irrelevant as far as their costs were concerned. What I wanted was probably futile. Perhaps all I was really angling for was a statement of recognition from Pat that I was accommodating his romantic gesture despite the possible financial ramifications for me.

I hoped that Robyn also appreciated the lengths Pat was going to for her – from dreaming up the whole Land Rover scheme and beyond. In many ways I had to marvel at his actions. We are so used to looking for romance in tokenism: gifts, hackneyed Valentine's gestures, stock phrases, petty compliments, that we don't often appreciate the grandiloquent expression.

CHAPTER 18 | Divide and Rule

What a lot of things we think of on these monotonous marches! What castles one builds now hopefully the Pole is ours!

Robert Falcon Scott,
Scott's Last Expedition: The Journals of Captain R.F. Scott

The next few days all fused into a blur. Again I dwelt, almost all day, on the thought of arriving home. In one vision Annabel was at the airport to greet me, heavily pregnant. In another I was late. In still another I was sipping my first ice-cold beer in the hot sunshine. Ice-cold beer may be an odd subject for a fantasy but somehow the condensation on the glass and the golden fluid inside were iridescent of warmth and luxury. In fact, when I did return, no real beer was ever half as good as those I had already tasted in my head.

Again I got frostnip, this time on the bridge of my nose, despite my nose guard. I had been wearing a neoprene Hannibal Lecter-style mask, but fortunately there was no one to scare. The mask froze to my beard so that it was impossible to take it off in a break. The wind continued to blow in our faces.

Whenever the visibility deteriorated, negotiating the sastrugi was even worse. Sliding up and down the jagged, knife-edges was quite a balancing act. I was comforted by the thought that Amundsen's party, who were adept on skis, fell regularly in these new conditions and Scott himself badly damaged his shoulder.

Eventually, we passed the 87th parallel. I longed for the 88th degree. The South Pole was still too far to contemplate. It was far better to think of one day at a time. A day would always end. After a number of successful days it would be possible to look back and see what we had achieved – the achievement might otherwise have over-faced us if we'd looked it squarely in the eye.

I kept telling myself, like some tinpot dictator: 'Divide and rule'. I had to divide the expedition up into manageable portions and, having done that, break the day itself up into even smaller ones. Joe Simpson, in *Touching the Void*, survived his ordeal by fixing landmarks ahead of him as he crawled in agony, and giving himself strict time limits to attain them. My mental catechism went like this:

'If I can just keep pulling until Pat takes over the lead.'

'If I can just endure until the break.'

Then at the break, when my body temperature cooled and my hands started to complain, I'd look forward to starting again – and so on.

Until the last session. As we skied the last half an hour, the tent – Eden – loomed larger and larger in my thoughts until, finally, I could think of nothing else.

Paul would always lead the last half of 'happy hour'. It was skied at a prodigious rate mainly to achieve a final boost to our mileage when fatigue or sweating were not as important given that camp beckoned. If the visibility was good, each of us could go at his own pace since there was no danger of getting separated. In reality, it was impractical to dawdle. Since I carried part of the tent, if I arrived late it only delayed pitching camp and caused the others to get cold.

As the clock wound down we'd all be on our chin straps, using our very last reserves of energy. If my watch told me the half hour was up, I'd be begging Paul, internally, to stop.

'Come on Paul, you bastard' (and much worse), 'stop now, come on, stop now.'

I'd paced myself for that period. At the end, Paul would slow down to look for a suitable flat place to camp. Was he stopping? Was that it? Yes, he's definitely slowing down . . . There it is, he's prodding the snow with his pole to his left and right, checking the consistency. Oh! Blessed relief! Today's marathon was over, the finish line crossed – until tomorrow.

After only 20 minutes of unpacking, putting up the tent, digging blocks of snow to secure the snow skirt and for the pot, I would be in heaven. The stove would hiss in the background while I languorously changed into a slightly damp but comparatively clean fleece and donned a new woolly hat. Each day was like this, a violent oscillation between heaven and hell.

We tended to lead in the same order to make navigation more efficient. Each of us would therefore become familiar with the angle he skied to the sun during his session. So, aside from variance in wind, sun and sastrugi, only tiny events distinguished the days.

One day stood out because my boot froze irrevocably to my ski. I had to sit on my pulk at the breaks with one foot in the ski and then, finally, bring it into the tent with me for the night. It sat next to my sleeping bag, the boot still snugly fitted, as if poised to ski away without me, until it had defrosted and was banished.

Another day was distinguished because I had to crap publicly and uncomfortably during my break.

The following day was remarkable for something as slight as enjoying a double ration of shortbread.

Before I arrived in Antarctica I naïvely thought that I wouldn't take a mini-disc player with me – an iPod was useless as the battery life in the cold was minimal – because I thought that the music might distract me from the purity of the experience. If Scott and Amundsen hadn't listened to music, why should I?

This is a difficult ethical path to ski down. If you have a preference for the ancient over the modern, to establish a greater coincidence with the old explorers, it is difficult to know where to stop. Should I eschew satellite contact? Did Gore-Tex give me an unfair advantage? Perhaps our lighter tent should be swapped for a thicker, heavier one with an awkward centre pole? The further you move down this route the more the experience becomes one of masochism rather than endurance. These questions tend to be ones asked only in the comfort of a living room during the planning stage. Once out here you take any comfort you can. It would be like a hungry dog deciding to voluntarily skip a mouth-watering rump steak. If anything, psychologically it is harder for today's adventurers who voluntarily renounce feasible and commonsensical comforts, as they know that there could have been a better alternative.

In Antarctica, despite all my initial pretensions, a mini-disc was essential. The rhythms helped me to ski and distract me from pain. In moments of comparative comfort the lyrics were poetry that I could properly listen to. Instead of inhibiting free association, music enabled my mind.

I hadn't had time to record lots of albums as it had been low on my list of priorities – so inevitably I borrowed those of the best-prepared member of the party, Paul. Paul is a rock freak. His self-confessed favourite occupation would be being a roadie for the Rolling Stones. His Rolling Stones mini-discs were sacred. He would let us borrow them but you could see, if you looked hard enough, the tiniest flicker of reluctance in his eyes – like a child allowing another toddler a turn on his new bike and then watching his shouts of enjoyment with a shy jealousy. He reserved the Stones for special days, like arriving at the Pole, whereas we would profane them by listening to them on any given Sunday.

In addition he had mountains of Springsteen, Fleetwood Mac, U2, the Eagles, Van Morrison – the list goes on. Not all of his collection would necessarily have been my first choice but generally these classics, being lyrically based and with such a clear structure, were truly inspiring. Good musical days helped, bad ones hindered. Stuck with an old-school Bob Dylan folk mini-disc, with him whining in unmelodic undulations all day, combined with cold hands, mountainous sastrugi and frozen goggles, would be enough to send me to an asylum.

On the other hand, pondering life on a still day, while the Eagles implored me to 'Learn to be Still' with the sun's rays refracting through the ice crystals of the air, was bliss. It seemed good advice, too: learn to be happy with what you have – don't always seek restlessly for some new, needless affirmation of what you are and what you are not. It is said that happiness is the absence of the striving for happiness.[1] I recalled the message preached to the band of drunks in *The Iceman Cometh*:

1 Chuang-Tzu, from the *Chuang Tzu*.

After you're rid of the same damned guilt that makes you lie to yourselves that you're something you're not and the remorse that nags at you and makes you hide behind your lousy pipe dreams about tomorrow. You will be in a today, where there is no yesterday or tomorrow to worry you.

I had long worried that desiring to traverse Antarctica was just an unrealisable fantasy that I indulged to take me away from mundane life and allow me to believe I could be someone else – an exotic philosopher-explorer, a Laurens Van der Post, a Scott, a Thesiger. Here, now, I was in this quiet expanse of whiteness, like a gigantic padded cell. Was this the place where there was no yesterday or tomorrow to worry me? Each day was like the last. Every day was today. Yesterday and tomorrow were all the same to me, a grand recycling of experience. I was living wholly in the moment: after all, each one was practically identical.

Paul told us, revealingly, how he had found this trip to be totally different from his other polar expeditions from the point of view of his mental life. As he had just undergone a divorce from his wife of 20 years, Matty, he now had all day for the tough emotional ramifications of that decision to percolate through his mind – whether guilt, sadness or hope. On previous expeditions, he confessed, he pondered and recreated the past in technicolour detail, reliving old holidays and old decisions, but now, with this dramatic change in circumstances, he found that increasingly he was dreaming about the future. It was an exciting and new imaginative space to be in, even if partially filled with these other conflicting emotions.

Dave, on the other hand, started the day by looking for shapes in the snow and imagining what they were, like a boy contriving cars out of clouds. Then, as if dying, he'd vividly relive scenes from his life, which would fly before his eyes like a kaleidoscope. He'd be wandering down the corridors of his junior school or find himself lying on a beach during a wonderful holiday. Then he'd be listening to music in his room 15 years earlier. It seemed interesting that David, the youngest, would think a lot of the past, and Paul, the oldest, the reverse. I spent the majority of my time musing on the future; I didn't know if that made me imaginatively bankrupt or forward thinking, but now, inspired by David's suggestion, I also had the whole of the past to roll around in. Suddenly I was looking forward to tomorrow, as tomorrow I'd travel back in time and rummage through some fond memories.

Tomorrow rolled on its petty pace and proved a tough windy day with no time to daydream.

The Inuit apparently have 50 different words for snow and we must have crossed over 30 of them. In the space of a few yards the terrain changed from soft- to hard-packed and back again, through every texture in between. We saw sastrugi in all their different stages of creation a few feet from each other: from foetus-ripples to fully adult waves, from Neolithic stones to post-modern sculptures.

The camp ground was very hard and I dug away at the snow in the wind with the shovel, like chipping flint from a quarry. Once inside the tent, worn out and despondent, we had a good heart to heart. Paul spoke up first: 'I had a really rough day today. I felt like Eeyore from Winnie the Pooh – stiff and ragged. I think we're working incredibly hard – perhaps too hard – and we're in danger of burn out. We are still very high. We mustn't be too hard on ourselves.'

All of us were ravenously hungry. Our snacks were divided into bags to last six days. It was up to each of us to divide up our own chocolate and nuts to last that time. It became an excruciating temptation not to start to chip into the following day's ration while sitting in the tent, even after eating a full meal.

'The pulling is harder than anything I've experienced on Hercules to the Pole,' Paul continued.

So far, either the sastrugi had been vast or, when there was no wind, the snow had frozen into a hoar frost, like sandpaper, over which the sleds refused to slide. Scott and Amundsen both complained of a similar phenomenon at approximately the same latitudes – with Scott, evidently frustrated, returning to the theme again and again in his diaries.

I felt a wave of relief as Paul told us how hard he was toiling over the miles. I recalled one session during the day where, starting 100 metres behind the others after a pee, I just couldn't catch up. I could hear my heart knocking frantically in my chest and was panting with the effort. I convinced myself that my heart would be strained if this continued.

As I came into the break, still a couple of minutes behind, I felt that someone would have seen how hard I had found it, would take me to one side and tell me that I was slowing the team down and would have to be evacuated. In all probability, no one had even noticed. It's almost impossible to hold each other up unless you physically stop them, as we hauled in a procession and if you arrived late, you just got a shorter break. However, in a state of virtual exhaustion, expending supreme effort all day, your mind works on your insecurities. I was often my own harshest critic – during my lead, for example, I always feared that I was behind the mark, usually pushing for all I was worth, grunting determinedly.

Now, imagining Paul tired as an old slack-jawed donkey from the effort made me feel better.

'I think we need to eat more,' he said. 'Otherwise we'll dip and won't recover.'

I felt as if I was already dipping.

He had brought along some houmous powder for a treat. We hadn't brought vegetable oil to mix with it but we melted some snow into it instead. Paul mixed the lumpy gloop up with a spoon as we all stared at it, before dipping his finger into the bowl and licking it with a smile. He put the bowl down between us and we all tucked in straight away to make sure we got our fair share. It wouldn't have made pretty viewing.

Now that Paul had admitted what he had been feeling, we all opened up a bit.

'I have to confess,' he continued with his mouthful of houmous, 'the issue about the resupply is beginning to be very stressful for me. I don't think we can continue to debate with ALE every morning and not know each day and every mile whether our food will be there or it won't. We have to resolve this.'

We nodded in unison, one eye on Paul, the other, askance, on the houmous bowl.

Pat chipped in. He told us how gutted he was that it didn't look like Robyn would get to the Pole. He doubted that ALE would manage to fly her there in time. If the resupply came earlier, which is what Paul wanted, he'd miss Robyn. If she came later, where was the incentive for ALE to get her there to coincide with our arrival, especially with the vagaries of the weather? The rest of the team had now left Antarctica with Martin. She remained on her own at Patriot Hills in a little tent with the small prospect of seeing Pat fading. He confessed that this occupied his thoughts for many hours.

We sat there putting our beating hearts on a platter. It was like an AA meeting, except that we were now solemnly passing around the dregs of the whisky.

In addition to my concern about Annabel, who now had less than a month to go until the birth, I admitted to feeling guilty about Steve Cotton, a member of the Land Rover team and an old friend. I felt that perhaps he hadn't got everything out of the expedition he could have and that I had lured him into an unrewarding project. Now he was on his way home. No doubt he'd be finding it hard to face family and friends without having fulfilled all of his intended goals. Personally, of course, he had nothing to be ashamed of but I felt responsible.

Discussing our feelings openly might not have been very 'explorer' but it was good and very interesting to exorcise some of the matters we had been fretting about, instead of letting them fester inside us.

Dave just listened.

'I confess to coveting Al's Galaxy bars,' he added with a smile.

CHAPTER 19 | Heat Miser

. . . that which we are, we are
One equal temper of heroic hearts
Made weak by time and fate, but strong in will
To strive, to seek, to find and not to yield.

Alfred, Lord Tennyson, 'Ulysses'

After our session in the confessional, we took it a little easier the next day. It was an incredibly enjoyable day. The wind had lulled and somehow, at the cost of less than a mile, the implicit consensus not to strain every sinew really paid off. I wasn't panting so hard and even found the time and the inclination to dwell on the beauty of the surroundings, although for most of it I just stared in a trance at the two karabiners that swung like hypnotic pendulums on the back of Paul's pulk and let my mind drift. Oh, that all days would be like that!

The next day reverted to type: cold and gruelling. I felt a strange sensation, a bit like a premonition. My nose felt foreign, as if it wasn't quite attached. I couldn't stop thinking about it for the first two hours and kept trying to check with my clumsy thick gloves that my nose guard was covering it. During a break I asked Paul to have a quick look at it. Pulling up my balaclava, he took a quick peak, before exclaiming without a hint of British reserve:

'Holy shit!'

I was looking for 'Don't worry, it's fine' – this was definitely less comforting. As my water bottle was still comparatively warm, I rolled it over my nose and then put my fingers on the white, waxy tip until they became too cold to do any good. I needed to coax the tip back to life and get the blood into it. The distressing thing was that it *had* been covered. I knew that any mental peace I had hoped for today was lost.

I couldn't help thinking of lurid scenes from the film *Seven*, in which the villain cuts the nose off a model to spite her face, knowing that her vanity will ensure that she kills herself rather than face the ignominy of ugliness. I kept telling myself not to worry. Minor frostbite shouldn't cause lasting damage. I just had to make sure I kept catching it in time. Amundsen's team all kept their noses even though they report that their time was a good deal taken up by repeatedly thawing them out.

Breaks, in general, weren't that relaxing – although they obviously improved if there was no need to thaw frostbite. It was more about trying to eat and drink as much as possible. I found that the intense cold inhibited the movement of my facial muscles, making it difficult to speak clearly.

'Does anyone find their lips don't work properly, you know, because of the cold?' I lisped.

'What?'

'Do you find your ears don't work out here?' I tried.

I explained how sometimes I had to move my lips out of the way with my fingers to avoid chewing them, hoping to find some comfort in the fact that this might be common.

'No,' Pat muttered, his mouth full of chocolate.

'I had a friend once', Dave piped up, 'who woke up one morning to find he couldn't speak properly. He had some scary double-barrelled syndrome. Maybe it's that?'

Pat smiled. 'Perhaps it's the first symptom of twisted testicles . . .?'

I couldn't help smiling, even as I forced frozen chocolate through the part of my rigid mouthpiece that wasn't blocked with ice.

We were at the highest point of the plateau now. The silence of the waste land, sometimes so stark it almost pressed on my ears, was interspersed during our breaks with the sounds of munching and with violent hacking coughs. All of us had them. The cough materialised mysteriously in the breaks and then vanished when we skied. A similar phenomenon happens on Everest – known as the 'Kumbu cough'. There it's mainly to do with breathing bottled oxygen; here it was connected with the dryness of the scarce air and with using our lungs rhythmically for hours and then suddenly stopping.

Our routine was very settled now. It just so happened that my lead always coincided with midday. At that time, due south followed the line of my shadow. It was an odd concept and a metaphor for life: you lead by following yourself. There was always something soothing and mesmeric about the session. If the expedition itself was self-punishment, then this session particularly offered me an opportunity to stomp all over myself.

I made an effort to think about something other than frostbite: today, 94 years ago, Amundsen reached the South Pole. Although we had climbed Mount Betty on the same day as he had, we were now exactly 106.4 nautical miles behind him.

If that was a milestone, the following day was even more historic. With only half an hour of our skiing day still to go, we arrived at 88.23 degrees – Sir Ernest Shackleton's furthest south. Dave's knee was again giving him trouble and he was in a lot of pain, so the decision to stop was an easy one to take. It had been the coldest day of the expedition so far.

I hadn't read tales of Scott or Shackleton as a boy. The first time I ever heard of Shackleton was about five or six years prior to Alex's death. Dad mentioned him during a conversation, explaining that he had once been stuck on an iceberg for nine months. I was flabbergasted. Why wasn't this story more widely known? I went out and bought his biography immediately. I vividly remember reading it while listening to Massive Attack's *Protection* album and specifically the song titled 'Heat Miser'. The song's rhythmic beats are punctuated by sounds of heavy breathing mediated through some sort of gas-mask. It conjured vivid images of awesomely strenuous exertion, which fitted perfectly the story of rowing over the high seas and man-hauling in the bitter cold.

Shackleton's actual story was even more amazing than Dad had intimated. I devoured it. It is a gripping tale of adventure. Even when I closed the book with a mixture of awe and admiration, I never, not in any imaginative version of my future, considered that I would one day spend so long striving to capture something of what he experienced and that I would eventually listen to that song camped at Shackleton's furthest southern point.

We pitched camp at that desolate place with a sense of real awe. Paul said a few words in honour of the man and stood outside his tent for a few moments soaking up the Antarctic silence. Shackleton was the first man to venture through the Trans-Antarctic Mountains and to discover the high polar plateau, thus opening up the way for Scott and Amundsen. Shackleton took the brave decision to turn around at this exact point, with only 97 nautical miles remaining to the virgin Pole, justifying his decision to his wife with words that would have made any self-respecting Roman turn in his grave: 'Better a live donkey than a dead lion'.[1]

Those 97 miles diminish in length the further you travel from Antarctica. Shackleton has been represented as turning around with the prize all but in his fist. In fact, 97 nautical miles, taking into account the round trip, represented more than a fortnight's travel. As it was, even turning around when he did, Shackleton only managed to get back to his base camp thanks to incredible good fortune with the snow conditions, unbelievable stoicism and a final, brutal 33-hour skiing marathon without sufficient supplies. After some 120 days of expedition, his ship – thinking him dead – was already half out of the bay: those extra 194 nautical miles would have meant certain death. To put it into perspective, Scott himself died having managed to get back to within 11 miles of base camp.

Shackleton is, however, rightly held by posterity in the highest esteem. Amundsen stopped here too, to honour the man and to hoist the Norwegian flag on his sled in recognition of the fact that every onward mile from then on was new ground:

> We did not pass that spot without according our highest tribute of admiration to the man, who – together with his gallant companions – had planted his country's flag so infinitely nearer to the goal than any of his precursors. Sir Ernest Shackleton's name will always be written in the annals of Antarctic exploration in letters of fire. Pluck

---

1 Shackleton said this about himself. From Roland Huntford's *Shackleton*.

and grit can work wonders, and I know no better example of this than what that man has accomplished.[1]

Sitting in the tent now, Patrick read out some of Shackleton's words. It was truly inspiring to hear them at any time, but sitting here, almost exactly where he had been, was a privilege: 'We have suffered, starved and triumphed, grovelled down yet grasped at glory, grown bigger in the bigness of the whole. We have seen God in his splendours, heard the text that Nature renders, we have seen the very naked soul of man.'[2]

If ever a poet trod this path, it was he. We talked in the tent of how excruciatingly hard his expedition had been. He hadn't taken skis, he had been starving and had suffered acutely from the altitude.

We decided that for most, it wasn't that hard to cope with these conditions for 10 or 20 days, rather it was keeping on and on when everything is hurting and your face is a mess. I could now dimly grasp what it must have been like for them. At least we had comparative safety assured. I can't think what it must have been like with the constant uncertainty of survival.

Scott took a copy of Tennyson's poetry with him and the extract from 'Ulysses' at the start of this chapter was inscribed on the cross that his men erected for him. The sentiments recorded are a powerful summary of the ethic that drove him on. The words of the poem closely follow Ulysses' speech by Dante. Ulysses is punished in the eighth circle of hell, the circle reserved for the worst offenders, being only one away from the very centre of hell itself, the ninth. The explorer is arguably seen by Dante as the epitome of recklessness. Interestingly, starting at the equator, all world maps band the globe in concentric lines of latitude every 10 degrees, which makes 90 degrees south, the Pole, the ninth circle. Appropriately for me, Dante's Ulysses left his wife and child in order to roam, attempting to pass the divinely ordained limits of the world, the Pillars of Hercules, on a voyage of southern exploration:

> No tenderness for my child, nor piety
> To my old father, nor the wedded love

1 Roald Amundsen, *The South Pole.*
2 Sir Ernest Shackleton, *South.*

That should have comforted Penelope
Could conquer in me the restless itch to rove
And rummage through the world exploring it
All human worth and wickedness to prove
So on the deep and open sea I set
Forth, with a single ship and that small band
Of comrades that had never left me yet.[1]

Our little band pressed on over the next few days. The sandy snow continued. It was still merciless pulling even though our pulks were now relatively light. The wind had all but died away but this meant the turgid hoar frost was not hardening into a smoother crust. It was clear and sunny around us but ahead we could see an ominous belt of cloud covering the whole horizon.

My toe was increasingly messy but remarkably it still wasn't infected. It really seemed now that the Pole was within our reach. For the first time on the expedition I saw that it could be a concrete reality – just a matter of days and hours away.

As I daydreamed, I experienced for the first time the truly awe-inspiring sensation of a snow-quake. With a deafening boom all the snow on the plateau for a number of miles suddenly settled an inch. There was an infinitesimal quaver in the ground, followed by a colossal bass-drum smack. For a split-second, not expecting it or having heard of it before, I thought that a giant crevasse was giving way beneath my skis.

The sheer scale of Antarctica, the arbitrary power shown in its avalanches, gaping crevasses and sudden snow-quakes can't help but induce a sense of menace. It is like a slumbering giant, whose occasional snores or shifts of position hint at the awesome strength beneath you. Many mountaineers who manage to climb a grand peak such as Everest claim to have 'conquered' it. The greatest climbers, however, have always recognised that you cannot conquer Nature and that they triumphed only because Nature in a calm mood, suffered them to bow their heads for a fleeting moment of communion at its very apex. The longer I spent away

---

1 Alighieri Dante, 'Inferno', Canto XXVI, translated by Dorothy L. Sayers with the substitution of 'child' for 'son' in line 1.

from society and in a Nature that was powerful and glorious, the more I started to be affected by the power of the pristine. It is a quality of uninterrupted mountain views and open spaces that teach us about our weakness rather than our strength. It became obvious to me that instead of trying to conquer, climb, haul or progress to its zenith, we should be striving to be in harmony with Nature. If the world does merely reflect to us the soul of man – the outer revealing the inner – then it is clear that the materialism at work in our souls has an unhealthy manifestation in the pollution of the world, in global warming, soil erosion, water contamination, increasing toxins, commodity scarcity and population growth. Now, in this altar of whiteness, I felt more keenly the dirtiness outside it.

Pat often called Antarctica 'God's great ice machine'. There is no doubt that for the entire expedition we all experienced something of our own tininess in relation to its implacable forces. The experience was a useful, albeit short-lived, tonic for the ego-centricity of man. Anything that humbles a person generally makes them nicer to be around.

The problem is that the basis of our own society glorifies the man who stands outside the mould, who wants to silhouette himself. Celebrity of any sort is admired. Indeed it could be said that the 'I' inside all of us longs even more nowadays to be saluted. Ego-centricity is demanded by our culture for success.

In the past, enduring Antarctica, like climbing Everest, became a badge of honour. Receiving plaudits for enduring privations and hardships rubbed directly against the beneficial effects of humility and weakness acquired when on the ice. You come back privately humbled only to be publicly puffed up. It's no coincidence that polar explorers – the real ones as much as the impostors – have enormous egos.

In our age of accessibility, as the world gets smaller, it is possible for more and more of us to 'play' at being an explorer. It's no longer necessary to go and spend three years and over-winter in order to traverse Antarctica. We live in the age of the video game, of nano-gratification. Answers can be supplied instantly over the Internet, laborious research in a library is redundant. Celebrity can be conferred without talent by being prepared to make a fool of yourself on television. Expeditions are growing as short as our attention span and are increasingly undertaken by non-careerist adventurers. Even the most extreme undertakings have now become a glorified reality show as the protagonists are accompanied by an invisible camera crew or otherwise record their every utterance on a video diary. Even in the short period since this expedition, a commercial race, stacked with celebrity entrants, has been staged for the first time in Antarctica.

Our age is one of increasing narcissism. It isn't easy to unpick precisely why this should be, there are a myriad of contributing factors: over-indulgent parents; the population explosion and the corresponding increase in the competition to succeed and therefore the need to stand out; the fact that many of us marry later and so have more time to focus only on our own gratification as adults instead of the demands of family (which forces us to learn patience and self-denial); the vacuum produced by the lack of ordered religion in many of our lives, a hole into which has been sucked a new and sinister twin-headed deity – Money and Fame; the fact that we are what we read, and we devour the same inconsequential scribblings, flicking past the depressing, dutiful and repetitious reports of disasters and war and feasting on the addictive and spirit-sapping social pages. We aspire to the beauty portrayed. We mistake fame for notoriety and in the web of celebrity confuse true talent with spin. So, when reading about an adventure, we are unsure whether the conqueror of such-and-such a desert is authentic or a mere pseud. By what criteria do we judge this anyway – the intention (a romantic odyssey or a publicity stunt); the ability (the blundering ingénue or the resourceful man of granite); the length of time; the hardships endured; the column inches?

Whatever the answers to this riddle, as more and more people seek the poles of the earth, or to cross major deserts or are helped to climb impressive peaks, the world becomes further inured and the respect for the feat fades. Maybe this, in itself, will allow the positive effect on the spirit to endure longer and force people to journey for private rather than public reasons, because, beyond all the fakery, there are certain absolutes that don't go away. The wind, the mountains, the snow and the sky are constant. Alone in a vast wilderness, buffeted by storms, it is genuinely possible to feel very small, afraid and not a little repentant at thinking you were strong enough back in your comfortable armchair, reading books of high adventure, to take on any dragon.

This feeling of weakness can be confused with religiosity. I never identified Antarctica with God, but skiing along under the immense blue vault of sky and cringing at the tremors of the ice was a little like worshipping at a shrine to the greatness and power of Nature.

For nearly 40 days, such a biblically significant period, we had been plodding painstakingly through this wilderness, hoping to get the chance, looming in a matter of days, to arrive at our Promised Land – the point about which the whole world turned.

I recalled all the moral dilemmas and fund-raising cul-de-sacs I had encountered before I got here and how the Pole itself had become a similarly wished-for apotheosis that had taken hold of me. Finally, I felt it was within touching distance.

CHAPTER 20 | Travelling Without Moving

The quest has taken me through the physical, the metaphysical and the delusional and back, and I've made the most important discovery of my career, the most important of my life: it is only in the mysterious equations of love that any logical reasons can be found. I am only here tonight because of you. You are the only reason I am. You are my only reasons.

John Nash, from the film A Beautiful Mind

A few days from our goal, we finally received confirmation that the resupply had been depoted. Paul, for one, now slept better.

Passing the 89th parallel, we decided to extend our travel time further to try and make the final push for the Pole as quickly as we could. Almost as soon as we had made our decision we were enveloped in cloud. The sun, which hung behind us, shone dimly through the mist like an icon's halo. It cast no shadow and once again forced us to rely on our compass. With my mask, the extra effort of navigating in the cloud and the sudden jolts caused by unexpected sastrugi, I struggled to keep my head cool. My goggles fogged up and froze, turning negligible visibility into total obscurity. Eventually I was forced to remove my frosted visor and rely on pulling down my woolly hat and squinting through clenched eyes to try to cut out the glare.

Despite these little trials, which were now just part of the daily routine, I was getting more and more excited about the looming milestone. Normally I phoned Annabel as we all sat around eating breakfast but this time I padded over to Paul's tent so I could be on my own. Forgetting about battery concerns and expense for once, I had a profligate 20-minute conversation with her rather than the usual five minutes. Although I had nothing particular to hide from the others, it was wonderful to talk in private.

'It's so lovely to hear your voice. God, it feels so long since we've talked properly. How are things – how are you?'

'Oh I'm fine, same old. I want to hear about you rather. How's the frostbite? Are you coping?'

My voice started to break as I admitted out loud the fear I had been suppressing inside me: 'I—I . . . I'm not sure that I am really. I'm just not sure. It's so hard. Each day, all day – just this hard, hard pulling; I don't know if I'm up to it. Everyone else seems so strong. It's so difficult. I don't think anyone can ever really know what this feels like.'

'It's bound to be as tough for them as for you. It must be.'

'I tell myself that but I can't believe it's true. Every minute of every day I feel like my mind is screwed up like a clenched fist with the effort of just keeping up, of making sure I'm not left behind. And there's no respite. It never ends. I just wish I was away from here – even for five minutes – just for a change. I miss you so much. Oh God, I miss you so much.'

The tears started to flow. I couldn't help myself. I felt so weak and so vulnerable in the tent. I wished I was anywhere but there.

'Baby, I miss you too. I think about you all the time. When I'm doing something here, I often catch myself for an instant and think about what you're experiencing and how it must be the opposite from me in nearly every way. Do you think about that ever? Do you ever think about me?'

'All the time. I barely think about anything else. It's so lonely here. Of course we're all getting on well but all day they're just figures in front of me – as separate as cars on a motorway. We don't talk. Each of us is spun in our own cocoons. I spend all my time dreaming of new lives for us, what we're going to do, how our children will be. I can't stop thinking about the moment we'll see each other again.'

'When will that be?'

'It's different each time. Sometimes I make it back and there you are at the airport, all pregnant and smiling and crying. Other times, it's your dad and he picks me up and tells me I'm just in time, the labour has just started and then we rush off together in the car to the hospital. Then, in others, I'm too late and you're at home and you won't look at me.'

'It won't be that way. It won't be your fault anyway. What happens, happens, darling. How's your face?'

'Pretty bad. Bristly, ugly, scabby. I wouldn't imagine me if I were you. I just hope I'll come back to you in one piece. I don't really know anymore. My body just doesn't seem to handle the cold like I thought it would. It's funny, I've never really been bad at anything before – and now I am. I hope you'll still love me.'

'Of course I will. More. I love you so much, sweetheart, it won't matter if you're changed, if you get there or you don't. I just want *you* back.'

I needed to hear that, her soft words washed over me as I cried.

'It's all so pointless. I wonder why on earth I'm here, away from you. It sounds so stupid but I think about Alex all the time. Every day I dream about calling up Richard and Fiona to tell them that Alex's flag is at the South Pole, that their son's flag is at the Pole. Somehow thinking about that moment makes it all worthwhile. It's not enough anymore just to want to do this. It – the Pole – seems so far away now, so far away, out of reach – and that's not even the end. How are you, anyway, are you all right?'

'Most of the time I cope fine and no one would know. I suppose I'm even proud you're away. At antenatal classes, all the husbands are there. The instructor always gets me up at the front and then demonstrates whatever she's teaching using me – because I'm on my own. Everyone knows why you're not there. It makes me feel good to be different. I feel special. Then, suddenly, occasionally, I hit a wall. I'm lying in bed alone and I imagine you coming back. You're bored with me and with our life and don't want us anymore.'

'Babe – it couldn't be less likely to happen. Believe me, this grind is overrated. I won't change. Thank you for being so strong for me.'

I paused for a moment to try to collect myself and refocus on where I needed to be – on Annabel.

'Is everything OK, you know, with the pregnancy? Are you OK? Is the baby fine?'

'Yes, if anything, too fine! The baby's big, healthy and kicking like mad. The doctor doesn't think I'll go to term as it's so big – not to stress you out or anything but we should be prepared in case it comes early.'

'That's what I'm scared of. Can't you just keep it in!? Sit still? Cross your legs or something?'

'Oh sure! No problem! Why don't you just click your fingers and get some decent wind to blow you back to me a bit quicker!'

'What am I missing?'

'Don't worry about that, Mum's taking a picture of me every week – so you can see how fat and disgusting I look – and I'm keeping a diary, too.'

'Will you hate me if I don't get back? I can't help it if I don't, it's really playing on my mind. I know I promised but I just can't see it all fitting into place. I think it was naïve of us to even think I would make it.'

'No, darling, I won't resent you. I love you. Just be careful, come back safe to us. I've thought about it a lot too and I know I can do this. I can do it on my own if I have to. It won't change anything. I promise I won't hold it against you.'

I needed to hear that, even if it wasn't true. I just so badly needed to hear that.

I had a good cry, it was different from the various outpourings I had had in the confines of my mask as it was an explicit and intense revelation of my feelings rather than a mental soliloquy.

It was so important to have that chat. Although I missed her even more, I also loved her more for her big heart and her sensitivity. I had needed to talk so much and felt much better for it. I hoped she did too. It was wonderful to connect with her again, something that had been more difficult in our intermittent, short and stilted satellite link-ups. I came away sure that a full reconnection would be effortless when I returned and was giddy at the prospect of having time to spend with her. With absence making the heart grow fonder and all the positive mental resolutions I had made (and I guess she had, too), I really felt that our life and marriage could be all the better for this experience. The last few weeks had had little aesthetic recompense and in many ways had exhausted my appetite for physical hardship. I longed for home.

So much time thinking on my own was making me more resolved to be a good husband and a good dad. The different challenges were helping me to shrug off my obsessional pipe dream. Perhaps it'd leave me happy to be myself and able to accept that, whoever I was, it wasn't Sir Ernest Shackleton. I was looking forward to being at home with people I loved and who loved me. This current life was simple in many ways but now I yearned for a different kind of simplicity: love, warmth, food and safety. I hoped I would never undervalue any of them.

Thinking about Annabel the next day as I skied made me reflect on marriage. It is an incredible but scary institution. When you agree to spend your life with someone – and try to honour the arrangement by communicating fully and wholly with the other person – it's impossible to hide anymore. Suddenly you're exposed. On your own, you can hide your faults from the world, hide your laziness, hide your fear and hide your lack of resolve. If your ambitions and dreams don't come true, who needs to know? Now someone would always be my witness.

I imagined our future together: there would be days when we faced new challenges and we'd both know if we shirked them, we'd both know each other's successes and failures in all their nakedness – even before they had life. If Annabel confided her hopes and fears to me then I would be aware of any little dream during that hazy, mysterious period before it hatches into a plan that either soars or sinks – and I would know if and why she had stifled it in its infancy. It's scary to live up to the pressure of being what someone wants and hopes you'll be, and yet it's also beautiful to be able to discover and explore each other. Each time I articulated how I wanted my life to pan out, Annabel would know if I matched up to what I claimed. With honesty and communication, marriage was going to be a humbling but incredible adventure. We could look forward to journeying through each other's valleys and summits, becoming intimate with the relief of our characters and each wading through the other for a lifetime, with no map other than intuition and shared experience.

I thought about our children. I knew that we'd both strive to imbue them with confidence, that we'd constantly encourage them to be what they wanted to be and shower them with praise. At some point, however, we'd have to release them into the world where, in all probability – although incredible to us – they'd have to confront the fact that they might be unexceptional. As that word suggests, only very few can fall outside the common mould. How would they react to life then? Would they be happy with (or just insensitive to) their mediocrity? Having been brought up on a diet of praise and encouragement, would they be happy with undistinguished anonymity. Understanding and accepting our ordinariness (even our insignificance) is one of the least acknowledged private struggles with the ego that most of us go through. It's not an accident that our society has put celebrity on a pedestal, as it's where most of our own egos ache to be. I was starting to understand that this whole expedition had been born out of a fear that I was just unexceptional. It had been conceived as a spasm against a mediocrity that I would in all likelihood return to. The desire to get out into such a lonely wilderness – where no one else was – was perhaps just a wish to reinforce, graphically, a sense of my own difference to other people, to prove to myself that I was not the same. However, my inability to transcend the daily trials and tribulations and fulsome sense of physical weakness just seemed to confirm my worst fears.

I later read about that call from Annabel's perspective, which showed me how strong she had had to be to support me while hiding so many of her fears:

> He was incredibly emotional – I really hope I have made him feel better about everything. I think he needed to hear me being strong and determined. He spoke of being worried that I would not love him when he got back all grisly and changed – he could not be more wrong, I am literally longing for the day he comes back – he must know that. I am worried that he will think I am boring and domestic – so we both have our sets of fears. He says he cries a lot and I can imagine why – it must be mind-numbing. In some ways, though, I am not worried about him missing the birth as I feel we will have so much to deal with as a couple and it might all just be too much for me: having him back, dealing with the birth, being a mum for the

first time – it's all utterly terrifying, daunting and emotional. Just having Al back in one piece is going to be scary. I want to be able to be the best wife and give him the most attention that I possibly can and yet having a baby as well is going to divide me so massively. How can I be all things? I hope I can do this as well. I am sending him so much positive energy. I hope he is getting it all now.

I was. The day itself turned out to be one of the best in Antarctica. I only needed one pair of goggles (by concentrating on breathing through my nose) and even removed my balaclava for the last two sessions to enjoy the sun on my face during the breaks. Listening to some great music, I let my mind roam free.

Will all these thoughts of marriage, expeditions and love, I couldn't help George Mallory coming to mind. In his first expedition to Everest in 1921 he described the wonders and rigours of his experience in letters to his beloved wife Ruth, finding time to think of her frequently: 'But most of all, I was delighted to find Kingcups; in delicate variety rather smaller than ours at home, but somehow especially reminding me of you – you wrote of wading deeply through them in the first letter I had from you in Rome.'[1]

Now it is not uncommon for people to accompany their other halves on outlandish expeditions. Just within our own parameters there was Patrick and Robyn, Paul and his family, and on Matty's expedition, Conrad and Hilary Dickinson (and in subtler ways, I felt that Annabel was with me). Furthermore, with the blurring of gender stereotypes in our generation, women often outdo their husbands in endurance. In fact, in many ways, explorers' wives have always outdone their husbands – it's just that their feats were less acclaimed.

In earlier eras, a wife would have had to stay at home and endure stoically both her fears and her husband's prolonged absences. Female fortitude was taken for granted. Many women worked all day and raised their children alone while their husbands were away fighting. Until recently this lot was commonplace and unremarkable. In fact, it shows how far cultural mores have changed that I should now be so concerned about the possibility of arriving home just a

---

1 Peter and Leni Gillman, *The Wildest Dream*.

few days late for my child's birth when my grandfather, away at war, missed my father's arrival by more than three years without criticism or particular guilt.

Ruth Mallory, an extreme representative of her generation, had to contend with George's long absences when he was fighting on the Western Front, during his three Everest expeditions and through various lecture tours. However selfless and devoted she was, she must have struggled to keep a stiff upper lip in line with prevailing Edwardian expectations. She wrote to George after one wartime farewell: 'I did part from you cheerfully in true British fashion, didn't I?'[1]

I recalled my parting from Annabel at the airport; she was heavily pregnant, a picture of beauty and vulnerability. David had covered her bulging stomach with 'Fragile' stickers. She was trying to fight back the tears. Neither of us had been very British.

It is thought that Mallory confided in a friend that he didn't expect to come back. Although I hoped and expected to return, just before I left for the ice, I wrote Annabel a letter from Punta Arenas with some words for our child in case I didn't. I later read about the effect of that letter in her diary:

> It's 6.00 a.m. and I have just read Alastair's letter again for about the tenth time. I think I know it all off by heart. What if he doesn't come back? He will be at the end of a gruelling day, no doubt. I feel like I'm going quite mad with anxiety and boredom. I had the most horrific dream last night. I cried the whole way, I can't really make head or tail of it, but Al had been away for many years and I was not sure when he was going to return. I was in this terrible place. I was rationalising everything, my life, morals, future, my desperation and disappointment at myself, at my strength and reserves – it was truly horrific. I don't think that I have ever cried so hard in real life. This big test!

I had felt torn whether to write that letter or not. In many ways I felt it was a little overdramatic and was bound to upset her. On the other hand, if something awful happened she would have something tangible to show him or her about my love, my regret and

---

1 Peter and Leni Gillman, *The Wildest Dream.*

my expectations. It did trigger an outpouring of emotion, however, that must have made a situation that was already very trying a little harder.

By way of response, Annabel asked her doctor to write the sex of our child on a blank piece of paper and put it in a sealed envelope. She then carried it permanently in her handbag. That way if something happened and she had the opportunity, she could let me know what our baby was going to be.

Being so newly married and with something so momentous for us unfurling, I thought constantly about Annabel and our future. I often considered how paradoxical it was that she must have been absorbed with Antarctica in her imagination while I was envisaging the greens and browns of Cape Town, where she'd gone to be with her parents for the birth. In a very real sense, for much of the time we must have swapped places. Spending so long dwelling on the future conjured the intriguing possibility that in fact I might only ever have been imperfectly present.

Annabel was certainly often with me. In her daily text message, a luxury unavailable to the likes of Mallory or Scott, even the tiniest detail – that she had had lunch with two well-known friends, for example – could give me ammunition for a whole day's reverie.

All of the team had, more than likely, spent years, months or weeks dreaming of the ice; once here, ironically each of us passed as much time as possible being transported imaginatively elsewhere. Then, when we returned home, in all probability we'd be nostalgically reliving parts of this expedition for the rest of our lives. Paradox-ically, we seem to be most satisfied in a place only when we're not actually there.

If I had gone to Antarctica for simplicity, then all the complexity I had left behind had been heaped on Annabel. In my eyes, her experience was as much, if not more, of a journey of tribulation and endurance as mine. There were uncanny parallels. While I risked the uncertainty of our route and pressing timetable, Annabel faced the possibility of complications in her pregnancy and, of course, the uncertainty of its painful conclusion. As my face swelled from the altitude and my feet got frostbite, Annabel's stomach, ankles and feet also swelled up. As she put on weight, so, in counter-balance, it slipped off me. Just as so much in Antarctica, especially the weather, was out of my control, so *everything* was out of her control – the development of the baby, when I'd phone (she couldn't phone me), when I'd be back or if I was in trouble. She was unequivocally facing her own South Pole.

We both kept a diary because, being absent for so long, we were keen to be able to share every iota of the other's experience. I wanted her to be able to read to me what she felt and thought during her pregnancy so that when I returned I could catch up on what I had missed. Likewise, I wanted to be able to read her every detail of the expedition so that she could feel and know that she was with me every step of the way, ever present in my mind, and thereby had experienced it all too.

CHAPTER 21

The South Pole

The goal was reached, the journey ended. I cannot say – though I know it would sound much more effective – that the object of my life was attained. That would be romancing rather too barefacedly. I had better be honest and admit it straight out that I have never known any man to be placed in such a diametrically opposite position to the goal of his desires as I was at the moment. The regions around the North Pole – well, yes, the North Pole itself – had attracted me from childhood and here I was at the South Pole. Can anything more topsy-turvy be imagined?

Roald Amundsen, The South Pole

With a miserly 28.5 miles left to the Pole, the day started cloudy. Paul took the first shift as usual, the conditions requiring him to don the compass girdle. Miraculously, after a few hours the day cleared and became beautiful.

Windless, we had superb travelling conditions except for deep snow and the thick hoar frost that Scott had loathed so wholeheartedly. When the sun came out I just couldn't stop myself taking off my balaclava. There was no wind. It just was so calm and quiet. All the others had their hoods down and had replaced their goggles and nose guards with sunglasses. Unfortunately, my nose was so sensitive now that it got frostbitten almost straight away. With the conditions so still and quiet it was hard to appreciate that the ambient temperature, at around -30°C, was still threatening.

Camping that night, with only one day's march remaining, Paul was in a mood of calm excitement. He told us that he wanted to stay up late that evening to make sure that he recorded all his sentiments at reaching the Pole again. I had expected that, as he had accomplished this feat twice before, it would have been old hat. He already knew what he was capable of. Pat intuitively picked up on Paul's subdued energy and went out to fetch the video camera. We were lucky to record the moment as he gave a unique and memorable interview. He spoke beautifully and eloquently. Listening intently, I felt privileged to be on an expedition with a man of his character and achievements.

He talked about the beauty he found in the landscape, a landscape of sublime austerity that he was irrevocably drawn to. His words had a great considered authority. His whole life had been played out in the snow and the wind. It was only right that he should notice and love the subtleties of its varied palette and be so much more acutely attuned to it than those of us who were just 'explorers for a day'.

He articulated how today he had noticed the sun clear out from the sullen clouds to reveal the full intensity of the snow until he felt as if he was skiing on a carpet of crystals, untouched by man.

He talked about how he felt a strong sense of history on this side of Antarctica that he had never connected to on his previous expeditions. Here we were camped barely a few miles from the final campsites of Scott and Amundsen. He described with humility the kinship he felt with them and his identification with the conditions that they had encountered.

He continued describing how hard he had found the Axel Heiberg Glacier and that, although the four days that Amundsen took to climb it was simply awe-inspiring, our 10 days (12 if we counted the two days we had been snowed in halfway up the icefall) would be seen as quite an accomplishment without dogs – and good luck to any team that tried to emulate it.

He went on to portray how immensely proud he felt that his children, Eric and Sarah, who were going to arrive at the South Pole from Hercules Inlet in the next few days – as the youngest man and woman respectively, unsupported from the edge of the continent – and that, in all likelihood, he would be there to welcome them. Even though he was gutted not to have been able to share that experience with them every step of the way, now at least he would be able to watch with unconfined joy the incredible moment when they emulated (and in some ways outstripped) the feats of their parents and could truly share with him the wonder of Antarctica.

His speech made me forget the hardships for a while and I felt ashamed that I had focused on them to the exclusion of the serenity and beauty that lay all around me.

Paul felt that this was the most excited he had ever been about reaching the Pole because, for the first time ever, it wouldn't all be over. He admitted a profound dread of the end of an expedition. On return, no one ever really understood what he had gone through. The onus on him was to reintegrate into other people's lives rather than the other way around because it was very rare for anyone to expend the effort really to get under the skin of his experience and its myriad challenges and significances. He felt that he ended up asking what had happened while he was away rather than the other way around. He often felt acute loneliness after returning from a big expedition as he was suddenly thrown back into another sphere that wasn't such a cauldron of mutual dependability and that vacuum, that emptiness, was filled with loneliness.

Inspired, my own feelings seemed somewhat prosaic. I felt great relief that our man-hauling was probably at an end. I felt relief in making this tangible milestone that hundreds of miles further back, stuck in a blizzard with frostbite and threatened with evacuation, I had hardly dared believe I would attain. I felt pride at the prospect of dedicating the achievement to Alex and I was looking forward, with the greatest relish of all, to the thought of 36 hours' rest. We had been out here in this freezer for 52 days. I had changed clothing only once. I was looking forward to a fresh set!

As to what lay ahead, I had mixed feelings. In some ways it seemed totally inconceivable that it might all be over in a little less than one more month – even though we still had two-thirds of the continent to cover – and yet that period of time seemed an aeon. And, of course, I was becoming more apprehensive of the Herculean labour that we still had to accomplish – harnessing the South Wind.

Over every rise, down every fall, we expected to see our goal. Just at the point at which we thought it might come into our field of vision, the weather completely set in. So much so, that with only two nautical miles to go there was still absolutely no sign of it. Even though we were navigating by compass, the miles, unusually, seemed to fly by. We were all infused with collective energy and purpose.

Now, coming across nothing, we suddenly all experienced minor tremors of doubt. Could it possibly be that we had got the declination (set manually on the compass) wrong? The magnetic South Pole was behind us, to the north, many miles distant from the geographic South Pole. The difference between the two is only academic in northern Europe but here it was fundamental. So a compass, unless altered after complex calculations, will send you in entirely the wrong direction.

We had got the relevant information from our GPS, but if we had entered the coordinates erroneously, it was faintly possible we had missed the Pole entirely. Common sense told us that we just couldn't have made an error that basic – especially as we had navigated mainly by the sun itself. However, wandering in the cloud was like walking down a dark alley at night – sometimes the mind imagines problems for itself. We suddenly doubted our methods. The problem with navigation by intuition in this disorientating wilderness, without any outstanding features, is that if you don't know exactly where you are – and therefore what the local time is – even the sun will only bear false witness.

Dave was the first to spot some specks on the horizon through the fog, which seemed at first to be five figures approaching us, like Scott's team resurrected – phantoms of the polar waste land. As we got closer we saw that it was only a cluster of flags – our first taste of the outside world for many weeks. On seeing one cluster in the distance we could suddenly see others. We suspected they were markers for pilots or for scientists on field duty to guide them into the Pole. Getting still nearer they appeared in more and more random groups, like flags on a field of Antarctic mini-golf. Their over-abundance and arbitrary placement was to become a good trope for the Pole itself, which had no apparent planning in its haphazard lay out.

I half expected, as Amundsen in the recesses of his mind perhaps had half hoped for, that the world would just fall away into some exotic hanging cliff, suspended above an abyss leading to the very bowels of the earth. It was slightly anticlimactic that the end of the earth was much like any other point.

David, like a hairy and bearded Robinson Crusoe spying the spoor of Man Friday, excitedly pointed out a footprint. Then, suddenly, we popped out of the cloud and into a bright day. And there it was in front of us: an enormous, pisted snow runway, bordered by flags, wide enough for a jumbo jet, leading towards . . .

I couldn't believe it – the most ugly airport terminal imaginable, a hideous carbuncle, a disgraceful disfiguring wart on the beautiful face of this continent. With no apparent order, trucks, wooden crates, pre-fabricated buildings, snow-mobiles, flags and masts splayed out in front of us.

I felt betrayed by my romantic fantasies. This over-filled dumping ground was a far cry from the emptiness that greeted Scott, in both the mental and geographical sense and yet I identified, although obviously in a less complete way, with his disappointment. His diary reads as a study of deflation. There is a palpable and tragic sense of wasted effort.

> It ought to be a certain thing now, and the only appalling possibility the sight of the Norwegian flag forestalling ours.
>
> The worst has happened, or nearly the worst . . . It is a terrible disappointment, and I am very sorry for my loyal companions . . . All the day dreams must go.
>
> Great God this is an awful place and terrible enough for us to have laboured to it without the reward of priority . . . Now for the run home and desperate struggle. I wonder if we can do it.

Amundsen, approaching the point, despite his usual ice-cool demeanour also admitted to something approaching jitters:

> None of us would admit that he was nervous, but I am inclined to think that we all had a little touch of that malady. What should we see when we got there? A vast, endless plain, that no eye had yet seen and no foot yet trodden; or – No, it was an impossibility; with the speed at which we had travelled, we must reach the goal first, there could be no doubt about that. And yet – and yet – Wherever

there is the smallest loophole, doubt creeps in and gnaws and gnaws and never leaves a poor wretch in peace.[1]

Of course, Amundsen had originally intended to travel to the North Pole. He had provisioned his ship and enlisted his men on that basis. He only announced his intention to the world and his own crew after leaving port and sailing in the other direction, bound instead for the southern ice in a ship ironically called *Fram* (Forwards). Scott received a telegram in Melbourne, Australia, well on his way to Antarctica, saying curtly: 'Beg leave inform you proceeding Antarctic. Amundsen.' It was the rudest of shocks. The British believed that they had a divine right to explore the globe and any rivalry was taken as an affront. Especially with regard to the South Pole – the prior exertions of Scott and Shackleton had branded a searing 'GB' onto the hide of that great continent – it couldn't and shouldn't be hustled now.

Victorian mores dictated that, while the Great Game itself was important, what was more significant was the spirit in which it was played. The whole of Britain believed that Amundsen had traduced that notion of fair play. To Scott, right there and then, it must have seemed doubly unfair. For Britons, for many years, despite Amundsen's audacity and brilliant accomplishments, their view of him was irrevocably clouded. It perhaps helps to explain a little why we were the first to follow in his path.

Among all the debris, we struggled to make out the Pole itself: a tiny, well, pole – striped white and red like a Venetian mooring post and topped with a slightly dented mirrored ball that had certainly seen better days. The marker was almost impossible to discern since the Americans were in the process of constructing a new base, which they had chosen to position so close to the Pole itself that they had made it seem comic in proportion. There was precious little deferential space around that little pillar, which has taken on a cultural significance and symbolic value that bears no relation to its dimensions.

The new base, made of steel and coated in plywood, was boxy, cheap looking and ugly. The construction workers had decided to

---

1 Roald Amundsen, *The South Pole*.

hold an ice-sculpting competition around it, so, weaving our sleds in between high-heeled shoes, martini glasses, an Easter Island *Moai*, a melted clock and other surreal scenes that could have been plucked from the imagination of Dali, we finally attained the Pole. I would have awarded the first prize, however, to some of the other-worldly sastrugi we had passed on our journey.

There we paused for a second before each putting a fist around one of Paul's ski-poles and planting it, in unison, into the very bottom of the earth.

It was another piece of ritual that Paul had clearly borrowed from Amundsen. It helped to give a solemnity and significance to the moment, as well as emphasise the unity of the team:

> . . . we proceeded to the greatest and most solemn act of the whole journey – the planting of our flag. Pride and affection shone in the five pairs of eyes that gazed upon the flag, as it unfurled with a sharp crack, and waved over the Pole. I had determined that the act of planting it – the historic event – should be equally divided among us all. It was not for one man to do this; it was for all who had staked their lives in the struggle, and held together through thick and thin. This was the only way in which I could show my gratitude to my comrades in this desolate spot. I could see that they understood and accepted it in the spirit with which it was offered. Five weather-beaten, frost-bitten fists they were that grasped the pole, raised the waving flag in the air, and planted it as the first at the geographical South Pole.[1]

Then and there, resting my hand on top of the mirrored ball that reflected a distorted figure of myself, the melted clock sculpture we had just passed took on a heightened significance. All the earth's lines of longitude, which determine differences in time, coalesced at this point, forced together into a single dot: the death of time. I walked around the world, passing every time zone in those few shuffled steps and for just one moment in this busy world I stood quietly at the still centre of the carousel.

We pitched our tents on the far side of the Pole, miles of uninterrupted space on one side and the Amundsen–Scott Base

---

1 Roald Amundsen, *The South Pole.*

glowering over us on the other. Clearly there were no amenities for us. There was a rigidly enforced rule of non-fraternisation. The base commander came out to meet and congratulate us and was much friendlier than we had expected. He invited us to come into the old base the following day for an hour's lecture on the science being performed there and a cup of coffee. Otherwise, he explained, we were forbidden from entering the facilities.

The territory we had just entered, as that was how it felt, had a strong scent of America. The site was supposed to be one of international significance – although even more so for the Norwegians and British. The Antarctic Treaty reserves Antarctica for all nations and yet we immediately sensed a total lack of deference for any of the principles supposedly espoused by that document.

It is said that possession is nine-tenths of the law. Certainly, at the Pole the various actions of ownership that are signified by possession were in abundance. The US is the only nation to have a base there; there has been no attempt to memorialise the Pole other than with a paltry placard. Many factors, including the rubbish, the joy-riding and the close proximity of the base to the site itself, represented clear signs of the territorial marking of a dominant animal. Metaphorically speaking, the Americans were cocking their national leg on a daily basis and urinating on the tree stump that was the Pole. Indeed, the dwarfing of everything international by everything American on the site could be seen as an appropriate symbol by some for prevailing aspects of American foreign policy.

Settling into our tent, we melted snow and cooked our usual evening meal and, after ringing family and friends and talking to the press, we finally turned in at around 2.00 a.m.

The following morning, 23 December, we were woken by the sound of revving on skidoos. From the base, US staff sat on high, eating eggs, bacon and fresh toast while they watched each of us in turn dig a hole and suffer the indignity of defecating in front of them – on what was effectively their lawn. It was a little disconcerting knowing that there were potentially 241 pairs of eyes watching me perform my ablutions.

Talking to Robyn the evening before, Patrick had heard to his delight that, if the weather was clear, after all the uncertainty, she would fly in on an ALE flight scheduled for the next morning coming to pick up a last-degree expedition – a group who had flown to within 60 nautical miles of the Pole and then skied the remaining distance. She would have a window of around 45 minutes to see Patrick.

I stayed in the tent while David and Pat went out to greet the Twin Otter. David regretted his decision a little when, with Pat and Robyn locked in an embrace, he suddenly felt like the proverbial gooseberry. There wasn't exactly anywhere to hide so, giant that he is, he just went and wrapped his arms around both of them, like an iced-up Mr Tickle.

It must have felt like the time vanished before it had even begun. After two months apart and having talked shop on the satellite phone throughout the expedition, now together – but barely alone – they must have wanted to say so much. There had been lots of speculation at Patriot Hills (relayed to us by the radio operators on our 'sched' calls) about possible marriage declarations. However, after taking photos together at the Pole, hearing about episodes from our adventure, talking first-hand about the Land Rover team's experiences, as well as unavoidable, inconsequential chit-chat, the moment for any real romance escaped them.

Watching the Twin Otter fly back up into the wide sky left Pat feeling more hollow and upset than he had done at any other point on the expedition. He sat on one of the ice sculptures, a kind of coffin or altar, with his head hung low, deep in contemplation, a picture of desolation – like patience on a monument. The moment had clearly weighed heavily with him, even though in many ways it had been the culmination of weeks of difficult negotiation over the satellite network. Time had evaporated quickly, leaving so much unsaid. Any long-desired moment will always struggle to compare to its perfect twin, indulged and spoilt for many hours in the imagination. Wonderful as it had been to see her, not having had any private time to share the thoughts and feelings that had been building up inside must have been very anticlimactic. Without an outlet, the pressure of that emotion now welled up into a kind of empty frustration.

Paul, in parallel, had also been looking forward to seeing his own loved ones at the Pole. He knew that they would be sleeping now barely 13 nautical miles away and that they would haul towards him that very night, to arrive where he stood on Christmas Eve. The promise held great excitement but it also must have held the potential of a certain awkwardness, since he would be reunited with his ex-wife Matty at the same time. Briefly, everything would become as it might have been – all together, celebrating. In itself that would be difficult for either or both of them. Then, of course, Paul would have to enact the pantomime of separation as he left them once again to continue north on his own. It was a powerful metaphor for the changes in their lives, of the arrival of his children at their own maturity and of a new phase for all of them as they headed back out into the wilderness.

If this expedition had occurred at a crossroads in my own life – or even was the very junction itself – the same was true for both Patrick, Paul and, to some extent, Paul's family. David, too, had been making commitments in his mind to projects and decisions that he would act out on his return. It was further proof that the Antarctic journey was, for all of us, a journey of the interior, of the self, that we were the both the way and the wayfarer.

22 | Leaving the End of the Earth

Moving on, making progress, wondering if we may prosper there rather than here – these are necessary conditions both for many kinds of individual achievement and for the collective achievement of our social order. More than ever before, this order seems to depend on restlessness. It urges that moves be welcomed more fully, more quickly. The process is speeding up . . . We are the new nomads . . . Thus we experience our exile from Eden.

Hugh Brody, The Other Side of Eden

Given that the South Pole had represented such a sought-after Eden, I had expected to experience a shoulder-sagging lethargy at having to leave. I didn't, however. In fact I felt the opposite: I was longing to leave the Pole – it had been very far from relaxing. The continuity of the expedition had suddenly been interrupted, the uncomfortable yet comforting routine had disappeared and the rest we had coveted had totally escaped us. I was restless and wanted to leave. That was Adam's curse: exile. Adam's surviving son, Cain, is the ultimate literary symbol of that wandering exclusion, the first real nomad. Some would argue that man has never shaken off his curse and that we are all born to roam – perhaps forever searching for a lost Eden. It is an Eden, however, that we are unlikely to locate anywhere but within ourselves.

Keen to move on, we soon located our resupply thrown by ALE into a clam tent pitched by the side of the runway. The bags were in a chaotic jumble, showing that they had been bundled in with a contemptuous lack of care. Several bags of powdered milk had split and had now spread over the other contents, covering them like a snow shower. At some point in the last two months the tent in which the rations had been stored had obviously been heated by the sun above freezing point – our high-fat salami had gone rancid: perhaps the most expensive 'saucisson' in the world, at a freight cost of US$196 per kilo to fly in.

We checked through our kiting kit. We found our stiff, shiny new boots with their promise of fresh blisters, our body armour, helmets, skis and spare bindings.

The air was so still it seemed hard to imagine that the wind would ever reappear. It had vanished during our last week of hauling. We had also heard from our scheduled calls to base camp that Matty's party approaching the Pole from the other side hadn't had a breath for nearly two weeks. After repacking our pulks, we could barely shift our loads. Paul reckoned them to be well over 100 kilograms each – heavier than he had pulled in his life. Maybe we would be becalmed here in the doldrums? If the wind didn't arrive soon we were in a quandary. We debated what to do. Paul, as usual, was coolness and pragmatism personified.

'If the wind blows we can do lots of miles without huge physical effort. If we have to pull it will be torture.'

'How far could we go each day if we have to pull?'

'With these loads, in the thick snow; seven or eight miles a day – a maximum of 10. We're weaker now.'

'With kites?'

'It depends on the terrain, the wind, our skill – but anything between 20 and 100 miles.'

We were expecting the next 120 miles to be deep snow and light winds. If the winds never came or were too light to tow us, then we were clearly in trouble. If it took us 10 or 12 days to haul off the plateau then we'd only have 12 days left to kite the remaining eight degrees – some 480 nautical miles. Worse, we had heard that Matty had encountered a belt of enormous, virtually impassable sastrugi as soon as the plateau ended – at 87 degrees of latitude.

'I vote we stay at the Pole for wind. There's just no point in pulling. We'll make that distance in a few hours if it comes. Why kill ourselves pointlessly?' Paul stated matter-of-factly.

Dave was happy to go along with Paul's decision. Pat and I just couldn't bring ourselves to wait. We voted, as a matter of pride – despite the futility – to man-haul out of the Pole as far as we could until the wind came. That way, if it never came, we could still claim we had given our best as well as increasing our chances of finding the wind the further we moved from the Pole.

We agreed that we'd stay at the Pole for a maximum of 48 hours and then haul out anyway – unless the wind came first, of course. So, ready to leave at a moment's notice, we were escorted by US officials into the old Amundsen–Scott Base, a silver dome straight out of a seventies science fiction thriller. It was the only aesthetically pleasing structure in the whole complex, partly as it was weather-beaten and decrepit but mostly as, nearly drifted over by snow, it was being inevitably reclaimed by the continent. Its decay was a fitting symbol of Antarctica's power and that was why we all liked it.

Stalactites hung from the supports. Inside its hollow, iced-up maw towered three double-storey red rectangles resembling containers for ocean-going cargo ships. There were no windows. They were heated to room temperature. Walking inside we broke out into an instant sweat and had to remove almost all our layers.

We were treated to a talk, from the affable staff, about the science and astronomy conducted at the base. They started pontificating on sub-atomic particles that pass through space and even the earth itself without disruption. Details of the core-sampling experiments and complicated astrophysics shot like meteorites over my head. For months I had been filling my mind with whimsy – physics was way beyond me.

I could see David eyeing up a plate of biscuits as he nodded drowsily in the heat, salivating slightly.

Paul and Patrick were also struggling to keep their eyes open, occasionally wiping sweat from their brows. The only time everyone seemed to nod – with understanding rather than sleep – was when, in a moment of laxness, the officials admitted to focusing much of their equipment, through the earth, onto China. They told us unguardedly that from the base they were able to detect nuclear activity there by the subtle changes in the tiny particles that they measured on their flight through the earth's core.

Even though the continent was supposed to be devoted to peace and science, the veil dropped for a moment and we could see that the science itself, at least to some degree, had an ulterior function.

Amazed by the sophistication, disingenuously we asked how many scientists carried out these complex experiments.

'Nine.'

'So how many people are at the station?'

'Two hundred and forty-one.' A ratio of 25 staff to each scientist.

'Then what on earth do all the others do?'

'Construction workers, doctors, technicians, cleaners, cooks and general support staff for the scientists,' came the reply.

The new base even had a basketball court and a special, humidified greenhouse for growing salad (at least I think it was salad . . .).

It transpired that during the Antarctic summer, between two and seven Hercules were flown into the base each day to bring in pieces of the jigsaw that was the new pre-fabricated base. The Americans made little effort to hide, warehouse or store their supplies as only a handful of spies – like us – would ever witness the chaos.

For a station premised on science and boasting 24-hour sunlight for the part of the year that it was most fully staffed, shamefully there was not even one solar panel. The station ran on something as old-world as diesel. There were scores of semi-circular corrugated structures, like half-buried piping, housing huge generators, all belching out diesel fumes. The fuel was all flown in by Hercules, which themselves burn tons. Considering that diesel cost around $2,500 a barrel in Patriot Hills, before taking into account the extra cost of being airlifted into the interior, I shuddered to think of the bill for this wasteful operation.

After cheering in Paul's family and Hilary and Conrad, we shared some truly touching moments watching Paul joking and laughing with them in their tent. Despite the conviviality, I was starting to get increasingly restless. I was seriously behind time for Annabel and only miracle winds could really come to my rescue now. I was desperate to press on.

The following day was Christmas and I wanted to be back together in our tight unit, not waiting in this strange city-camp. I feared that slowly, with the increased comfort, I was being jolted out of the robotic and concentrated mindset that had been essential in overcoming the rigours. I didn't want to be softened up only to be sucker-punched over the next month.

Every direction on leaving the South Pole is north. Given that every degree of a circle would take us to a different point on the coast of Antarctica, there was only one correct direction but our GPS was unable to supply it. Nevertheless, we headed out of the base on almost the opposite bearing we had arrived from, heading towards a ring of electric wiring that surrounded part of the perimeter. We thought it would be useful to wait on the other side of these wires so that we wouldn't have to negotiate them with our kites when the wind came. Away from the confines of the station we could also slip back into expedition mentality.

The measly distance to the pylons felt like leagues. Once we gained the perimeter, feeling like escaped prisoners-of-war, we pitched tent to rest and eat so we would be poised to put in some big hours. We wondered if the winds would ever blow.

As luck would have it, contrary to all expectation, we didn't have to wait long. The wind started to rustle our tent almost as soon as we had licked our bowls clean. Minutes later, we were taking it down again and forcing gnarled feet into pristine ski-boots, bristling with adrenalin and anticipation.

It is a little-remarked fact that Scott himself withdrew from the South Pole under sail. He found a discarded sledge runner left behind by Amundsen a month earlier, which Scott reckoned marked the very Pole. So, commandeering the Pole itself, he used it as a yard for a floor-cloth sail. It was almost as if, unable to claim priority, at least he could take possession. Thus under sail, the wind blew his sledge along at a great rate until increasingly heavy drift snow stuck to his runners and finally brought him to a standstill. This deep snow was also going to be an issue for us. It was reassuringly soft in the case of a bad fall but required enormous force to shift us.

Amundsen, despite having dogs to pull him, also recognised what an asset the wind could be. He, too, rigged a sail onto his sled and his diary paints an idyllic picture of his almost effortless return that must have been a far cry from Scott's increasingly strained journey: 'Wisting in full sail, with his dogs howling for joy, came close behind.'[1]

Having only kited at the top of the Axel Heiberg, we were all a little rusty and it took me a while to gain confidence. I wasn't leaning aggressively against the puffed-up weight of the parachute canopy, preferring instead to swing the kite gently to and fro just to get a feel for its character and eccentricities. I practised following Paul's tracks to prove and test my control.

I had dressed much warmer than normal since I wasn't man-hauling but the concentration, fear and adrenalin caused me to sweat profusely. In less than an hour my undershirt was wringing wet. I took off all my outer layers at the next break. My bottom layer, exposed for a second, turned white before my eyes and stiffened into a plank. I put a thinner fleece on top and opened my down jacket to my waist to allow the condensing sweat to pass out. Until the frost melted again, I moved with the elegance of an ironing board.

In the tent, when we eventually stopped, everything, including my ski-boots, was wringing wet. Cloud passed overhead and I was robbed of the warming radiation of the sun on the tent. My fleece trousers and down jacket were particularly sodden. Unlike Gore-Tex, both materials are hard to dry at the best of times. They were still uncomfortably wet by morning.

The night's travel had yielded us a spectacular 36 nautical miles: it was more than we had travelled, as the crow flies, for the entire two weeks on the glacier. It had taken us 12 hours. Now, the wind was light and we had to saw back and forth with our 11.5-metre Sabres[2] to try to generate enough power just to move at all. We were so tired on making camp that we forgot that we had missed Christmas entirely. It only occurred to me subsequently how patiently and magnanimously Paul had adhered to our wish to get going and that without complaint he had missed a once in a lifetime opportunity to spend Christmas with his whole family at the South Pole.

---

1 Roald Amundsen, *The South Pole.*
2 We each had four kites with us, all made by Flexifoil: a 7.5-metre Sabre, a 9.5-metre Sabre, a 11.5-metre Sabre and the most powerful, a 10.5-metre Blade. Paul also had with him a 4-metre Bullet as we had damaged a 7.5-metre in an accident at Patriot Hills. The stronger the wind, the smaller the surface area required. The Sabres, due to their design, were more docile than the Blade and the Bullet.

Instead of locking into the invariable routine we had used before reaching the Pole, we now kited when the wind allowed and stopped only when tired or conditions demanded. With 24-hour sunlight there was no logical twilight hour to encourage us to put up the tent. The only inconvenience to our erratic schedule was the effect on our body clocks – although sleep was never that hard to procure.

We still took breaks to take a swig of water and munch a chunk of Mars bar but the timing was much more arbitrary. Sometimes a fall would mean the other three would have to wait, cooling rapidly, while the unfortunate faller tried to untangle his knotted kite. Normally, stiffness and chill would cause one of the waiting party to lose his rhythm and make him fall immediately afterwards. Alternatively, his kite lines would snag on some sastrugi while it bounced impatiently on the ground and on launching it, the kite would just haul the skier over and start the frustrating process of waiting and untangling again. It was very challenging to move efficiently all at the same time and to keep one's patience.

We each wore a helmet and a lightweight motorcycle back protector. Pat and I also used knee pads for protection. David, resembling Robocop, donned full body armour.

Protective clothing was necessary because of the sheer power we needed to pull our pulks. Kiting in Antarctica is risky. Foremost is being hit in the back by a 100-kilogram sled attached to you by a rope. When travelling at speed a square hit can easily break your back. Second, the chances of hitting our heads on hard sastrugi or taking a nasty tumble, which can wrench a knee or break a wrist, are high and would mean evacuation.

We also feared being dragged. If this happened it would be almost impossible for the others to stop the wayward kite. Equally dangerous was the risk of the kite uprooting the skis that we used to peg it in the snow during a break and fanning off over the horizon.

Losing a kite this way – or through wear and tear – meant that the team couldn't all sail at the same pace in the same winds, since one of us would have to use a different-sized kite. Paul was already using our one spare kite (a 4-metre Bullet) as a replacement – in the highest wind, he would already be differently equipped.

We reasoned that hidden crevasses shouldn't be a huge issue as we were travelling fast on skis and therefore much of our weight would be spread over the snow, as well as being lifted upwards by the kites. We thought we'd be very unlucky to break the surface of anything but the lightest snow bridge. We were wrong, as we would soon dramatically find out.

The second day, the wind dropped to such a level that we could barely progress at all. Intimidatingly, we launched our most powerful kite, the 10.5-metre Blade. It is a very high performance kite – easier to launch and bring down than the Sabres, but much more powerful and harder to handle in the air. By the end of the second day we had already skied a degree from the Pole, leaving a further nine to go. Having missed it yesterday, we intended to celebrate Christmas, but having slept for barely a few hours the previous night; we just couldn't keep our eyes open. We put on some paper hats to get into the mood, whooped a few times with false enthusiasm and were soon all fast asleep, drooling into our empty bowls, our brightly coloured headwear making us look like weary fools rather than excitable revellers.

I noticed over the next few days that Paul was a little more irritable and quieter than usual. On the second day, he grew very upset with Dave and Pat for tearing off ahead and then following the wrong bearing, sacrificing direction for speed with their typical élan. We weren't able to catch up to tell them that the bearing was wrong, as each time we got within a safe distance they'd kite on. Paul told them in no uncertain terms that it was dangerous to travel so far apart and with such disregard for navigation. Pat and Dave fidgeted uneasily as Paul chided them. He was entirely correct but his usual calm, admittedly with provocation, had momentarily slipped.

It wasn't that hard to surmise the true cause. Although we had all bonded into a very close group, blood runs thicker than water and Paul was clearly, and understandably, missing his children. As we slept that night (or day) we heard their team kiting past us – they were also kiting back to Hercules Inlet. They stopped to shake our tent and halloo. It was a strange experience, heavy with sleep, to hear other voices when we had just re-acclimatised to the vast voids.

Having left the South Pole six hours after us, the winds had picked up without them having to man-haul to the perimeter. They used that extra time to kite on a further five or six nautical miles than we had. In turn, the next day, we swooped past their tent. This tagging continued until Dave had lost their trail. Paul was now so close and yet so far from them. Being out of synch with their travel only served to emphasise his separation. It was he who had instilled in them a love of kiting and now they were following that passion in kiting back from the South Pole without him.

I became anxious that our two expeditions didn't provoke a pointless rivalry that would become detrimental to healthy and safe progress. We started to measure our success by how much we improved on their day's progress. Perhaps the most quietly competitive of the team, I found myself unable to rest easy if I knew they had outstripped our total. I wanted, selfishly, to have Antarctica totally to ourselves. I didn't like the idea of following their tracks or vice versa and found it a little depressing that another team was attempting the same feat. My preference was to ditch their tracks as soon as we could and get back to being a team again, mentally.

Feeling a similar competitive pressure, unknown to us, they had shifted their 'sched' call with the radio operator at Patriot Hills to five minutes after us, so that they could learn our coordinates rather than the other way around, allowing them to focus on beating our daily mileage.

So, having lost their tracks for the time being, we decided to travel north along a different longitude and to shift, where possible, onto night-time travelling so that we wouldn't have the sun in our faces. Paul's chances of seeing his kids again until we reached Hercules Inlet faded with the loss of their trail.

Having severed the emotional umbilical cord, we saw Paul slowly perking up and rejoining us emotionally – although it was still a while before I felt we had him with us wholeheartedly.

Annabel was due in almost 20 days. I needed, I reckoned, about four or five days, weather permitting, to fly back. We still had 524 nautical miles to go: an average of about 35 a day to make it – more if we encountered the inevitabile calm days. But it was still possible. In my mind, the race was on.

With this target in mind, only steady and unspectacular progress followed. The winds hovered just over the threshold necessary to permit travel. For the majority of the time, we had to saw the sails through the air – slewing violently towards the kite with each power-stroke, and then using the surge of speed to turn back to our true direction. It was inefficient, slow, exhausting and meandering progress. Each time we skidded around, the pulk would jerk us in the belly and then follow on behind like a reluctant child.

The days became, in a different way, reminiscent of plateau hauling: each tiring experience was only differentiated by small details. Day three was very similar to day two except for the fact that halfway through we were swept into a large, surreal boulder garden. The terrain was soft and flat but every 20 or 30 yards enormous round snowballs provided benign bollards to race around, helping to vary the monotony of the scene. We had intruded on to the white baize of the gods: they had scattered abruptly on our interruption and had left unfinished their heavenly game of billiards.

If we travelled a little upwind, we found we could 'park' the kite and relax against it, getting some real speed up. Moving further downwind we had to work harder to keep up progress. It led to another debate on direction. Rather like on the Axel Heiberg, Pat and I were keen to take the faster route – after all, we were barely making 30 miles a day at present. If we moved upwind, I argued, we would move onto a longitude of about 86 degrees but be travelling swiftly. Then, if the wind lulled we could always drift back downwind – which was very easy – to our current longitude.

I was overruled in favour of continuing on the present tack, on which we had better information on the condition of the terrain.

Again and again our progress was hindered by periodic incompetence. In those early days it was nearly impossible for all of us to proceed without a hitch. One fall, one knot, one complication and we'd all have to wait. Starting on time was the hardest. Invariably one, or all of us, would unravel our kites to find them badly tangled – often caused by a fall late the previous evening or a hurry in packing them away to get out of the cold. Yesterday's haste was always tomorrow's delay. No sooner than we were all ready than one would fall while launching. It often took us over an hour to get moving.

Waiting to start was often a blessing for me. As we were now only wearing ski-boots, consistent ambient temperatures of around -25°C – although a little warmer than we had experienced on the higher plateau on the southern journey – was still far too cold for these boots. The outer, plastic shell was like a fridge. My inners, still damp from the first day, sucked all the heat from my feet. Soon after putting them on they often felt like lifeless blocks of wood. On the fourth day in particular, I was minutes from frostbite. If we had got away on time, with my legs working less hard kiting, they might never have properly revived. The waiting, though, gave me time to run aggressively on the spot for 20 minutes until I started to sweat. This and further constant stamping on the spot, eventually forced blood into them and they started to warm up. I felt pins and needles starting and, instead of the lumpy stiffness, they acquired a less-worrying numbness. Although I feared that I may have been too late, having waited an hour already, I didn't feel I could make the others put up the tent again to inspect. So we pressed on.

For most of the day I was distracted by the superb scenery. The sun meandered in and out of dappled clouds. One moment it stood naked, the next it glowed in a perfect sphere through a soft white veil of cloud, like a beautiful woman with her legs silhouetted through a linen dress.

That night in the tent, I took off my socks with a little trepidation and a lot of interest. If I had saved them, the feeling I had had today would be a good benchmark for how to avoid the problem in future. They both seemed fine – thank God – and my frostbitten toe unchanged.

Pitching camp so late meant we decided to sleep a bit later than normal. The problem was that this would affect our routine the following day; we'd finish later and the cycle would continue.

Having managed another 30 hard-fought miles in light winds, the next day, while yielding the same result, felt very different. Our main concern to date had been getting off the softer snow of the plateau; now as we started to drop down gradually, the snow was getting increasingly harder packed. With less resistance our problem became one of control not power.

Paul was deliberately the slowest. He was very controlled. His tactic was to try to force us into a slower and more careful progress.

Pat was kiting superbly and therefore getting the most frustrated. He managed to regulate his mood by telling himself that we were still moving significant distances, the terrain was abominable and it was hard to point the finger at any one culprit since so much of the delay was also caused, paradoxically, by waiting for the waiters: expeditions are great levellers. As soon as you are about to explode with rage and impatience, and your mind is wholly taken up with these wasteful emotions, you can guarantee that a bad accident is only seconds away – it naturally follows from your distraction. We all ate many, many spoonfuls of humble pie.

The Blades, which swooped in huge ungainly arcs over our head, generated fearsome rushes of speed but, being so big, they were slower to react to our commands. Flying them became increasingly hard as the sastrugi rose in size and frequency and we were forced to steer an intricate and hazardous path.

With the wind directly behind, the only way to minimise speed was to fly the kite high above our heads. Swinging it down in front of us would open the full face of the parachute to the wind and catapult us forward. The massive upward lift would pull my harness up under my arms and squeeze all the air out of my lungs. It was either that or a similar effect between my legs; it wasn't hard to work out why I had chosen to take the waist rather than the seat harness. I felt totally overpowered and a little scared.

By the first break on this harder terrain, we had made an amazing 12 nautical miles in only two hours. I was desperate to change down to a smaller kite but, given the scintillating progress, none of the others wanted to. We had managed to keep together efficiently without mishap and this suggested we should keep the system as it was. Paul, however, still ticked us off for going too fast. He had been bringing up the rear and pointed out that all our pulks had been fishtailing wildly. Flipping them over would delay us and on this terrain we were asking for a bad fall.

Paul was still somewhat silent and aloof. Quite apart from worrying about his children, more than ever before he was feeling the responsibility of guiding. It only took a couple of no-wind days, which were inevitable, to put a big strain on our resources. The time pressure we were under had never eased significantly since the first days on the glacier. Paul had never had anyone in any of his expeditions fail. It was an unmatched record in polar circles and, rightly, a source of pride. He was desperate that none of us took unnecessary risks. I knew that he was passionate about kiting but I feared that the strain of shepherding such irresponsible sheep was preventing him from enjoying it wholeheartedly. It was incumbent on us to eke him back to himself.

After that first session, I made a few adjustments to my kite and ate my snacks on my own pulk rather than carrying them over to the others' so we could munch together. I just didn't feel in the mood to talk. I knew that I would only try and argue them round to a less powerful kite.

The next session was a disaster. The terrain became very uneven, littered with monumental sastrugi, deep ditches and corrugations. It became increasingly difficult to keep the kite in a slow zone. Each time I had to put it down to wait for someone, it got snagged on the jagged ice. When I tried to launch it again, the brake lines caught, causing the kite to spiral like a diabolical corkscrew without breaking free from the ice until it had tied itself into a mad tangle. If I kept it aloft it was almost impossible to stop and wait. Just looking behind would cause my attention to falter for a second and the kite to whizz into the power-zone. If I did manage to keep it above my head (the least powerful place) it would lift me off the ground and pull my harness up under my ribs, crushing them.

Accidents tended to happen so quickly. Ripping along, I felt a sharp jab in the belly, causing me to exhale violently. I looked back briefly to check that my pulk was the right way up and not stuck in rubble. During that brief instant of inattention, one of my ski-tips dipped into a trough, snagged on the curling wave-tip, and catapulted me into a somersault.

I remember seeing my pulk, then my kite, then the sky and then the snow all from different, whirling perspectives, like a trip through a kaleidoscope. All the images were shattered on landing.

For a split second, there was calm silence and my guilty load skidded into my shoulder, missing my back protector, and causing a stinging crack of pain to bolt down my arm. Within that brief instant I recalled I was still attached to a massive kite. I desperately tried to claw at the handles, which were lying haphazardly in front of me. Too late. The kite hit the ground with a sickening thud and then spun around, dragging me forward on my belly over the bumps and crags for a full 30 yards, jolting all the air out of my lungs, before I finally managed to manoeuvre both handles the right way around and yank the brake lines taught to rein in the runaway.

Getting my breath after a mouthful of snow, I noticed that both my skis were lying somewhere in my wake. Now I had nothing to secure the kite with. Instead, I managed to clip my pulk trace to the kite's brake lines and, thus extricated, I limped back to get my skis, swinging my arm gingerly to see if my shoulder had been damaged. The others waited impatiently, trying to decide by my body language whether it would be a long wait and therefore whether they should set down their kites. With all my kit retrieved, I started to determine where the knots were and how I'd set about untangling them in this freezing wind.

If I had had the same accident with any of my other kites – a Sabre instead of the Blade – I would never have been able to secure the kite to my pulk for fear of the whole load being dragged over the horizon. The Sabres were prototypes and consequently they hadn't been quite perfected yet. Part of our role was to test them for the makers and we had found by trial and error that in strong winds they were much easier to fly but much more difficult to land and to keep docile once grounded.

The others had to wait for half an hour, getting increasingly cold. Both Pat and Dave snagged their kite lines as soon as I caught them up, causing me, in turn, to wait for them: just retribution. The continual irony was that the mere act of waiting for someone that had fallen was itself likely to cause an accident. Hence, if progress was smooth it was very smooth but if there was one hiccup, it would concatenate. A fall or a tangle, like a ripple on water, was a catalyst for a chain reaction of incompetence.

In that session we only managed to complete 5 nautical miles and at the next break, not before time, we decided to change to smaller kites. Moving two sizes down, we all felt like spirits released from purgatory. It was the first time we had used this particular kite since the top of the Axel Heiberg but now, with more experience, it seemed like a little puppy rather than the minotaur that had given all of us, and David in particular, such a rough ride. We had to remember that it wasn't ever the kite that ran slipshod, though, it was always the wind – sometimes in league with the terrain or the mist. The kite was just the messenger, the blameless agent.

For an hour I felt ecstatic, I was in complete control. The ground was more manageable. Totally confident of the chute, I found I could look around me. Earlier in the morning I had been focused doggedly on my kite, looking for every tell-tale twitch and ruffle that would demand counter-action. Now I noticed that the sun was ringed in a halo of light: an infinite rainbow, circling around and around the sun in imitation of Saturn. My elation was as strong as my frustration had been earlier, scudding along on this supernatural frozen sea, harnessing the silent wind and watching the other kites undulating in front of me.

Kiting, like Antarctica, can change in an instant. One moment you are as happy as a condor on a jet of warm air and the next, a lack of concentration, neglecting a brake line or hitting an unexpected obstacle can cause you to plummet back to earth. Likewise, soft snow gave way to perilous sastrugi, sun to cloud, wind to calm, and calm to storm with the same capriciousness. As we moved off the plateau, descending inexorably to the sea, the air was becoming denser. With more molecules per square metre, our kites were becoming correspondingly more powerful in the same winds. Now at a modest remove from the Pole and as the height dropped off, the katabatic winds would come into play. All this, with the harder snow, was ramping up our speed – and our risk.

Shortly afterwards I was shaken out of my ecstasy. We entered a field of the biggest sastrugi we had yet encountered. They seemed bigger than anything we had hauled over, even if it wasn't. It was hard to compare as we covered the ground much quicker when kiting, particularly the open ground between each trough, and so the surface felt more dense with hazards. Previously, it would take longer to arrive at each sastruga so our perspective of the contortion of the landscape had been different. Indeed, hauling with my head down, concentrating only on labour, my field of vision had been restricted to my ski-tips and it had been harder to appreciate the bigger picture.

For Dave, kiting through this broken land must have been particularly painful. For the last few days one of his ski-boots, which were a shade too narrow for him, had been rubbing on the side of his foot. A very nasty purple spur had formed that resembled an abscess. The more it swelled, the tighter the boot became and the worse the bunion. By day three, he had abandoned the usual inner lining of his ski-boots and cadged my cross-country ski-boot inners. He placed these inside his ski-boots but clearly they weren't designed to fit and must have placed a different and very uncomfortable strain on his feet, given that we were kiting for so many consecutive hours. From now on, he was always the first into the tent to take off his boots. As we dug snow around the tent, we listened for the moan of release as David pulled his feet out of his plastic outer shells.

CHAPTER 23 | North

It is not the critic who counts, not the man who points how the strong man stumbles, or where the doer of deeds could have done better. The credit belongs to the man who is actually in the arena, whose face is marred by dust and sweat and blood who strives valiantly, who errs, and comes up short again and again, because there is no effort without error and shortcoming; but who does actually strive to do the deeds, who knows the great enthusiasms, the great devotions, who spends himself in a worthy cause; who at the best knows in the end the triumph of high achievement, and who at worst, if he fails, at least fails while daring greatly, so that his place shall never be with those cold and timid souls who know neither victory nor defeat.

Theodore Roosevelt

On 28 December I managed to get through to Annabel. She had two weeks to go until the birth and had hit a wall. I had just been away too long now. She'd been really miserable. A factor in her present mood must have been the post-Christmas 'cold turkey' – the comedown after a festive and upbeat distraction. All her family would have been around, there would have been excitement, presents, fun. With the commotion over, it must have dawned on her more forcefully that I was missing and what she was, in all likelihood, about to go through alone.

It was becoming more and more difficult for me to imagine her. She would have changed so much physically, and her experiences in the interim would have been so distinct. It was almost impossible for me to sympathise completely with what she was experiencing.

Inevitably, she would also be having to explain my absence at drinks parties, dinners and antenatal classes and was probably totally bored of the whole topic. I doubted that she would ever want to discuss it again.

Checking the website for progress and sending a daily message meant that she regularly confronted my absence whereas I pondered our separation only as often as it occurred to me. It wasn't forced on me by extrinsic events. Kiting absorbed all my concentration, leaving me less empty mental space than I had had man-hauling. Annabel, on the other hand, was forced into passivity by being heavily pregnant. Passivity creates a better platform for anxiety, fear or frustration.

We knew that we were due a day of minimal progress after our steady mileage. It came the following day. By the time we had got our kites up, the cloud had descended. Peering through the fog, all balance evaporated. Our knees, instead of absorbing the hits like shock-absorbers, took them rigid and tense. After about 10 minutes Dave was becalmed in the relatively light winds and pulled out his Blade. Inevitably, it came out all tangled. This was on top of a long wait for Pat to unknot his kite at the start of the day. Finally, just as everything comes around in a cycle, it had been *his* turn to hold us up.

Soon, what wind there was died. Pat and I, on the Sabres, couldn't move and none of us could see anything. Paul had been suggesting for a while that the team needed a rest day. We had resisted his advice while constant wind prevailed and we were still on the plateau. Now, considering that there would be only further delay while we changed kites, we camped after a miserly 2.8 nautical miles.

Even though it was beneficial for our bodies to rest and recover, I couldn't help but think of the missed mileage. Even though it was cloudy, the sky looked incredible. It was dappled with dark clouds and the sun shone through: a bright dot glowing in the middle of those black splashes. A thin belt on the horizon, below the clouds, shone orange-pink, silhouetting the jagged outlines of imposing sastrugi that lay somewhere in the bleak distance.

Lying in the tent, Pat read us a quote from *Captain Corelli's Mandolin* describing the light in Cephallonia which he felt was wonderfully apposite to Antarctica:

It is a light that seems unmediated either by the air or by the stratosphere. It is completely virgin, it produces overwhelming clarity of focus, it has heroic strength and brilliance. It exposes colours in their original pre-lapsarian state, as though straight from the imagination of God in His youngest days, when He still believed that all was good . . . Once the eyes have adjusted to the extreme vestal chastity of this light, the light of any other place is miserable and dank by comparison.[1]

Caught in the moment, Dave thumbed through his journal. He had written to friends before setting off, asking them to send him something inspirational, personal or amusing for him to reflect on while he was away. He cut and pasted each reply into his journal so that he could read a different one each day. Today he read aloud the quote at the head of this chapter.

In a more reflective mood, snuggled up in our sleeping bags, we turned on the satellite phone to download any text messages. I couldn't believe what I read. There were two from Annabel. The first one told us about a huge tsunami that had hit Indonesia, Thailand and southern India. An estimated 12,500 people were dead. The next, sent a day later, increased the toll to over 125,000 – a figure that even later we found still to be wildly inadequate. How strange that a few digital characters could change our mood so completely. It was incredibly sobering on various levels. Here we were stagnant in the middle of nowhere, while somewhere on a more populous side of the globe hundreds of thousands of people were fighting vast, chaotic forces for their very lives. However harsh Antarctica had been, it suddenly seemed benign and indulgent compared to the destruction that Nature could reap elsewhere. However challenging what we were doing seemed in our eyes, it imploded into nothingness before these terrifying statistics.

I also knew that my parents and two sisters were spending Christmas in Kerala, southern India and had flown on Boxing Day. For all I knew at the moment that was in the epicentre. The following morning, refreshed physically but more than ever aware of our remoteness, we found the winds blowing again. After

---

1   Louis de Bernières (1995), *Captain Corelli's Mandolin*, London: Vintage.

untangling our inevitably knotted lines, we set off with our biggest Sabres aloft.

In a little over one hour, we made six nautical miles. Pat stopped to take some footage since the conditions seemed so good that we felt we could afford the time. Today we were convinced we would travel as far as some of our better sessions had promised. There was an incredible, eerie half-light wafting over the snow as spindrift dusted over sastrugi and then fogged the air. There was still contrast on the terrain but the skiers in front would, from time to time, dangerously disappear into a cloud of snow. We had to keep close together.

The hard snow-waves came and went and occasionally gave way to soft, velvety snow, gently sloping downhill with the occasional large ice boulder, about four feet high, to avoid. All of these fantastical formations were made from the wind. In some cases it felt as if we were skiing through a prehistoric meteor garden shrouded in dust-sheets like a disused house. We skied into a patch of smooth snow, lit with a golden sheen from a sun glimmering through the spindrift that thronged the air. I couldn't help myself pumping my fist into the air and whooping with exultation, exclaiming spontaneously and without inhibition how perfect and beautiful it all was. I was floating on a blanket of cloud on top of a frozen sea many kilometres thick. It was surreal and wonderful.

As soon as Antarctica had showed us her smiling face, the grin snapped shut into a hideous scowl. In a matter of seconds the wind increased by a further five knots, the soft snow that had been such a pleasure to ski over was whipped into a frothy torrent and we were suddenly enveloped.

Paul, the only one of us using a Blade, was overpowered in an instant and we looked back to see his kite twisting violently in the wind. Then, in cinematic clips, each time I looked over my shoulder I saw a further instalment: Paul being thrown to the ground, getting up, falling down, staggering forward against the wind until he was lost to sight, wrapped in cloud.

We all dropped our Sabres, but in wind like this it was no easy matter. As soon as they hit the ground, they'd slew around to present their full face to the wind, even fully braked, and drag us over the snow until we unhooked ourselves and took our weight off the power-lines. It was a farce each time it happened. Soon all three of us were skidding forward on our bellies further away from the stricken Paul but luckily still all together and in sight. I couldn't come to a halt and was being dragged on before the storm. Dave's kite was twisting and thrashing. Pat had managed to get his down and was running to help Dave.

I took off a ski as I slid, held it aloft like a javelin and shoved it into my brake lines to halt my kite and enable me to unclip. Pat then ran over to jump onto my kite, which was still bucking and weaving in the wind like an Iberian fighting bull pawing the ground.

Seconds later I heard a yelp from him above the roar of the wind.
'Holy Shit!'

The wind had yanked both Pat's skis out of the ground and his kite was hurtling off into the distance. I sprinted after it as fast as my ski-boots, the deep snow and the altitude would allow. Without skis it was like running through treacle. I hoped there weren't any crevasses. I threw myself on his kite, returning the favour of a few minutes before, panting with the exertion of the sudden action. Into this scene of chaos, Paul emerged from out of the gloaming, a shadowy figure, shrouded in mist, his skis on his shoulders, heaving his pulk behind him.

With only 10 nautical miles travelled on such an initially promising day, it was time to set up camp and sit out the blizzard until visibility improved.

I managed to get through to my sisters in India that evening. Thankfully, they had been in the air during the worst tidal waves and had only experienced minor after-shocks in Kerala, where they were totally cocooned from the tsunami chaos all around them. There were dead in the not-too-distant vicinity but they had been unable to do anything to help. They stayed where they were, feeling lucky and a little guilty to have somehow escaped all trace of the Indian Ocean tidal waves.

CHAPTER 24 | The Winds of Change

Midway in the journey of our life I came to myself in a dark wood
For the straight way was lost.

Dante Alighieri, 'Inferno'[1]

On New Year's Eve we passed the halfway stage of the expedition in terms of mileage. We had also passed 60 days on the ice since arriving at Patriot Hills. Once again, feeling overpowered in difficult terrain and in search of real progress, we drew out our Blades.

The names of our kites and the strangeness of our landscape made it easy to imagine that we had been transported into some chivalric epic or mythical testing ground. Indeed, a common coincidence of the various classical myths and literary epics is the descent of the protagonist to the underworld.

In Dante's 'Inferno', the wind has a prominent role. It drives before it those sinners who have succumbed to the pressure of lust but, most strikingly, it is found to emanate from the wing-beats of the devil himself in the heart of the ninth circle. It is this diabolic wind that has frozen hell. In reality, of course, the katabatic winds do emanate from the still heart of Antarctica.

With our biggest kites unfurled, we soon hit a downhill run with barely a single obstacle. My pulk, flying hot on my heels like a vengeful harpy, almost overtook me. Trying not to brake to ensure I outstripped it, I moved so quickly that it flipped twice and a bag

---

1 Alighieri Dante, 'Inferno', Canto I, translated by Dorothy L. Sayers.

came flying out of the back. David, following right behind, swooped down impressively with one arm outstretched, like an eagle on a vole, to retrieve it.

Then it was his turn. He flipped his pulk, and I had to pull up suddenly behind him, to avoid running him down. As I waited, he tried to flick his stricken sled back over on its belly while continuing to fly his kite. As he reached behind him, the kite swung back towards me, wrapping itself like demented ivy around my lines, sending my tangled kite crashing to the ground. The rest of his lines settled dangerously around my neck, head and arms.

It was as if I had run into a spider's web, like an episode from a surreal myth, and I just couldn't get shot of the lines. Dave and Paul came rushing over to free me before I was seriously injured. I may have misheard the apology for nearly decapitating me with the cheese-wire sharp lines after I had just helped him, but it sounded remarkably like: 'Don't come so close, you bloody idiot.'

As it was New Year's Eve, we celebrated with another instalment of Paul's powdered houmous and crackers, which were exactly that – powdered – after taking a heavyweight pounding in the back of our pulks as they smacked over the lips of the snow-waves.

I woke up to a glorious New Year just seven miles short of the 87th parallel. I called in home to celebrate. A load had been lifted from Annabel's shoulders since our previous conversation. She had discussed the birth of our baby with the doctors and they had suggested that, as the baby was large, it would be inadvisable to wait to have it naturally and so, after deliberation, she had decided that the birth would be a caesarean. It would take place three days earlier than the due date, on 12 January 2005 at 12.00 GMT.

So that was it. Early. I wasn't going to make it back in time. We were behind time even for the previous date – three days earlier was impossible. The hope I had carried with me, day in, day out, had been extinguished.

In vague, unarticulated ways, I was disappointed that the birth wasn't going to be natural, yet I was relieved that it should be less risky and at least I would be able to listen to the whole saga as it unfolded, live. It was only remote involvement but I would still be the first to know whether we had had a boy or a girl and the first to hear the baby's screams. It was strange to think I was going to be a father in exactly 12 days and yet nothing out here would have changed at all. One day I would just be me; the next I would be a father, without having seen or experienced anything. I would be a bystander to the biggest event of my life.

As we all thought about home, Pat described the wonderful sensation of colour and smell on arriving back. He remarked particularly on the softness and variety of the colours after this starker palette. He told me that the everyday smells seemed so dramatic. In Antarctica, by contrast, many of the fragrances were dulled by frost – which was probably a good thing.

I wondered if New Year's Day would be auspicious. With a brisk 14 knots, checking if we were all ready, Pat put his thumbs up and unhooked his brake lines from his harness. It was as if he had suddenly stepped onto a bronco at a rodeo. Released as if by a trigger, he lurched from side to side and then was spun onto the snow in a matter of just a few seconds. He should have held onto a bigger handful of mane. I launched straight afterwards and, finding that my lines were also twisted, was spun to the deck before I had even stopped laughing.

Once we were away, the wind gusted stronger and stronger. Soon it was over 18 knots, rising to 20. My pulk flipped on a piece of sastruga and, foolishly trying to copy Dave's manoeuvre from the previous day, I tried to flip it over while keeping my kite in the air. I should have learnt my lesson. As I leant down it swooped violently down, flicking me over and dragging me along the snow face first – like a lifeless Hector, my pulk bobbing along behind me.

Dave, meanwhile, had also fallen and his kite was spiralling up in the air and hitting the snow then launching again before plummeting back down brutally – 'thwack!', five times, each harder than the previous one. I was sure the air pockets would rend. His harness had been pulled down around his legs so that, trussed up like a kidnap victim, he was powerless to do anything until Pat and Paul ran over to help.

With all the excitement, at least my frozen feet had warmed up. I lay panting on the ground and slowly got up and flipped my pulk back over. It had another slash in the canvas. All of our sleds were bruised, with rips and dents hastily bandaged by gaffer tape. We did need to be careful not to trash them completely: inside were our life-support systems.

Changing down to our smallest kites, our luck resurfaced. We hurtled forwards, racing over incredible virgin snow, with enough obstacles for chicanes to keep us on our toes. Beautiful spindrift blew a fraction over the surface. The sun hung low on the horizon and the ground rose and fell in enormous bowls. Wherever there were sastrugi, our sharp skis skimmed over the top to leave flattened edges that glinted like knife blades in the sunlight.

That session was incredible – speed, adrenalin, beauty, progress, synchronicity, spindrift, light. What a way to spend New Year's Day. I wondered if anyone was doing anything more sublime and beautiful anywhere in the world. While many would have had a hangover, here we were surfing across the unpisted grandeur of the last great wilderness.

Needless to say, as was beginning to become a pattern, all good things soon came to an end. The wind died very suddenly and we made our last seven miles with the Blades. In one day we had used our biggest and smallest kites; we had crashed; we had sped and we had crawled; we had whooped and we had cursed. A life in a day.

In the bright sunlight, with barely four knots of wind, we camped. At this lower altitude the weather suddenly felt almost balmy. It was noticeably milder. We were finally coming down off the heights and breathing more easily. What a joy! We took our time setting up the tent, enjoying the sensation of being out and warm and comfortable instead of cold, tired and wind-harried.

For the whole of the next day the wind stayed the same. We had nearly 400 nautical miles still to go to the end of the continent with 16 days of rations remaining. I didn't feel we had gone quite far enough yet to ease the tension. One big day and my shoulders might start to unknot.

Come, wind. Blow!

Everything about our current location seemed to suggest it was permanently in the doldrums. The snow was luxuriously deep and soft. As we lay and read, talked and played cards in the tent, nothing altered.

25 | Touching the Void

Words wasted into the snow and wind, shouted to no one in particular in a shaking fury of bitterness and grievance. Idiot words, as meaningless as the hissing empty wind around me.

Joe Simpson, Touching the Void

The devil was in a sleepy mood and showed little sign of ruffling his wings. Not a breath stirred. The sun shone in the middle of a cobalt sky. Inside the tent it was hot. At about midday of our second rest day, Paul suggested a plan to invigorate us. Although we weren't entirely optimistic, he hoped it would get us out of these calm waters.

He took the lines off one of our Sabres and tied them to the Blade. With this alteration, our biggest kite could fly on whopping 50-metre lines, double the usual length. The theory was that we could tap into higher wind, which was generally stronger. The difficulty would lie in launching the kite. There followed the subtle challenge of flying them without the canopy sinking to earth like a fluttering sycamore seed. There would also be a significantly delayed response to any action of the pilot.

Each of us helped the others to throw the kite up into the air but the last person, Paul, had the challenge of trying to launch himself. We tried desperately to keep the sails aloft. We sawed our way painstakingly forward with what little wind there was high up, but it was still preferable to hauling. Dave, towing a heavier pulk, had real trouble moving until we redistributed the weight and unknotted the even denser tangles resulting from the long lines.

After several hours, we noticed the terrain changing and the breeze steadily increasing. Before we knew it, we were travelling – really travelling. The terrain was still relatively soft and smooth with only occasional ramps. I was now massively overpowered, we all were and we found ourselves drifting east with the wind.

Pat, who had for many days now taken on the burden of navigation while, for safety, Paul brought up the rear, had been finding it especially hard to kite at this rate and check our direction (which, anyway, was a distraction from the fun). He attached the compass to his sleeve and consulted it by extending his arm out in front like a parody of Superman, letting go of his handles for an instant and then hurriedly regripping them to yank the canopy back through the power-zone. He had become very accomplished at this one-handed kiting, sometimes holding a video camera in one hand to try to film our progress from something other than a static perspective. Once he even strapped the camera to his helmet but had to abort the experiment when he started to suffer from a monumental crick in his neck and a beguiling squint, since, to focus the camera straight at something he'd have to look 20 degrees to the left. In the tent after a day's filming we were sure he was cheating at cards since instead of looking at us straight in the eye, he'd be staring innocently over our right shoulders.

We made out three little nunataks on the horizon. As we progressed they rose up into spectacular mountains: the Thiel Mountains. Positioned some distance ahead, they were the practical halfway marker of our return. Our spirits soared that they were even in sight. We veered west to repair some of our navigational carelessness and cruised powerfully in parallel with the up-rising mountains. With minimal sastrugi and the wind now directly behind us, we could tack at leisure and we swept like synchronised swimmers back and forth along the plain, zig-zagging across each other's tracks. What a way to travel!

The going was so fantastic that Paul skied ahead to set up a camera shot, asking us to kite past him one by one. Behind him was a bank of what looked like bigger sastrugi. He asked us to ski as near to him as we could manage.

I followed directly behind Pat. Picking up speed for a dramatic photo, slewing towards him, I jumped a couple of big corrugations and swept past Paul. Ahead, Pat was yelling something barely audible that I couldn't hear above the wind, my thudding pulk and shwooshing skis.

'Al, put down your kite . . . NOW!'

I skidded over a bank of snow and there in front of me was a wide crevasse covered by a snow bridge.

'Shiiiiiit!'

I careered over it, thudding on top of the bridge and skating up the compressed lip on the far side. Over and safe, I pulled my brake lines violently and skidded to a halt, my kite falling into another chasm that lay in front. Suddenly, I noticed that what we had taken to be a field of enormous sastrugi was in fact tortured, violently cratered ground, littered with crevasses. Some had lips snarling 20 or 30 feet into the air. White on white, they were nearly impossible to make out from a distance.

Dave, seeing the commotion, stopped on the far side. Paul told him to wait while he went to examine the crevasse that Pat and I had just flown over. The winds had been rising steadily all afternoon. They were now very brisk but we still had our Blades on double lines. Dave must have thought that since Pat and I had gone over the crevasse it was safe. And so, while Paul took a closer look, he inflated his kite. Large crests rose out of the plain in front of him.

Leaning aggressively against the wind, which was blowing him inexorably into trouble, for every yard of forward progress he slid three towards the gaping holes ahead. Realising that he was just being dragged further into the crevasse field rather than coming out towards us, he turned quickly back around but the act of turning itself used up further metres and drew him closer to the heart of danger.

Paul looked back, outraged to find his instruction ignored, and watched in horror. David threw himself onto the snow to stop his kite and rolled to a halt in front of the first bank.

Paul marched forward purposefully, without skis, to give Dave a piece of his mind. Two figures inclined against the wind, talking in animated terms. Paul evidently told David to fold his kite up. He angrily took hold of Dave's pulk trace, slung it over his shoulder and stomped back upwind to southerly ground. His bent figure hunched against the wind and with each step he sank deeper into the snow. It was reminiscent of an earlier phase of the expedition and a graphic reminder of what we would have been forced to do if we hadn't had the wind.

I watched Paul towing Dave's pulk from the other side of the crevasse I had just crossed. I flicked back to Dave but I couldn't see him at all.

He had totally disappeared from view.

I scanned the horizon to right and left.

Nothing.

If I hadn't have been wearing goggles, I would have rubbed my eyes and blinked like a cartoon character. Dave's kite still lay fluttering on the ground where he had just been standing. With the troughs so hard to make out accurately, and with scale (as always) so deceptive, I assumed that he must be kneeling down, winding in his kite lines in a little hollow. He didn't appear for a while and I started to get worried. I was powerless to run to him since a vast crevasse separated us. I would have broken through the crust like a stone through water. I was only dimly conscious of time; the penny of cognition hadn't dropped properly. Suddenly, it occurred to me that he had fallen through the snow. Could he? Oh, my God . . .

Time froze. Still nothing.

Then I saw his head only. He waved an arm and shouted something indecipherable over the wind. Behind me, my kite started jumping aggressively in the wind and pulled me backwards. I grabbed my skis and shoved them into the brake lines to stop it, like staking some beast. Looking back, I saw that David was on his feet and staggering towards Paul.

Pat and I skirted the crevasse northwards until it petered out and we rejoined the others. Looking at Dave, I could tell by his eyes that he had had a profoundly disturbing experience. His pupils were dilated, wide with fear. A piercing green, they are usually calm and steady but now they were flicking from the ground to each of us and back. He shook his head. It was as if he had seen a ghost or witnessed a car accident. He was in a state of disbelief.

'I was rolling my kite away,' he stuttered, 'and then I just . . . sank in to my knees. I wasn't sure what had happened, it took me a split-second to realise that I was standing on a crevasse.'

We all listened in silence.

'Then I kind of felt this crumble and a slight rush of air and just fell through the snow. I stuck out my arms by instinct. The next thing I knew I was suspended by my arm pits.'

He paused.

'My legs were just dangling, hanging there. I didn't have a rope. I wasn't attached to my kite. There was just nothing to stop me except this thin crust of snow under my arms.'

He paused again, staring at his feet, as if imagining them hanging.

'I looked down and saw this space beneath me.'

'Was it deep?' asked Pat. 'What would have happened if the snow had given way?'

'I saw a ledge, say 12 feet or so lower but I could see blue light shining up from underneath, through the snow. It was empty on either side. I don't know how deep it was under that. It just doesn't bear thinking about. I thought I was gone. I was definitely gone.'

We had jettisoned our crevasse rescue gear and ropes at the Butcher's Shop. We would have had to fabricate something out of kite lines – that was if he was still alive and we could even locate him.

'The worst thing', he continued, 'was that no one could hear me. I just shouted and shouted but no one came. I shouted for Paul over and over again. Paul! Paul! Paul!' David mimed with a hoarse, strained cry. 'I just couldn't believe that no one was coming to help.' He looked at us with evident emotion in his eyes.

Paul, upwind and angrily cursing David as he hauled his pulk, would have heard nothing.

'How did you get out?'

'I just hung there screaming. It seemed like an age. As my legs dangled they hit the back of the crevasse wall. It was sheet ice. I pushed against it with the soles of my feet and managed to lever myself out without putting too much weight on the snow. I sort of shuffled out into a heap by the side.'

Dave had seen his life flash before his eyes. He was freaked out. He agreed to continue so that we could all extricate ourselves from the collective hole we were now in – it showed his strength of character and resolve. We hauled our pulks back south and set up our kites some 200 metres away from the main body of crevasses.

Paul told us that he would launch his kite first, then I should follow, then Dave, with Pat bringing up the rear. We'd move east. There was still some evidence of disturbance, so it looked as if we'd have further obstacles to clear.

I hoped there were no further crevasses to test Dave's nerve. The double-lined Blade was now seriously overpowered for this delicate work. Changing would have taken a further half an hour. We were all dog-tired. We had already covered 52 nautical miles that day and it was 2.00 a.m. Although we had hoped to accomplish a degree, we had already spent over an hour in this predicament.

Paul launched; I followed. Not having much room, inflating the kite from where I was meant putting it directly into the power-zone and then trying to zip it up above my head as quickly as possible. However, doubly slow to respond, by the time it got there I had already picked up lots of speed and was sliding back north again. In front of me, Paul suddenly spotted another enormous crevasse in front of him. He carved around, was thrown up into the air as he turned and snapped the carbon fibre poles that he had decided to use to keep his pulk from running into his back. By the time I had skittered to a standstill I was a further 50 metres downwind and nearly back in the main field again. Luckily, the others hadn't launched yet.

This crevasse tapered wider and wider. At the outset it was barely a crack. Its lips grew increasingly more pronounced, starting as a ripple and becoming a bank until the snow bridge in between them finally collapsed and its maw gaped, toothless and open, like the lair of some mythical creature.

I needed to approach it at right angles. Other crevasses lay further to the side. I had to keep my course as much as possible upwind and make sure I wasn't blown into them. My kite would still be in the power-zone as I hit it so I'd be travelling at maximum speed.

Paul screeched over it. I had less room. I watched him leaning almost horizontally against the kite and edging as hard as he could to gain ground. If I had been in a car, it would have wheel-spun, burning rubber from a standing start. I lifted my kite and floored the pedal. It yanked me powerfully forwards.

The others watched nervously from behind. I scorched over it. My skis thumped down the lip, causing a small chunk of the snow bridge to fall away. From further back, the others attempted it with the added adrenalin of having watched us go first. It must have seemed like madness for Dave that, once burnt, he should be putting his hand back into Nebuchadnezzar's furnace so quickly. Pat led, regulating his speed with more control than I had managed, crossing near enough to my tracks to see the part of the snow bridge that had come away where I had crossed.

A little shaken, we continued more sedately south-east in a silent procession, passing further disturbances but no more crevasses, until we were safely a mile or two north of the field, which lay like a snarl behind us.

The tent was pitched by 4.00 a.m. and we drank a hot chocolate that felt more like a double martini given our euphoric elation at the excitement, the danger, the twisted ice, our near escape, the mileage and the awesome mountain vista.

26 | Mutability

Such . . . is the state of life, that none are happy but by the anticipation of change; the change itself is nothing; when we have made it, the next wish is to change again.

Samuel Johnson, Rasselas, Prince of Abyssinia

Over the following week the same tumultuous to-ing and fro-ing of our fortunes continued. Whenever we thought that we were about to accomplish a huge travel day, something bad would transpire. Our progress oscillated between the mediocre, the passably good, the amazing and the depressing. Each day had its own dramas, frustrations and elations. Again we encountered every snow surface, every wind, every setback and every excitement. Trying to keep on an even keel emotionally was trying. The hope of making it back home for the birth had, of course, gone but now our urgency was determined by the food we had. We were keeping abreast of that target – just – but there wasn't a lot of room for error.

On the first of the ensuing days, perhaps still recovering from his shock, David had a nightmare. Almost every kite he pulled out was either tangled or broken. As the wind meandered between the ranges, all day was spent either changing or waiting.

Paul gave Pat a talking to, telling him that if he couldn't wait patiently we'd set up camp immediately. Pat had said nothing but it must just have been exhibited in his body language. The kiting was altogether more trying than the man-hauling in terms of the team dynamic, especially now, after 66 days together.

Typically, it was my turn to cause trouble the following day. Although we made good progress, between us we chose three different kites, perhaps trying to second guess any changes before they happened. I decided to copy Paul. Unfortunately, he chose my least favourite kite, the Blade on long lines. It was a constant battle with speed and control, spending most of it fishtailing, weaving and bobbing uncomfortably over the uneven ground. The constant obstacles meant it was almost impossible to brake until a rare flat patch enabled me to dig in my edges for a split second, lean back and haul the kite back above my head. My knees cried out for me to stop. I was feeling bruised and weary from being dragged at near-suicidal speeds over ramp and ditch. It was incredibly hard to stop, and then waiting made me intensely irritated.

It seemed we were copying yesterday's formula for frustration. Dave started with a short-lined Blade. He had trouble moving, while I was overpowered; I took some weight out of his pulk. Then he stopped to change to a long-lined Blade. Then we all stopped to change to 11.5-metre Sabres as the wind increased. Antarctica was supposed to offer us steady winds – where on earth had they gone?

The winds of the world have many gorgeous names, which have been celebrated in poem and song: the Harmattan, the Sirocco, the Mistral, Boreas, Zephyrus – but there has never been a paean to the Katabatic. It is a fickle beauty, ferocious one moment, stubbornly unmoving the next; now driving the snow before it, now barely coaxing our sledging flag out of slackness. To me it is the very essence of Antarctica, its spirit, its breath. Indeed, the mutability at its core is the hallmark of the continent. The continent seems locked in a frozen dormancy but it is all illusion. It has a beguiling lack of stasis that is bewitching; nothing there is quite what it seems and what *is* there soon changes. In seconds, the soft light is eclipsed, contrast vanishes, the cirrus clouds scud in, the sky moves from cornflower to matt grey and the witch cackles.

Checking over my shoulder that we were keeping together, I watched the gorgeous Thiel Mountains retreating behind us. The sun shone through the partial cloud cover and cloaked them in gold. They are five jagged rock peaks, like perfect triangles – mythical mountains of the imagination – side by side. Sheer rock faces and ice walls divided each mountain. Behind, it was possible to discern a col out of which a beautiful glacier flowed down the hollow behind the peaks. The cloud cover that caused the breathtaking refraction off the mountains also led to poor contrast in front of us. Our knees took the punishment that compensated for this beauty.

After covering 50 nautical miles, despite our many delays, Dave, uncomfortable and unbalanced on the longer lines, stopped to take them off again. I should have followed suit. Instead, unwisely I made my feelings known.

'Can't we just all use the same damn kite? Then we could all bloody travel at the same speed.'

Paul looked at me sternly.

'It's far better we're all comfortable. The terrain and the visibility are dangerous.'

The dominant dog had nipped me back into my place in the traces.

With worn nerves and hating my kite, I was just striking out aimlessly. But having made an issue, which must have made Dave feel I was getting at him, I couldn't now follow suit and change kite. It would have emasculated my tirade. Of course, this was foolhardy hubris.

We were determined to make a whole degree. Tired and overpowered, I had a tremendously bad fall a few miles further on. I had stopped to wait for the others. Starting again, I careered forward and hit a lump of sastrugi awkwardly. Flicking over in a somersault, I left behind my skis, one of which got crushed by my pulk, breaking a binding, but luckily diverting the sled past me at warp speed. I looked up, dimly conscious of the kite swooping through the air before noticing with horror that the rope connecting the kite handles was still hooked into my harness. I braced myself and was lifted many feet into the air, my pulk jerking my back as the slack trace suddenly tightened, sending my feet and arms forwards and pulling my waist backwards like a crash-test dummy. I was thrown back onto the ground before being dragged a full 20 metres by my wayward kite – over all manner of jagged sastrugi – until the kite came to a standstill.

Unseen powers had punished me for my impatience at Dave's legitimate concern.

The others were all waiting for me on the horizon. I was dragged again and my skis were so far away by the time I got my face up out of the snow that I was unable to use anything to pin my kite to the ground while I unhooked myself. Unless I let it go completely, which might have been irrevocable, I couldn't get out of the system to retrieve the pulk. I was in a Catch 22 situation. I decided to wait for one of the others to walk the 400 or 500 metres back to help. The kite thrashed and kicked in front of me, smacking the ground violently. I dug my heels in against it. Every few minutes it'd rock me forward and drag me a yard before I re-established a semblance of control.

It was odd waiting for so long for someone to come and help as I lay on my belly, getting colder while my kite jerked in a frenzied motion. Despite the surreal wrestling match, my weary mind just disconnected from the struggle. I noticed the colour of the sun on the horizon and the beauty of the bizarre outlandish shapes of the sastrugi, the undersides of which had been cut away by the sharp wind, forming a series of huge pointed noses that kept above the light chop of an unruly sea and sniffed at my predicament.

I finally skulked into camp. That was that for the day. I had prevented the full degree. Despite the circumstances, the guys – particularly Dave – made no recrimination.

We were still owed a day of uninterrupted travel. Sadly it didn't come the next day either. Pat's lines were in a jumbled mess. It took him two hours to unravel them and eventually, such was the freezing wind, we had to set up tent again to continue the disentanglement inside and allow him to take his gloves off and all of us to warm up.

Once ready, for a heaven-sent two hours we swirled with the snow but the wind mounted steadily until the visibility just vanished in the powder that the increasing gusts blew up around us. Standing still was quite impossible. Pat and I moved in front and Dave and Paul brought up the rear. Luckily, Pat looked behind him and managed to catch a glimpse of Paul wrapping his kite around Dave's and bringing them both down. Then they disappeared into the driving snow. Pat hollered something inaudible and slashed his hand across his throat. I could barely see Pat by the time I had wrestled my kite to the snow, buried it so it stayed deflated. The wind had now risen to a gale force 29 knots.

The scenery was magical as the spindrift blew against the sastrugi, shadows from the sun making their shapes even more dramatic, while the cirrus clouds, split into a herringbone formation by the wind, were tinted yellow by the low-lying sun. As I trudged closer to where I thought they were, I finally made out three bent figures working on the kite lines with dog-fur hoods up, huddled together to break the wind. It was incredibly frustrating to have to pack away again, on what, only 30 minutes before, we were certain would have been an astonishing day.

The next day the high winds continued to rage. Someone had untied the silver cord around Aeolus' mythical bag and the winds that had recently been imprisoned now swirled uncontrolled. We were right on the threshold of possible travel. We decided to risk it again.

Pat's kite seemed to have an unidentified glitch and it seemed that he had damaged it in the chaos of the previous afternoon. His canopy seemed to fold in the power-zone, flutter to the ground and then pop open suddenly, sucking air into it and throwing him forward with the uneven dart of a jellyfish.

Again Pat checked over his shoulder through the spindrift to see if Dave and Paul were following. Losing focus on his kite, I watched in absolute horror as it swooped earthwards. Trying to stop it hitting the ground, Pat pulled aggressively on the bar, fizzing the kite back into air so that it hoisted him up like a rag doll. His whole pulk was lifted clean off the snow and left hanging by his trace behind him. He must have been some 18 feet off the ground. His legs parted and he came down primarily on his right leg.

I was pleading with him internally to put his legs together, just as you are trained to do when landing from a parachute jump. He didn't. I watched it crumple beneath him – it was broken for sure.

As soon as he had landed, his kite smacked the ground, spun around and relaunched again, spinning him upside down. His helmet smacked the ground as his legs got thrown up, limp and lifeless. He later said that his back protector had ridden up and had got stuck up behind his helmet, locking his neck rigid, and this stroke of luck had stopped it from whiplashing. He lay on the ground motionless as his kite bounced in front of him.

Watching this with a macabre fascination caused me to lose concentration and the same thing almost happened to me. I managed to pull my kite down but, taking the full force of the wind as I did, it sent me surging forward. I crashed over sastrugi, heaving on my brake lines with all my might. My pulk flew over the massive troughs, ripping open the Velcro straps and spraying the contents over the snow. I screeched to a halt 100 metres away, buried my kite and rushed back to Pat.

Mercifully, stiff and bruised, he was in one piece. Understandably, he had had enough and after a miserly six nautical miles we put our tent up in the hissing wind. Another precious day wasted.

We heard on our 'sched' call that there had been awesomely high winds all over Antarctica. Patriot Hills itself had been lashed by incredible 50-knot winds – even stronger than the blizzard we had sat through at the top of the Axel Heiberg – and our base camp tent had been blown away. Paul told us that the two previous times he had been to Antarctica the winds had been relatively constant and invariably between 10 and 16 knots. Now it seemed to be swinging all over the place and spending a good deal of time over 25 knots. I had only used my mid-size kite twice, which told its own tale of the extreme fluctuations.

Sitting in the tent while the storm played out, Pat and I had a great heart to heart. We talked about the expedition, the future and our emotional state generally. We discussed how we felt that the expedition had been so unyielding. Antarctica had never seemed to let up for us. We had never been able to coast. We were always up against time pressure and now, having made such paltry mileage again for the last few days, the same grim spectre remained. If it wasn't the time pressure, it was financial negotiations with ALE, a blizzard, sastrugi, deep snow, the icefall, a hectic period at the South Pole, injury or some other trying decisions. Pat compared this to his last trip from Hercules Inlet to the Pole. Then he had known what he was getting and, more or less, he got it. The conditions had been more comfortable, with many less variations.

He confessed to getting a little irritated over the past few days at our progress. The greatest patience was exhibited by Paul and Pat. Pat had to navigate, which included the responsibility of looking around like a school prefect to make sure his file were following and then braking to ensure even progress. Paul also bore the bulk of the irritating assistance he was often called to give to a stricken kiter, given that he was the last in line and the most experienced.

We both talked about being broke, what to do for money when we returned, where we wanted to live and why we had decided to come on the expedition. The last was a hard question for Pat to answer. He was sure that taking on and succeeding in this challenge would cause him to hold an intangible confidence in his own decisions and give him a backdrop of difficulty against which he could define who he was. He felt that many people saw polar expeditions as ticking a particular extreme box and were therefore mystified by his decision to return to the ice again – but that just showed that they didn't understand what for him was the real lure: the love of actually being in this austere land, the closeness of friends, the sheer thrill of swooping over this fantastical terrain, the fact that you don't always have to have a reason – it was just enough to want to.

We certainly agreed on one other thing – we were due a big run. The next day, finally, we got it: soft snow, electric speed and perfect high wind.

Paul's little kite flapped like a torn rag in a gale, whizzing through the air as if it was on steroids. Pat was a little quieter, nervous after his accident. We surged forward like greyhounds out of the traps. My kite was still filled with snow from burying it the previous day and as it glided through the air, snow sprinkled out from the grill like sugar through a shaker.

The terrain varied, generally improving in stages – better, a little worse, even better, less bad – until we hit a broad section, uncharacteristic for this time and region, where the snow was soft and we weaved our kites in beautiful, clean figures of eight and flew over the snow. We all felt a vast weight of tension lift off our shoulders. The miles – all 72 of them – drifted past in a blur of perfect motion as our kites sliced through a serene sky.

Travelling by night and day, with all our internal clocks screwed up, I had to continue checking the date. The clock was ticking until Annabel would give birth and I didn't want to call 12 hours too late. With 24-hour sunlight, the very concept of time had lost all meaning. I was utterly disorientated. We had little fixed routine. It was all about distance. Annabel was right to be a little worried that I might lose track.[1] Life here passed in miles and yards, not minutes and seconds, as time itself metamorphosed into a journey.

The next day we covered, unquestionably, the hard yards. It was a pitiful, miserable, painful day. There was no contrast on the ground. If you were a glass-half-full sort of person, the ground, all things considered, was very flat. If you weren't, you would have grumbled about the sastrugi that *were* there, which we clattered into blind, and about the wrenching on our already delicate knees. The only positive moment was a brief clearing of the sky. Pools of light momentarily dappled the snow. For a split-second we could see. Ahead was a low-slung stratum of clear sky beneath a roll of clouds. We hit that luminous patch for the briefest of instants before the vaults of heaven snapped shut with a boom.

We camped with exactly 120 nautical miles to go to the end of the continent. We all suddenly sensed that the end, after all, was now in sight. We could almost smell Patriot Hills ahead of us.

---

1 Amundsen seems to have had a similar problem: 'With most of us the ideas of day and night began to get rather mixed . . . The date was hopeless. It was a good thing if we remembered the year.' (*The South Pole*)

CHAPTER
27 | The Final Burst

We shall not cease from exploration
And at the end of all our exploring
Will be to arrive where we started
And know the place for the first time.

T.S. Eliot, 'Little Gidding'[1]

What a bizarre, surreal, hard, emotional, tiring, sublime day. I run out of words to describe it, as I haven't had, nor will I ever have again, a day like it in my entire life.

The wind was marginal and the visibility poor, like the previous day. We decided not to travel until the weather improved. We were three-quarters of the way down a hill that was pockmarked with sastrugi, which had caused us to stop the evening before. We hung out in the tent. From just before midnight the weather started to clear and I became itchy to move even though the others were in no hurry.

My goal, which I had mentioned to them, but not so directly as to make it unequivocal, was to push hard to try and do a degree in each of the next two nights. That way we could complete the traverse, for sentimental reasons, on the same day that my baby was going to be born – 12 January. Even though I'm not superstitious, it seemed preferable to finish the trip before the 13th. In the back of my mind, I was worried about my emotional state in carrying on. Would I

---

1 In T.S. Eliot, *The Four Quartets.*

have to down my kite, call in for the birth and then continue with the expedition, my head swarming with this new experience and my mind elsewhere? How would I motivate myself to continue? Of course, I'd want to get back to my family but I wouldn't have the appetite for the concentration required for kiting over rough ground, for hard travel and for not making mistakes. My mind would be in South Africa not Antarctica.

Musing over a map of Antarctica, I realised that the area of coast I was heading for, Hercules Inlet, was, in epochs past, adjacent to Cape Town. It is easy to look at a map of the world and see where the continents fit together like a puzzle to form the ancient world-continent of Pangaea. You can see where the kidney that is Australia, with its curved dip on the Adelaide side, fits snugly against Wilkes Land, Antarctica. You can see where the long peninsula, shaped like an up-stretched Elephant's trunk, from the tip of Antarctica connects with Cape Horn at the base of South America. You can see how Africa nestles against South America. It looked in my Pangaea puzzle as if South Africa fitted snugly into the indent formed by the Weddell Sea. Before the Ronne Ice Shelf formed, when the sea froze, Hercules Inlet would have been next to Cape Town. As I travelled, then, I moved closer to Annabel – it was only a question of time, not geography, that separated us. There they were lying at the end of my journey.

So, with many still-daunting miles to go, we waited for contrast. Finally it came; we broke camp and put up our Sabres. We pulled slowly away from the steeper ground and, as we did so, the sastrugi diminished. It was as if Antarctica was finally opening up for us and conspiring to help me with my goal. As the wind grew in force, the sun shone brighter. Soon, synchronised, our kites dipped and weaved in unison until, in a gorgeous blur, we were flying across the now-soft snow.

As we flew, elated, I would tack away from our little flotilla and race at 90 degrees to the wind and then swing my skis into my kite, gliding around on the smooth surface and swoop back towards the speeding nucleus of the group. That way I could change my body posture, give my knees a rest and enjoy the sweet sensation of speed across this most beautiful and vast moonscape. Our progress was symphonic in its beauty and silence. I could only hear the steady swooshing of the kites and the knife-sharp edges of my skis slicing the snow. Reaching the highest speeds of the entire expedition, my pulk glided behind me, relieved not to be smacking the sastrugi noisily.

Within four hours we had made an incredible 40 nautical miles. We were, suddenly, leaving ourselves a reachable target for the 12th. I could hardly believe that the conditions would hold and the snow would remain so soft; it was incredible that it was like this. Down here, near to the end of the continent, where the snow was expected to be hard, the conditions instead were similar to those of the plateau. I thought, fleetingly, of our Land Rovers and the unseasonal challenges they had had to face.

The spirit of Antarctica fanned me on.

The words for 'wind' and 'spirit' are the same in Hebrew and in Greek. It is also the word for 'blow' and 'breath'. Hence it is used in Genesis to signify God breathing life into the world. At Pentecost the same word is used for the strong wind that brings the Spirit among the apostles and it is also the breath of God that was breathed into Adam. Now I hoped that the same breath that was blowing me to the edge of Antarctica would breathe long life and health into my child tomorrow.

Since the start of the expedition, the birth of our baby and my homecoming had been inextricably intertwined. I didn't think of one without the other. Our strict timetable had taken on the characteristics of a race. All along I had hoped fervently that the wind, the snow and the ice would yield for me. It had become a race against Nature – not just Antarctica, but the creation of a human being.

Driven on, we soon saw the tips of our first mountains on the horizon emerging slowly from out of the snow, a group of three. Paul hadn't seen them on any of his other expeditions. They rivalled the Grand Tetons for splendour. As we glided on, further in the distance, the ground gave birth to further summits and the Independence Range started to reveal itself to us.

The going became tortuous. It was very slow work – the opposite of what we expected as we drew nearer to the mountains. We all removed our outer layers with the effort. Now it was daytime, we were kiting into the sun. It was almost impossible not to stare into that bright orb as I swung my kite over the golden surface. I blinked often, my eyes were now stained yellow where I had been dazzled. It felt warm on my balaclava, so I took it off. It was the first time I had uncovered my face for an extended period of exposure since early on the plateau, before the Pole. The pleasure of the sun on my face nearly drowned out the straining of my knees and arms.

After considerable effort (which I feared had eroded my companions' will to push on through the night) only 39 nautical miles remained. We discussed our plan in the open. Paul was happy to go with the consensus but leant towards a big push. I was definitely keen to continue. Although the winds were light, the sastrugi were big and these were easier to negotiate when going slowly. It was also sunny. Tomorrow was always another day in Antarctica and another day could always (and frequently did) bring different conditions.

The sooner we left, too, the more chance we had of making the continental edge before 9.00 a.m. (the birth time). It was now around 6.00 p.m. We had the night. If we slept now then I'd have to go through the drama of phoning in to listen to the birth in mid-travel. I didn't push my view, as I knew that everyone was knackered. At the same time, I was surprised that they didn't insist how important it was for me to free emotional time and space for this seminal event.

Paul asked me how long I thought the birth would take. I told him an hour – even though it would probably only take about eight or nine minutes – but I was astonished at the thought that it might, for the others, just be a matter of pausing for the allotted 'schedule' and that they even considered that I could just happily launch my kite and continue afterwards. I was probably being precious about it but I felt, somehow, that even though I was so removed from this strange experience of imminent fatherhood, that the others should still recognise the significance to me – even if, in reality, I *was* utterly peripheral to it.

We were split. Pat and Dave were in favour of camping. A little angrily, I blurted out, 'Look, for Christ's sake, can't we just make up our minds?'

'OK,' nodded Pat. 'We're going to camp for the night and try to finish the job tomorrow when we're fresh.'

I nodded, said nothing and trudged off to fold away my kite. My body language betrayed my annoyance but I didn't object overtly.

As I started to pack up, the others stayed talking. After a few moments, Pat called over to say that there had been a change of heart – we'd carry on but eat something first.

I'm not sure what changed their minds, whether it was my disgruntled stomping or the fact that completing the challenge would mean the most restful outcome for everyone – a final, stress-free extended sleep at Hercules Inlet. There was also the strong possibility of seeing Paul's family there. It was bizarre to think that both teams had arrived on the same Ilyushin on 1 November, got to the South Pole within 24 hours of each other and now, despite our very different expeditions, could finish at the same point at the end of Antarctica, again within 24 hours.

We had a couple of hot drinks, soup and some rice to rehydrate and fortify us. Dave, being in no rush, was understandably the most reluctant to leave. He dozed while the rest of us fought off sleep. We were worried that if we indulged narcosis we'd feel terrible after a brief nap or lose our conviction and give in to the inner urges to recuperate in the comfort of the tent.

The world runs slowly when you're in a haze of fatigue. You feel as if you're under water or in a dream, your mind moves so slowly that you can almost hear the cogs grinding. But there comes a point, like a drunk in a moment of precision, when the reel stutters and, within the numbness of your brain, you see clearly. As I sat there watching Dave nodding asleep, I flipped back through the bizarre twists and turns that my life had taken to bring me to this desolate spot, on the brink of the end of my adventure.

CHAPTER 28

An End and a Beginning

Montaigne believed the journey, in itself
Was the idea. Yet from this moving plane
I look down on the dazzle of the World.

Conscious of his words but wondering
When, when shall I be here, at journey's end?
The journey, *said Montaigne,* is everything

. . . It is too soon! The journey is myself!
Helen Bevington, The Journey is Everything

Getting out of the tent was terrible. The slow, tedious sawing of the kite to generate power in the light winds, the big sastrugi and the constant wrenching on our tender knees all added up to a nightmare cocktail. I felt like a zombie. We crept along infinitely slowly, jarring our bodies incessantly. I hardly cared about speed as long as we moved. I kept telling myself that it would be over soon. It was only a question of time. As long as minutes passed, the end – some end – would draw nearer.

I thought about our baby all the time. Just as I was ending my journey, he would be starting his. I went through my short-list of names and tried to fit them to different imaginary little people, each holding my hand on the way to school.

The expected winds around Patriot Hills didn't materialise. We crept past Three Sails, three distinctive nunataks, evenly spaced

AN END AND A BEGINNING | 227

a few hundred metres apart, resembling the fins on a buried dinosaur's back or a school of giant orcas moving beneath the frozen sea. Seeing them was a shock as we'd first seen them on the horizon at Patriot Hills, albeit from a different and disorientating angle but it now meant that we were nearing that camp and, psychologically, this was our first recognisable marker. Our goal was within touching distance.

As we progressed we could suddenly spy the camp itself: a cluster of blurred dots nestled into the mountains. It was night-time again. We'd been going for a further six hours; 20 miles remained. If anyone had looked out from their tents they'd have seen four kites moving from the south like ghosts, gliding silently up and down, in the icy air – and then we'd have been gone.

The surface stayed lacerated with vicious gulfs between the windblown ridges but the snow itself started to get softer in consistency and so the sudden lurches and drops became gentler on the body. The wind slowly increased. We headed on towards Hercules Inlet, marked out by the mountains to our west. Given the disorientating number of peaks and nunataks, the route should have been hard to pick out and yet it seemed very clear. There was an inexorability to those final hours, a simple equation: time plus perseverance equals success. How simple – but each minute passed so painfully slowly.

Way ahead we could see the ground slowly descending as if the horizon was the crest of a curve. It had a softness to its usual jagged edge. Dave stopped a few times with an upset stomach. As I passed him, he had his trousers down, crouching low and uncomfortably behind his pulk, being whipped by a strong ground wind.

Stopping became increasingly hard with the big kites. Soon it was gusting over 20 knots. The change had been so sudden. Putting my kite down to wait for the others, I snagged it on some sharp snow formations and it tied itself quickly and alarmingly into a bow tie before my eyes.

The others passed and were now moving out of sight over the horizon-dip, towards the end of the continent. Untangling my kite on my own as it thrashed in these relentless winds would take too long and I was weary now. I didn't want to test their patience and, being overpowered anyway, I drew my smaller Sabre. Ignoring the usual safety practice of putting my kite away properly to minimise delay – not thinking I'd use it again with only about six miles to go – I just stuffed it, tangled, lines and all into my pulk and unravelled my smaller kite. That wasn't knotted, thank God, and I was up and kiting in perfect power in minutes.

I made towards the one figure, Paul, that I could still see on the horizon. When I passed him, he was also squatting, crapping behind his pulk. He, too, must have also had an upset stomach from the exertion. It was around 5.00 a.m. We'd now been up and kiting all night, all day and all the following night. The others were also changing kites when I caught up. We all continued together down towards our goal and, for me, in a matter of hours, fatherhood.

As the slope gathered steepness, the brittle snow suddenly, without warning, ceased and we skittered onto an area of shiny, gun-barrel-smooth blue ice. Our skis gained speed rapidly with the lack of resistance. We started to outrun our kites and our pulks slid even faster than us. If we powered up to keep the kite ahead of us, then we'd move dangerously quickly down the hill.

I had survived nearly 60 days of expedition, and a further 14 in a wind-pelted tent at Patriot Hills; I silently prayed not to injure myself now. This fear had been insidiously eroding my confidence all day. It's strange that you can travel for so long and not think particularly about injury, but now, with the end so near, I thought about it almost constantly. Sliding out of control over this blue ice, I realised it was a matter of time before I took a nasty fall on this concrete-hard surface.

I glanced behind me to see Dave on his back, his skis up in the air above his head, sliding like an ice hockey puck straight towards Pat. Smack! – Pat's legs were taken out from under him. In the air, their kites had clashed and Dave's kite wrapped itself in a blur around Pat's lines; they came crashing to the ice in a twisted wreck.

I downed my kite and desperately tried to slow down so that I didn't slice the kite lines lying in front of me with my sharp skis. I stopped just short, but my pulk came whooshing past me and settled right on top of my lines. If the wind caught the kite again, with that huge weight resting on the power-lines, it would thrash to break free. All around me were thin cracks in the ice that looked suspiciously like small crevasses.

I knew enough about the polar landscapes to know that as the ice calved off the continent onto the sea hundreds of feet below, there were likely to be large fault lines. Paul, who had managed to cross the blue ice, had now tangled his kite on the sastrugi on the far side and it flapped noisily. We were all so tired. We didn't need this. The downhill slope got steeper in front of me and I imagined with dread trying to keep my pulk behind me. I packed away my kite gingerly as I was slipping all over the place on the sheet ice and some of the lines were now snagged on jagged lumps on the edge of the ice-field.

In the meantime, Dave and Pat had loaded their catastrophically jumbled wreckage of kites – one blue and white, one red and white – in an ungainly heap, like a crumpled Union Jack, on top of Dave's pulk. I took up my trace and ski-skated across the ice towards Paul. The slope was now steep enough to downhill ski, so we got out our ski-poles and started down. We were less than three miles from Hercules Inlet. The decision to ski proved farcical, as the sastrugi were too big to slide over pulling our pulks, with no additional power other than gravity to get their speed up.

Our heels were fixed in the back of our bindings so we couldn't man-haul and our shoulders ached with the effort of pushing on our ski-poles. We toyed with the idea of putting on our cross-country ski-boots and changing skis so that we could haul, but Dave and Pat had each broken one and lost the other. If we kited again, it would be very dangerous with the steep slope and the heavy weight crashing on behind us and, in any event, Pat and Dave's kites were ridiculously tangled.

It seemed such a black comedy to be so close to the end of the continent with no means of getting down there safely. If we walked down without skis, towing our sleds, we were in much more danger from the crevasses that were starting to appear, as the giant glacier that is the Antarctic ice cap shelved off onto the Ronne Ice Shelf.

Dave came up with the best idea. Each of the two untangled kites would act as a locomotive and we'd tie two pulks in series as carriages. Then a second skier would ski behind the last sled trying to slow down the train of pulks and keep them from sliding forward onto the kiter. The combined weight would put a huge strain on the kite so we hoped that the lines would hold.

Pat and Paul, as the best kiters, would each tow, while Dave and I controlled the respective trains. Typically and characteristically, Paul proceeded slowly and with control. Pat doesn't do 'slow' and raced off, swinging the kite skilfully through the power-zone, yanking me forward with each surge. The cross-country skis tied to the top of my pulk started to come loose with each violent tug and their sharp points skimmed my shins each time I careered forward; I prayed I wouldn't fall onto them. Each time there was slack in the pulk trace, I would dig in my edges and skid to the side and heave both sleds back so they didn't overrun Pat.

Once again we hit a stretch of unforgiving blue ice and sped like a runaway train across its corrugated surface. Then, with a vicious grating of edges Pat screeched to as rapid a halt as the ice allowed. I hauled on my rope, snow-ploughing violently on the hard surface. After more than 40 hours of constant kiting my aching knees sent shooting pains up my legs and my skis shuddered loudly on the ice. Ahead of us in the ice was a huge gash – a final crevasse. God, not here, not now! It was 7.00 a.m., two hours until the birth of my child, and here we were in an ice-field with an abyss to cross.

I let go of the rope and skated towards the edge, thrusting my ski-pole into the snow bridge to test its strength. I wasn't sure what 'good' was. The edge crumbled and the snow was soft but I couldn't see deep blue emptiness through my hole and the snow in the centre looked harder.

I looked at Pat.

'Trust me, it'll be fine,' he shouted over the wind, launching his kite before I could object. Ah – that familiar refrain: what a fitting end.

He skied parallel to the crevasse, digging in his edges as far as the hard ice allowed and skidding closer and closer to the edge, husks of ice falling away onto the snow bridge as we moved. Being dragged behind, I yanked the train of pulks periodically away from it with all my might every time they slewed towards its edge. Then Pat turned suddenly and scudded over it, taking me and the sleds with him. My skis smacked the edge and I rattled over the snow bride behind the shuddering pulks. We arrived safely and a little adrenalised on the other side. I wanted to bellow with relief. Paul and Dave followed. We all careered on, the two pulks fishtailing madly and flipping every so often as we bumped and twisted down the glacial run-off.

One mile to go.

A little further, the slope gradually started to lessen and the snow extended flatly on before us as far as the eye could see. Pat stopped and looked round at me. He smiled. I dimly realised that we were there.

We had done it.

There was no fanfare or party of cheerleaders. The snow under our skis was much like any other snow. Nevertheless, somewhere over the last mile, hundreds of feet below us, the sea had started. Ahead, the Ronne Ice Shelf floated on and on, clearly distinct from the mountainscape and the steep and uneven downpouring of ice we had just passed through. I was surprised and elated to see that, even though the exact finishing post was unclear, the end of the continent was so much more dramatic and definable than I had expected. The glacier had sloped down so evidently that it was almost like being on the Axel Heiberg again, and now, all around us, it was flat, flat ice, extending relentlessly on.

Pat and I collapsed into the snow and lay against our pulks. Pat unhooked himself from his kite and for once didn't even bother to secure it to the ground.

'Let it fly off!' he smiled. 'We're not going to need it again.'

It fizzed off a few yards and caught on a lump of ice.

'We've bloody well done it!' Pat exclaimed. 'I can't believe it, can you?'

We lay exhausted in the snow, muttering muffled congratulations to each other.

I was lost for words. I was too exhausted to speak sense anyway, but I wasn't sure what words to use. I had summoned the energy to whoop a few times but there's only so many times you can do that and repeat 'Oh, my God. I can't believe it' like a bewildered idiot. Besides I knew it wasn't really over for me and that if I drained myself of all emotion now I might not have any left to savour what would occur in less than an hour's time. Annabel would be having her epidural now. Boy or girl? I was about to find out. I silently prayed there would be no complications.

Paul and Dave, moving slower down the glacier slope, eventually joined us. We all hugged – or rather draped ourselves on each other wearily – we were too tired to celebrate with any genuine gusto. It all seemed so unreal. We had done it but it hadn't really sunk in. We hovered in a penumbral world, each in a cloudy haze, locked in a post-adrenalin come-down.

We crawled into the tent to get a brew on and enjoy that sweet moment of satisfaction when you know that your body can't go on – but it no longer has to. The task is done and only rest and relaxation lie ahead.

As the fear and concentration evaporated, they were replaced by a lethargic sleepiness. It was now 8.30 a.m. local time. Half an hour to go. I was almost nodding to sleep. We had now been up and on the move for some 46 hours, and in deep concentration for most of them. Yet I knew that in moments I was going to experience an even more emotional and momentous occasion than completing a traverse of Antarctica – and probably more draining. Soon I would be confronted by a heady cocktail of euphoria, worry, excitement, loneliness, joy and sadness.

'Hey, Al, don't fall asleep and forget to call in,' joked Dave.

'Yeah, right,' I said, with a forced smile. 'I'm just letting my eyes close for a second,' I lied.

Shortly before 9.00 a.m., I unzipped the tent flaps and once again went out into the bellowing wind. The sledging flags flapped noisily. I pulled them down so that I could hear the satellite phone above the wind without any distraction before going into Paul's tent for some privacy.

I had toyed with the idea of putting a video camera in the corner of the tent to film me listening to Annabel give birth. This moment had been such a talisman to me that it would have been logical to try to capture it. I had contemplated this point for three long months, dreamt about it, day in, day out. Imagining it had dragged me through some difficult days, so it was more than strange that it was actually about to unfold. But, now that I was almost there, I couldn't face the intrusion of the inanimate camera. I didn't want to feel inhibited by having an audience, silent and listening, at the moment I would be most exposed. And I was so, so tired.

The birth had almost been a figment: something I had used to escape from the present to motivate me, something to fill the spaces of the mind. Now that it was about to metamorphose from the imaginary to the real, I didn't know how I would react. My relationship to the whole process had become so distorted that I didn't trust myself to respond as expected. How could I show Annabel a film of me listening to the most incredible event of my life in which I was expressionless, nodding from sleep, feeling no emotion? My energy and nerves were already frayed and ragged, from the last hours in particular.

Most of us feel the pressure to conform to a conventional emotional reaction. Many would own up to feeling trepidation when attending a funeral, for example. It is no reflection on how upset we are or how much we loved the departed if, for some reason, we cannot shed a tear. We might even feel that the judgemental eyes of the congregation are assessing our response and feel ashamed. I decided against the camera. However I reacted would at least be authentic, private, naked. I sat there alone, nervous, excited and a little scared.

What if something went wrong? What if something was wrong with the baby? Would Annabel ever forgive me for not being by her side?

I dialled.

It rang three times. Lyndy, Annabel's mother, answered. It was that simple. I had got through directly from the ice just off the continent of Antarctica to the operating theatre of the Kingsbury Hospital in Kenilworth, Cape Town, South Africa. I sang a silent hymn to modern technology! They were five minutes behind schedule. Lyndy asked if I could call back so that I didn't waste the battery for the crucial period. I couldn't believe it – call back? What if I couldn't get back in touch? What if the satellite moved behind the horizon? My heart thumped.

I looked around me at Paul's sleeping bag and odd knick-knacks. My body felt so sleepy and yet my mind was taken up with the unreality. I didn't dare shut my eyes. I called again and got straight through to Annabel. She was in tears and sounded frightened and alone.

'I'm so scared, Ali, they're going to start in a couple of minutes.'

There seemed to be a lot of people rushing around but no one focusing on her. It was as if she, like me, was utterly peripheral to the whole procedure.

'I think they're starting, Ali, but I'm not sure. I can't feel anything.'

'I'm there with you, darling. I'm sending you all my love. I'm holding your hand. Can you feel that? Can you feel I'm there?'

'Yes, baby.'

'I love you, sweetheart.'

'I love you, too.'

'I'm so sorry I'm not with you,'

'You are here. They're starting, I think.'

Annabel let out a few stifled screams. I could hear the operating team exchanging instructions in the background then the surgeon talking: 'The head's out.'

'The head's out, Ali. Oh my God!'

I heard a yelp in the background and then, suddenly, some vigorous screaming.

'Can you hear that, Ali?'

'Yes.'

A huge, long-repressed wall of emotion just surged through me involuntarily. My shoulders heaved and I started to weep with every fibre of my being.

'It's a girl. We've got a girl. You've got a little daughter!' Annabel sobbed.

I just couldn't hold it in – those violent, choking tears and I cried my heart out in that tent floating on the sea ice, so many miles away. Whether it was relief, stress, loneliness, shock or excitement, I could barely get a word out through my heaving throat while my little girl's sobs melted with mine and flew out of my little tent into the desolate wastes of Antarctica to add a further tale of wonder to the other mysteries of the last continent.

'My beautiful girls,' I managed to splutter out. 'I'm so proud of you.'

'She looks long, Ali . . . Long! Long legs and arms!' Annabel cried.

Annabel wasn't allowed to hold her, though. The doctor took the baby away from her to be inspected, scrubbed, measured and tagged. She was then put in an incubator, which apparently is normal, without so much as being put in Annabel's arms.

'Is she healthy?'

'Yes, she's beautiful, she's perfect, Ali.'

I felt such relief and such sad-happiness. It's the most incredible mix of emotions I've ever known. Physically and mentally we were both shattered, we had been through this wonderful experience together, the most momentous of our lives, but it was tinged with the smallest iota of sadness of being apart and, for me, of not being able to hold either of them. I told Annabel I loved her more than anything, that we had just finished the expedition, that I was on my way home to her.

I sat alone for a while and cried and cried for not being there to meet her and witness her special arrival in this world – my daughter, our child. I guess I cried at the relief of it all, at the end of the tension and the worry and the fear and the uncertainty. It was as if all the anxiety and trauma of the last two years was all fizzling away into the windy ether.

I was a father. I looked around. There was no evidence of it. The tent rattled violently in the wind. Otherwise it was silent. I knew the wind would mean the others couldn't hear me. I cried out loud with blessed relief. No one need see, no one need hear.

I learnt afterwards that the entire operating theatre had been in tears. The anaesthetist, the surgeons, the nurse and the midwives. It had been such an unusual experience for them.

Annabel, too, had been so preoccupied with the phone call that she hadn't felt the operation. Only on hanging up did she complain about the pain and the pulling – they were putting in the last stitch. Her surgeon laughed, asking where she'd been. She could legitimately have responded: Antarctica! It was one of the easiest caesareans they had ever performed.

'It should be mandatory for the husband to be on the other side of the world and calling in by phone!' the surgeon joked.

I rang my parents to tell them the news: that they were now grandparents and that I was safe and coming home. Suddenly, having my own child, I got a sense of connection to my parents, as if they'd want to know I was all right, just as I wanted to know if my baby was all right. I called my sisters. I could only get through to SJ, but, having been strong for Mum and Dad, I just couldn't hold it together with her. I think she knew who it was from the heavy breathing.

'You've got a little niece,' I spluttered.

'Oh, that's wonderful – are you OK?'

'Yeah, I'm fine,' I cried. 'I'm—I'm . . . I'm just so gutted not to be there . . .'

'Don't worry, sweetheart, she'll love her dad all the same.'

It was useless carrying on as I just couldn't talk. What a wreck. I heard Pat come padding over the snow. He unzipped the tent gingerly and looked in softly, cautious that he was disturbing me at a crucial moment. They hadn't been able to hear me above the wind. I wasn't on the satellite phone now. My eyes were red and I sat hunched up, still clutching the phone.

'It's a little girl.'

'Congratulations,' he said and gave me a big hug. 'Shit. You're a dad! That is bloody amazing!!'

Pause.

While I had been in Paul's tent experiencing the most incredible moment of my life, the others had been using the spare satellite phone to tell our base camp we had made it.

'Look, dude, I'm sorry to disturb you now but we've just heard that ALE is going to send in a Twin Otter to pick us up. The good news is that we don't have to haul ass back up the ice cap to Patriot, the bad news is that they're already on their way. Are you ready? Do you need more time?'

Pat had drawn the short straw to come and tell me. No one knew how to break it to me, during the birth of my daughter that I had to hang up and pack as a plane was about to land, the winds were dangerously strong and we had to find a suitable runway if we wanted to fly out. The whole expedition had been like this: intense emotion smothered by the need to put practical necessities first.

Feeling was squeezed out until there was no room for it anywhere but inside your goggles.

We would have to break camp immediately and dig out the tents that we had just dug in, pack up our pulks and drag them a mile back up from the sea ice and prepare a runway.

Suddenly, out of nowhere there was a prospect of getting out of Antarctica that same afternoon. It all felt so weird. A mere three days ago we had been 240 nautical miles away, up around 4,000 feet high and very far from home – and now we were here, finished; a dad, going home.

Many expeditions traditionally conclude in death. I felt so lucky and privileged that mine had ended so emphatically in life.

Epilogue

Dismounting from the Twin Otter at Patriot Hills, the first person I clapped eyes on was Boris, the intimidating Chilean I had noticed on the Ilyushin on my way to Antarctica. He looked strangely altered. Then, it struck me: he had shaved off his magnificent beard. It was a casualty of a vodka drinking match. Without it he resembled a bald taxi driver with a middle-aged paunch and a shy expression – a peacock shorn of his plumage. His former original and grizzled image had fizzled away with his beard.

I wondered if he recognised me, all frostbitten and hairy – we had swapped places, if you like. It is amazing what appearance can do – not only for first impressions – but also for your own self-image. Put a meek little clerk with spectacles and thinning hair into a desert, give him a beard like an Iranian ayatollah and, even if he is the same humble person inside, he will be treated like a despot. Perhaps it *was* possible to be who you wanted to be – as long as you remember (as happened to Boris) that it is only as transitory as the next drink.

I had expected more time plodding around the camp, sorting out the wreckage of our kit, down-stressing, preparing myself mentally for colour, smell, darkness, money, commerce and ugliness after 76 days in the wilderness. Instead we prepared to be ejected into the rat race within the next few hours. Pat, in particular, was very disorientated at the prospect of such a sudden return.

'It's so odd for it all to be over . . .' he kept muttering. Of course, it was the end of the expedition but it was also a new beginning – both for me and for my baby.

* * *

The Ilyushin arrived at Patriot Hills that same evening but was delayed a further two days as high winds, gusting to 50 knots, prevented its departure. Arriving in Chile at 4.00 p.m., someone from ALE complimented me on my beautiful daughter. I could barely bring myself to acknowledge it. They had seen her face on the internet. I couldn't help but feel aggrieved – did everyone except me know what she looked like? I rushed straight to an internet café to see her for myself. Was she really mine? She looked nothing like me. It was a baby the same as any other. I struggled to bridge a continental divide of intimacy.

Still unshaven and unwashed in nearly three months, I walked across the road to the Lan Chile office to change my flight home. There were so many cars and people around! They managed to find me a flight to London leaving the very next morning; I suppose they didn't want me hanging around.

With one night left as a team, the four of us stayed up talking and gorging on everything we had fantasised over – steak, beer, soft bread, fresh vegetables, glistening fruit. A whiff of nostalgia was already setting in and we indulged ourselves with bright smiles and a sense of deserving. For once we didn't have to ration the whisky.

I arrived in Cape Town 36 hours later, just in time to take Annabel and our baby, Lily, out of hospital.

I walked down the white-washed corridor with the bizarre feeling that I was on a blind date. Inevitably we both felt our own private anxiousness at seeing each other again.

Would we pick up where we had left off? Would either of us have changed?

I put my head slowly around the door to where Annabel was lying. All she could see was a skinny neck and a shaggy beard. She smiled coyly. She did well to disguise how underwhelmed she must have been at the sight of me. We kissed with the strange shyness of teenagers.

There beside her was a small figure. I reached over and picked her up. Holding her to me for the first time, I matched her puckered little face to that strident voice I had heard in Antarctica. I couldn't believe how small she was; she almost fitted into the palm of my hand. The sense of dislocation I had felt in Chile just fizzled away. I just stared at her, my daughter. What relationship would we have? How would she turn out? We were irrevocably linked together now, forever, me and this cherished stranger. She, on the other hand, didn't seem that impressed. She wrinkled up her little nose (my first shower was already three days ago) and started to cry. It was probably what her mother had wanted to do.

Looking back, the effect of our experience on my relationship with Annabel was very positive. I think we ended up feeling a fuller and deeper love for each other, not so much because of the absence but due to a new respect at the qualities that we each showed independently of the other. I was drawn to Annabel even more by her courage and her generosity of spirit. Although I've faced some charges of arrogance and insensitivity for choosing to continue with my adventure despite Annabel's pregnancy, it's difficult to prescribe moral absolutes as the machinations of any relationship are private and no two relationships are the same. Whatever our thoughts on the avenues that two people choose to explore together, you can never fully understand their dynamics.

As for the others, Steve Cotton, Conor and Martin from the Land Rover team flew out of Antarctica roughly a month after they had arrived at Patriot Hills.

Martin continues to have many other adventures, flying all over the world with his stunning brand of extreme photography. Conor has gone back to teaching film studies in Ireland and is planning to return to Antarctica with the Irish expedition that he originally intended to travel with. Steve Cotton initially found the transition from the excitement and severity of Antarctica to the routine of life in the Home Counties a little difficult. The anticlimax of not fulfilling the vaunted aims of the expedition no doubt affected his pride, but, as time has passed, I believe that he has seen the experience for what it was: a fantastically exciting opportunity filled with camaraderie, uncertainty and a chance to see one of the world's most extraordinary places, and he is now agitating for more adventure.

Steve Jones stayed on in Antarctica after the other three departed and started working for ALE. He returned the following season to work for them as a field guide.

Matty, Paul's ex-wife, remarkably – after less than six weeks' recovery – went with Tom Avery to the North Pole with a team of dogs and managed to break Peary's long-disputed record by arriving at the Pole from the Canadian Arctic in only 37 days. Conrad, the Englishman who accompanied her in Antarctica, man-hauled to the North Pole the following winter with Canadian Richard Weber.

David caught the expedition bug in no uncertain terms. Barely two months after we had returned, he flew to Greenland with Paul, and Paul's two children Eric and Sarah, and together they crossed the Greenland ice cap by kite in a world record five days. Then, the following winter he attempted a crossing of the Arctic ice cap by dogsled with Paul, Sarah and Martin. The team was evacuated after an incredible 100 days on the ice, approximately 190 miles short of their goal as the sea ice melted around them. It was an extraordinary journey and, as David promised in our tent, he did it to publicise global warming and inspire change – it was the first in what he hopes will be a sequence of missions under the brand 'adventure ecology'.

Pat and Robyn, although they didn't get hitched in Antarctica, did get engaged while in Mozambique at the end of the English summer and are planning more ridiculous enterprises. Pat has written a novel based on his experiences in Tibet and, indelibly smitten by Antarctica, has now established a company, White Desert, flying people into Antarctica.

Pat and I continued to spend various months unravelling the expedition and organising the shipment of the kit before finally drawing the experience to a close by lecturing to a full house at the Royal Geographical Society in aid of the Alex Roberts-Miller Foundation and the Prince's Trust. Richard and Fiona, Alex's parents, were there but I don't think I ever told them what it meant to me to dedicate the achievement to Alex.

Whenever someone raises money for charity the common perception is that that person is supporting others in more difficult circumstances and that the gesture is generous and giving. Ironically, for me it was simply the other way around. For most of the expedition,

I leant on Alex's foundation as if it was a crutch. For a good many reasons, both emotional and physical – as you know – I kept asking myself in the considerably cold light of day (all 24 hours of it) what the hell I was doing. I imagined, time and time again, the moment that I would ring Richard and Fiona from the axis of the world and tell them that a flag with their own son's name on it was at the South Pole. The fact that I was raising some money for them through something that seemed in every other way so utterly pointless helped hugely to motivate me each day. I needed to pretend that it wasn't all just vain egoism. It made me feel better that Richard and Fiona might feel comforted that something positive was flowing from Alex still.

Sir Ernest Shackleton, in his epic adventure on the *Endurance* expedition, at a final knife-edge moment on South Georgia sensed a fourth figure travelling with him and his two companions, ensuring his miraculous, safe return. Religious commentators have picked up on this and even T.S. Eliot uses the idea in *The Waste Land*, probably the most important poem of the twentieth century.

> Who is this third who walks always beside you?
> When I count, there are only you and I together
> But when I look ahead up the white road
> There is always another one walking beside you

Of course, I'm not suggesting that Alex was there but I *am* suggesting that the good that Alex's foundation is achieving was helping push me along. I'm so proud to dedicate the adventure to Alex and I hope that this will be the first in many dreams and fantasies that are realised for him so that his death will cause a spiral of achievement to spin on and on.

As for me, with Antarctica behind me, I wasn't sure what lay in front. In that respect, I suppose I was returning to the same situation that I had left: rather like the ending of *The Iceman Cometh*.

The themes of that play are relevant in many ways. Hickey urges the drunkards who while away their lives fantasising about tomorrow to put up or shut up, to *do* what they've long been muttering about over their whisky cups. All their dreams, in the fullness of the play, represent the impossible and many of us, me included, can identify with that siren voice that constantly insists that we aren't capable of what we imagine.

I'm not triumphantly comparing my notionally successful experience to their failed pipe dreams, for, in the terms of the play, I fall into the same category. We are programmed by Hollywood to see 'fulfilling a dream' as an outcome, something that can be contained in a single sentence or reduced to a two-hour slot. He wanted to go to Antarctica; he went. *Veni, vidi, vici.* But what does the character do when the film ends? In reality, the consequences of attempting to realise a dream last longer than two hours. It is about changing your whole life to accommodate a new way of being, creating yourself anew and then maintaining (and evolving) that new posture all your life.

Before I ever set foot in Antarctica, I knew that I wasn't a polar explorer. I knew, like all other drunkards – sozzled on fantasy – that I would return from my walk outside and continue to prop up the bar. I don't want to continue going to the loneliest locations on earth for the sake of breaking, in new and subtle ways, meaningless records that have effectively already been broken. I don't want to risk my life to live up to a pseudo-image. After all, I visited Antarctica for other reasons – historical, cultural, personal and romantic.

George Orwell once tried to analyse why he wrote. He identified four motivations – sheer egoism, aesthetic enthusiasm, historical impulse and political purpose. Under sheer egoism he recorded:

> the desire to seem clever, to be talked about, to be remembered after death, to get your own back on grown-ups who had snubbed you in childhood etc. etc. It is humbug to pretend this is not a motive and a strong one. Writers share this characteristic with scientists, artists, politicians, lawyers, soldiers, successful businessmen – in short the whole top crust of humanity. The great mass of human beings are not acutely selfish. After the age of about 30 they almost abandon the sense of being individuals at all and live chiefly for others or are simply smothered under drudgery. But there are also the minority of gifted, wilful people who are determined to live their own lives to the end.[1]

---

1 George Orwell, *Why I Write.*

It is humbug for me, too, to say that egoism wasn't a motive for the expedition and, in part, for this book. Indeed, the desire to write a book and the desire to cross Antarctica were so linked as to be practically indistinguishable for they both drew upon the same forces. The tracks of my sled were a scratchy calligraphy on the blank page of the white desert, sketching out what I felt about the world and my place in it; my path soon to be covered in snow just as my words will be recorded in this book and then soon forgotten on a dusty shelf. Yet despite this, aesthetic enthusiasm and historical impulse were equally important. For me these motivations are both bound up in romanticism – the lure of dusty travel books, the lustre of adventure, the desire to make my life different and unique. Antarctica was the logical choice. Being in such a psychologically and poetically meaningful place meant it was connected in my mind to the psychedelic, other-worldly proving grounds of myth and legend. But any parallels of my journey to these or to the annals of Antarctic history haven't been made to elevate myself. Rather than showing what I *am*, they exemplified what I *felt*. This story shows that it still remains possible, whoever you are, to feel you are anyone, at least for a while. And there were times when I *was* traversing the underworld, hitching a ride on a phoenix and being guided through layers of ice by both Amundsen and Dante.

Our society (and many before it) has been soaked, rolled, sweated and baked in tales of exile, punishment, labour and love. We may not all have read these tales but they constitute the fabric of our literature and art and their influence has permeated our cultural values and moulded our attitudes to heroism and glory. It is hardly surprising that our society, through the laurels it confers and via a host of unconscious influences, encourages the emulation of those heroes (in as approximate a way as is now possible).

The reality of the expedition, however, except for isolated instances, was for the most part anything but a fairy story – although on return, strangely, the memories have been gilded – re-romanticised, if you like. It shows that romance has limited dimensions. It exists in the past and the future but never the present. This is one of the conundrums of happiness. Romance is a deceptive harpy that causes you to look and look and never be happy. But to ignore it is to shut out one of the most essential and beautiful pleasures of life and it must be indulged. The irony is that even though I know that so many parts of this trip were unutterably hard, now, in the security of my home, and despite myself, I just can't help but yearn for another adventure . . .

The graph of experience is made up of many different 'presents': a succession of different movies – some mundane and others exhilarating – beating out the jagged contours of a mountain range. This adventure was just one of those scratchy heartbeats on the line of my life. Home again, like all of us, I'm unavoidably scanning ahead for the next systolic up-rush (or the diastolic slump). There is always something new ahead – whether good or bad. The horizon presents an ever-changing tableau. Soon a new challenge will present itself, more real, more pressing and more urgent (because it is new) than anything I have ever done.

On an Antarctic journey, you are seduced for a brief moment into an unreal world where the horizon moves, yet is always the same – a hazy white line. You are under the illusion that your life has been put on hold, frozen, and that it is possible to suspend reality and escape time, moving on a treadmill without ever getting anywhere. It's make-believe, of course – eventually you do come home and return to the beginning again: the place from which you left.

For me, the challenge is to get the right blend between real life and fantasy, to strive to be adventurous, in the widest sense by continuing to exploit interesting possibilities, meet interesting people and do exciting things – however passive or active those are – in order to grow, learn and develop. And so, with this particular movie over, my life continues and perhaps no real resolution is possible.

Back in the real world, the first hurdle to deal with was the anticlimax of life at home. However exciting it was to be a father and wonderful to spend time with Annabel again, in many ways I had a tougher time coming home than I ever had in Antarctica – the struggle to earn money through part-time teaching and journalism, the weight of the substantial debt for the resupply, the constant administration of life, the late-night shifts bottle-feeding, the adjustment to a new emotional space. The contrast was absolute and I found a full and honest respect for everyone that manages all of it with equanimity.

I found the void between what I had wanted my life to be and what it was quite a burden. Now I understand that this reaction is quite typical. It's a type of moon-sickness. The astronauts who walked on the moon complained that confronting life on earth again was almost impossible knowing that nothing could ever compare. Apsley Cherry-Garrard, one of Captain Scott's companions, looked back touchingly and poignantly on his expedition with Scott for his whole life, agonising over whether he could have done more to save Scott and his companions, having turned his back, unwittingly, on them only a few miles away from where they perished.

I've quoted Cherry-Garrard various times in this book, including the first part of his famous line from *The Worst Journey in the World*: 'If you march your winter journeys you will have your reward.' This is not the whole sentence, though, it continues: 'so long as all you want is a penguin's egg'. Before I left, the significance of that concluding part was lost on me, indeed I thought it ruined the beauty and romantic promise of the first part. It is only now that I really understand it; polar travel may be heroic but, being a form of escapism, it is essentially futile. The penguin's egg is a cipher; it stands for your personal holy grail, however inconsequential that might be to other people. The egg also represents a symbol of birth, or rebirth. For me, the reward of the journey was not just the birth of my daughter but also the ability to understand myself better, perhaps even to create myself anew in the white wilderness and through the fire of physical exertion – as Gibran says, 'pain is the breaking of the shell that encloses your understanding'.[1]

It was while I was away that I came to realise that the expedition was partly an attempt to rebel against my own mediocrity. I now had to confront it again face-on. I became worried that the trip would be the one 'interesting' footnote to my life and that I would be forced to bore people rigid about it into my dotage even while, really, it signified nothing. For that reason I found refuge, most often, in the reverse: silence. Would nothing else of note happen in my life?

1 Khalil Gibran, *The Prophet*.

It may be more difficult to weave a story around the rump – what's left after the expedition – but that remainder is *life*. The rest is only a sideshow. I started to realise that life is where the true challenges lie, not in some remote windy desert: to nurture relationships, to be a positive person, to rise above the mundane, to seek the beautiful, to meet all the myriad tests of responsibility and, through it all, not to lose the capacity to dream and grow. And I now know that in the future I will experience moments of magic and wonder with Annabel, Lily and my future children that will surpass everything so far. Indeed, if anything, the conclusion to my winter journey was an authentic and dramatic meeting with real life that was more profound and emotional than anything I encountered on the ice. I look forward most to an even more exciting adventure through life with Annabel. I see in my daughter some incredible qualities that I can't wait to watch develop and I already have a bond with her that means her birth, and not the expedition, will forever be one of the most meaningful events of my life.

As I write now, a few years on, certain of the authenticity that led me to take on this challenge but distanced from the force of feeling I then had, it does lead me to see many of these traits not as exceptional but, regrettably, as the reverse: symptoms of my age and generation. I find it difficult to consider or admit it, but as I understand more about the times we live in – the tendency towards narcissism, the desire for publicity, the short-termism, the wish to receive the badge of an explorer without a lifetime's hard work, the growth of the 'guided' experience, the increasing accessibility of achievement, the drive to publish – I see many parts of what I undertook unavoidably exhibiting the tendencies of this era.

Is it ever possible to defy the zeitgeist? Is real difference possible? Rebellion itself is so conformist. Don't all rock stars follow the same stereotype – success, adulation, contempt for the music establishment, drugs, drink, an orgiastic surfeit of sex, repentance, rehabilitation in a well-regarded clinic, a come-back album (all played out publicly at the dictates of the star's publicist)? Of course following this path is partly an excuse to indulge in the hedonism most of us secretly covet but it's hardly novel. If real originality is impossible, then maybe all we can hope for is self-awareness?

What about all the resolutions I made out there, though: to seek happiness away from the material; to be a better person; to show people how much they mean to me; to make time to enjoy the present; to learn to be still? Could I keep them now? Had the experience ingrained these sentiments?

The truth is, not really. It's amazing how quickly I slipped back into the pace of it all. All you have to do is touch the whirring treadmill ever so slightly and you are catapulted back on among the other rats. Or if you just choose to sit alongside instead, you go mad with the sound.

It is only rarely now that I think consciously about the pleasure of being warm or lying in a hot bath or feeling Annabel's breath on my skin. The experience must have changed who I am and how I think, it must have given me a deeper perspective, but it's only rarely that I access that chamber.

There's no doubt that the experience of spending time alone with myself was revealing. I came face to face with many of my weaknesses but in other ways I enjoyed experiencing time as time – undistracted by anything extrinsic other than the wind and the cold. And I have returned a vastly more emotional person than I left – maybe because I now have a greater empathy for hardship and loneliness. And such an extended time exposed to the power of the pristine rather than to our prevailing materialism may have helped inject me with a more purposeful environmentalism.

By stepping out of a conventional existence and going briefly into unmarked land, I threw away the map I was holding. During my time away, I found that real life is every bit as difficult and unpredictable as any physical exploration – and none of us holds maps to tell us what to do, we just muddle through with some dead reckoning and an old compass.

Select Bibliography

The following is a selection of books that have all been important to me and which to a greater or lesser extent have inspired this book and in some cases have been the source for quotations.

Amundsen, Roald (1987), *The Amundsen Photographs*, edited by Roland Huntford, London: Hodder & Stoughton

Amundsen, Roald (2002), *The South Pole*, Edinburgh: Birlinn

Botton, Alain de (2003), *The Art of Travel*, London: Penguin Books

Brody, Hugh (2002), *The Other Side of Eden: Hunter-gatherers, Farmers and the Shaping of the World*, London: Faber and Faber

Camus, Albert (2004), 'The Myth of Sisyphus', in A. Camus, *The Plague, The Fall, Exile and the Kingdom*, London: Everyman's Library, Alfred A. Knopf

Chatwin, Bruce (1988), *The Songlines*, London: Picador

Chatwin, Bruce (1997), *The Anatomy of Restlessness*, London: Picador

Chatwin, Bruce (1998), *In Patagonia*, London: Vintage

Cherry-Garrard, Apsley (2001), *The Worst Journey in the World*, London: Picador

Dante, Alighieri (1995), 'Inferno', in D. Alighieri, *The Divine Comedy*, translated by Allen Mandelbaum, London: Everyman's Library, Alfred A. Knopf

Dante, Alighieri (1950), 'Inferno', in D. Alighieri, *The Divine Comedy: Hell*, translated by Dorothy L. Sayers, London: Penguin Classics

Eliot, T.S. (1961), *The Waste Land*, in T.S. Eliot, *Selected Poems*, London: Faber and Faber

Eliot, T.S. (2001), *The Four Quartets*, London: Faber and Faber

Emerson, Ralph Waldo (2000), 'Nature', in R.W. Emerson, *The Essential Writings of Ralph Waldo Emerson*, edited by Brooks Atkinson, London: Modern Library Classics

Emerson, Ralph Waldo (2000), 'Self Reliance', in R.W. Emerson, *The Essential Writings of Ralph Waldo Emerson*, edited by Brooks Atkinson, London: Modern Library Classics

Fiennes, Sir Ranulph (1994), *Mind over Matter: The Epic Crossing of the Antarctic Continent*, London: Mandarin

Fiennes, Sir Ranulph (2003), *Captain Scott*, London: Hodder & Stoughton

Gibran, Khalil (1992), *The Prophet*, London: Penguin Books

Gillman, Peter (ed.) (1993), *Everest: The Best Writing and Pictures from Seventy Years of Human Endeavour*, Little, Brown & Co.

Gillman, Peter and Gillman, Leni (2001), *The Wildest Dream: Mallory – His Life and Conflicting Passions*, London: Headline

Hancock, Graham (1995), *Fingerprints of the Gods: The Evidence of Earth's Lost Civilization*, London: Random House

Huntford, Roland (1996), *Shackleton*, London: Abacus

Johnson, Samuel (1995), *Rasselas, Prince of Abyssinia*, London: Penguin Classics

Krakauer, Jon (1998), *Into the Wild*, London: Pan Books

Lawrence, T.E. (1935), *The Seven Pillars of Wisdom*, London: Jonathan Cape

Macfarlane, Robert (2004), *Mountains of the Mind*, London: Granta Books

Melville, Herman (2002), *Moby Dick: Or, The Whale*, London: Penguin Classics

Milton, John (2003), *Paradise Lost*, London: Penguin Classics

O'Neill, Eugene (1993), *The Iceman Cometh*, London: Nick Hern Books and Royal National Theatre

Orwell, George (2004), *Why I Write*, London: Penguin

Rimbaud, Arthur (1998), *A Season in Hell*, translated by Mark Treharne, London: J.M. Dent

Saint Exupéry, Antoine de (2000), *Southern Mail/Night Flight*, London: Penguin Modern Classics

Saint Exupéry, Antoine de (2000), *Wind, Sand and Stars*, translated by William Rees, London: Penguin Classics

Scott, Captain R.F. (2003), *Scott's Last Expedition: The Journals of Captain R.F. Scott*, London: Pan Books

Seuss, Dr (2003), *Oh, the Places You'll Go*, London: Harper Collins Children's Books

Shackleton, Sir Ernest (1999), *South*, London: Penguin Books

Shelley, Mary (1992), *Frankenstein: Or, The Modern Prometheus*, London: Penguin Classics

Simpson, Joe (1997), *Touching the Void*, London: Vintage

Thesiger, Wilfred (1991), *Arabian Sands*, London: Penguin Books

Thoreau, Henry David (1999), *Walden*, London, New York: Oxford World Classics

Wheeler, Sara (1997), *Terra Incognita: Travels in Antarctica*, London: Vintage

Wheeler, Sara (2007), *Too Close to the Sun: The Audacious Life and Times of Denys Finch Hatton*, London: Vintage

Whitman, Walt (1986), 'Song of Myself', in W. Whitman, *The Leaves of Grass*, London: Penguin Classics

Woodhead, Patrick (2003), *Misadventures in a White Desert*, London: Hodder & Stoughton

Author's Note

This book tells the story about an expedition. It's a regrettable facet of polar journeys that for marketing and sponsorship reasons they all try and claim some 'first' and end up doing so by comparing apples with oranges, in ever more artificial and arbitrary ways. This aspect doesn't interest me at all – we did what we did and the truth of the route, and the 'living' of it, is told in these pages.

However, I would like to make one note on this topic for those people who consider such things important – concerning the fact that this was a west–east traverse. There have been other traverses, longer and more impressive – achieved by Alain Hubert, Sir Ranulph Fiennes, Borge Ousland, Will Stegers and Ann Bancroft, for example. There are Traverses and traverses. This expedition was a traverse with a small 't', in the sense that although we travelled from one edge of the continent to the other (where the land ends and the sea starts – underneath the sea ice), we did not travel to the water itself. There are various precedents for distinguishing a continental traverse from a full traverse.

The second point to note is that by convention, as Wikipedia states: 'Antarctica is divided into two by the Trans-Antarctic Mountains close to the neck of the Ross Sea and the Weddell Sea. The portion west of the Weddell Sea and east of the Ross Sea is called West Antarctica and the remainder East Antarctica, because they roughly correspond to the Western and Eastern Hemispheres relative to the Greenwich meridian.' Given this, anyone coming down through the Trans-Antarctic Mountains is, by definition, crossing the divide between east and west Antarctica, from east to west.

We were the first traverse, to my knowledge, going up through the Trans-Antarctic Mountains into East Antarctica (for good reason, as most people don't want to pull full sledges at the start of an expedition up mountains: they prefer to pull emptier sledges down them) . Therefore we crossed this east–west divide from west to east – so we have called this a west–east traverse.

Of course, the reality is even more complicated. First, because after going to the South Pole we then swung from there to Patriot Hills in a dog-leg, meaning we headed back into west Antarctica (west–east–west). Second, the truth is that 'west' and 'east' in Antartica are only an illusion: the only possible direction heading to the South Pole is south, and whichever direction you take away from it, on any longitude, you are can only be heading due north. I hope you'll see from the above that a claim is never simple, people will always disagree and the facts are not that interesting anyway!

Acknowledgements

With an expedition like this there are a lot of people who have contributed and I'd like to acknowledge all those institutions who believed in two breathless and naive romantics - Invesco Perpetual, Dunhill, Nikon, Group LCF Rothschild, the International Polar Foundation, Marketform, BPP Professional Education, Mumm Champagne, IPaccess, Burberry, Landrover, Mountain Hardware, Lifeventure, Puma, Berghaus, Brunton, Adidas, Snow&Rock, Specs of Kensington and Altamira Holdings.

Among the group of sponsors, I'd also like to particularly thank Rob Hain and Andrew Williams who took the vital decision on the title sponsorship that actually breathed life into my Frankenstein. Gratitude also to Lady Ariane de Rothschild and Alain Hubert of the International Polar Foundation, my friends Holly Bellingham and Simon Turner of Marketform who made being sponsored such a pleasure, and to Sir James Cayzer – who wrote the very first cheque that got the funding underway. Behind the scenes thanks also to Lewis Orr at JohnHenry.net and Rory Scott and Hector Proud at IdeaGeneration. Graham Nicholson, thank you for many things, you've been a great friend and mentor, supporting me in my career, writing and this expedition – it's not forgotten.

In many ways the book is a separate project and, like the expedition, it took some time and perserverance to bring it into being. Huge thanks to Tatiana Wilde at I.B.Tauris for taking me on, I'm so pleased you did. You were just such a pleasure to deal with in all respects;

thanks also to the rest of the team there – especially Jayne Ansell and Alan Bridger and also Steve Williamson and Jessica Cuthbert-Smith of JCS Publishing.

Bear, thanks for writing the generous foreword. You're such a big star now and yet it's amazing how much you're still your old self – I really appreciate you supporting me. Many thanks to Sir Ranulph Fiennes, both for being the patron of the expedition but also for spending precious time reading a book by an impostor and then being so kind about it. I'm also indebted to John Hare for taking time out of the heat to consider the cold and to Jonny Bealby for being a total star and my first choice for a beer. Martin thank you so much for letting me use your pictures – they are truly stunning and, as you would say, you are a 'top' man. Paul, likewise, thanks for the photographs, but more importantly thanks for keeping me safe and teaching me to see the ice as you see it: not hostile, but open and pristine. Dynamite Danger Dave, your capacity for humour at any time was, and is, astonishing. It was wonderful to get to know you. A big mention to Conor, Robyn and the two Steves.

Thanks also to my family – Mum for not worrying too much, SJ, Justin and George for love and support and painstakingly packing up weeks' worth of chocolate and peanuts into small ration packs and particularly Dad for being behind this idea even if it didn't look like being the sensible career track move – and also for looking after the expedition company while we were incommunicado.

Two people remain to be thanked (although I know there are so many more that deserve to be singled out). Pat – our expedition started two years before we hit the snow. We planned and executed it all together. We took every footstep in tandem. Getting to know you well, and to rely on you on the ice, was a privilege – thank you too for patiently going through my (even more) pretentious first draft and pointing that out to me so directly . . . I look forward to more adventures.

Lastly, Annabel – thank you my darling heart. I don't need to tell you in writing how much I owe you.